Becoming Physically Educated in the Elementary School

CHARLES B. CORBIN, Ph.D.

*Assistant Professor, Department of Health and
Physical Education, Texas A & M University,
College Station, Texas*

Illustrations by ELEANOR HANOVER NANCE

LEA & FEBIGER · 1969 · PHILADELPHIA

1

Preface

The fundamental purpose of any educational program for children is to help them to learn. More specifically, the basic purpose of the physical education program is to help children in *Becoming Physically Educated in the Elementary School*. The emphasis is on the child. The teacher, whether a classroom teacher, a physical education specialist, or a future teacher, is the agent responsible for helping the child in becoming physically educated.

This book was written to aid the teacher in two basic ways: (1) To present a sound basic understanding of what children need to learn in the elementary school, and (2) to aid the teacher in selecting physical education experiences which will most likely produce desired learning in children.

The first section of the text (Chapters 1 to 10) presents information concerning basic physical education beliefs, guidelines for learning, and the nature of the learner, with the specific purpose of aiding the teacher in "tailor-making" programs to meet the behavioral objectives of a specific group of learners.

Section two (Chapters 11 to 20) is basically a collection of diversified physical education experiences which can be selected by the teacher or the learner in helping the learner in *Becoming Physically Educated in the Elementary School*.

I have made a special effort to present scientific information to aid the teacher in clearly understanding the foundations of physical education. It is hoped that this sound foundation will help the teacher with little experience, as well as the master teacher, in making decisions as to what to teach in elementary school physical education.

I wish to express my gratitude to many individuals who have aided in the preparation of this book: To Mercedes Gugisberg of the University of New Mexico, who sparked my special interest in elementary school physical education; to Charles Renfro, director of elementary school physical education, Albuquerque, New Mexico, who guided me in my apprentice years and who contributed many fundamental teaching ideas; and to Virgil Morgan, a former classroom teacher and now a principal, who read the manuscript and provided vital insights regarding the practical presentation of information in this book.

Special recognition goes to Dr. Ruth Abernathy for her invaluable editorial assistance with the manuscript.

CHARLES B. CORBIN

College Station, Texas

Contents

Page

1. Becoming Physically Educated — 1
2. Developing a Founded Point of View — 5
3. Guidelines for Teaching and Learning — 19
4. The Learner — 31
5. Objectives — 46
6. Planning the Program — 65
7. Movement Exploration — 81
8. Helping Children Understand Physical Education — 96
9. Some Details and Policies — 104
10. Tips for Teaching — 113
11. Fundamental Skills and Fundamental Skill Activities — 123
12. Movement Exploration Activities — 143
13. Experiments and Discussion Questions for Use in the Classroom — 160
14. Low Organization Games — 180
15. Gymnastics and Tumbling — 206
16. Relays — 231
17. Sports and Lead Up Games — 241
18. Physical Fitness Activities — 280
19. Rhythms and Dance — 303
20. Evaluation — 330
Appendixes — 343
Index — 357

1

Becoming Physically Educated

The challenge to American education is to help every child learn to learn. In accomplishing such an enormous task, educators ask the questions: "What is an adequate education?" "Can Johnny read sufficiently?" "Is he physically fit enough?" Are these really the measures of the quality of our educational programs?

In educating each child goals must be higher than "adequate" or "sufficient". We must ask, "What can man become?" not, "How does man perform?" The goal of education is then to provide each individual the opportunity to achieve his or her own potential. The end product, "the fully functioning healthy individual" is something to be achieved. Challenging educational experiences coupled with a personal desire for achievement are necessary ingredients for the development of human potential. Fulfillment of human potential is not given, it must be achieved.

Physical education is charged with the responsibility of contributing to the development of the "fully functioning healthy individual." As a part of the education program, physical education is one contributor to attainment of this larger goal. Physical fitness and health provide a basis for the development of man's potential. Without these qualities man is limited in his ability to achieve. Thus we should not be content with "enough" or "average", the challenge is greater than that. In meeting the challenge, physical education should provide the opportunity for each child to achieve his potential, not only in terms of the physical but in terms of providing opportunities in which a contribution to the development of the healthy individual is made. Certainly each educational discipline will strive to accomplish certain specific educational objectives, but in addition each discipline will work to the development of the totally educated child.

The Teaching-Learning Process

Becoming physically educated does not merely occur, it must be attained. For this reason, it is essential that the teacher consider the process by which the individual is to "become" physically educated.

Since the teacher is the agent charged with responsibility for providing experiences through which children can become physically educated, it is essential that teachers become familiar with the teaching-learning process. The following discussion is organized around the model illustrated in Figure 1-1.

FOUNDATIONS

First consideration relates to professional foundations. This includes one's point of view, an understanding of the guidelines of teaching and learning, and an understanding of the learner. The teacher, as the agent in helping children become physically educated, must develop an informed point of view or otherwise he cannot organize an appropriate plan of action. He should be familiar with professional guidelines derived from scientific findings. The development of a point of view and the knowledge of founded guidelines provide a partial foundation for effective teaching, but only a real understanding of the characteristics, needs, and interests of the learner can complete the foundation. It is on the basis of foundations that objectives are established.

OBJECTIVES

Objectives are used to clarify what is going to be done for a group of students. These objectives must be based on the previously defined foundations. The definition of objectives becomes the second step in helping the teacher organize for aiding children in becoming physically educated. Objectives, then, are the blueprints based on the specifications prescribed within the foundations areas.

FIG. 1-1 *The Teaching-Learning Process.*

PROGRAMS

It is on these objectives that programs are built. Programs are the action phase of the process. It is through these programs that children become physically educated. These programs, as part of the process, are not foolproof, but are tools for increasing the chance that the desired outcomes of the program will be developed. It should be emphasized that these programs are one step in this dynamic, continuous process and are only valuable to the extent that they are a means to an end, rather than an end in themselves. Every activity, as part of the program, is selected to fulfill objectives. Rather than teaching an activity for activity's sake, the effective teacher uses activities as one step in a process designed for the achievement of specific goals. Contributions of programs should not be limited by objectives established for any one group of children. However, the physical education activity or tool that most likely will contribute to desired outcomes should be selected and concommitant outcomes that result from these programs will be extra fruits of one's efforts.

EVALUATION

The final phase of the process would be another step in the continuous process. This process is evaluation. Programs, objectives, and foundations are of little value unless the product is continuously evaluated. The teacher must consider the weighing of his objectives. If one follows a sound teaching process but excludes evaluation, he has excluded the one step designed to determine if program objectives have been achieved. It might be argued that evaluation, as part of the process, is not merely the final step, but the link which insures the continuation of the process. Evaluation provides the basis for understanding basic foundations and for establishing programs' objectives.

The Teacher is the Agent

As the agent for promoting learning in physical education, the teacher must be concerned with all phases of the process. Preoccupation with one phase may result in failure to accomplish desired goals in physical education. An example is the technician who is primarily concerned with the program phase of the process. The teacher, as the agent in the teaching-learning process, is concerned with all phases of the process, not only the program phase. If our ultimate aim is the development of the fully functioning healthy individual, we cannot expect fulfillment if children's characteristics, sound point of view, and other phases of the process are not considered. The teacher must be a technician and more if our objectives are to be attained.

Adherence to the teaching-learning process does not assure accomplishment of ultimate educational purposes, but it does improve the probability that these purposes will be achieved. The teacher, as the agent in this change, is wagering on the teaching process as a good bet to aid children in fulfilling their potential in physical education.

The ultimate goal of physical education is to help each child achieve his fullest potential in a sound learning situation, with the assistance of an effective teacher working through the teacher-learning process.

Bibliography

1. Association for Supervision and Curriculum Development, *Perceiving, Behaving, Becoming,* Washington, D.C., NEA, 1962.

2. Corbin, Charles B.: The Professional Process, *The Physical Educator, 23:*173, Dec., 1966.

2

Developing a Founded Point of View

The development of a founded point of view is paramount to the teacher of physical education. It is on the basis of this point of view that the teacher prepares a plan of action. The beliefs that make up a point of view provide a basis for the development of objectives and programs in physical education.

The founded point of view is built on more than opinion, it is built on beliefs based on established philosophical truths, scientific fact, and/or a progression of logical reasoning. In addition, the founded point of view must be systematized and internally consistent. In the final analysis it is the founded, systematized, internally consistent point of view which serves as a format for action. The following section of this text includes a discussion of important ideas which must be considered in the development of a point of view.

What is Physical Education?

Physical education has meant many things to many people, and most unfortunately it is often misinterpreted. Until teachers accurately define physical education, it is not likely that physical education will make its maximal contribution to the total educational program. Many misconceptions have been held concerning physical education, which makes it necessary to clarify the relationship of physical education to other educational areas.

Physical Education is More Than Recess!

Recess has long been the part of the elementary school day during which the children are released from the classroom to play in activities of their choice. The teacher is usually released for a "breather" during this time as well. Traditionally recess has been deemed a necessary part of the school day. With the recent emphasis on physical fitness, many schools have suggested recess as a time during which physical fitness should be developed. In many instances the recess period is held to be a period of physical education.

As part of the teaching-learning process, programs of physical education are designed to meet specific educational objectives. It is no more logical to assume that children will meet these physical education objectives effectively on their own than it is to assume that objectives in reading or mathematics will be met without sound programs specifically directed at the accomplishment of these objectives.

Physical Education is Neither Recess, Athletics, Intramurals, Nor Survival of the Fittest.

One often hears, "They have a fine physical education program; they won 15 and lost 3." Such a reference is to an athletic program and not to physical education. These programs, most often found in the secondary school, are part of the total physical education program, but only a part. Athletics are "interscholastic" programs or programs of competition between schools. Research and scientific evidence suggests programs like this have no place in the elementary school[1,2] (Box 2-1).

Intramurals is another part of the total physical education program. Like athletics, intramurals is one part and not the total program of physical education. This program includes opportunities for any child who wants to participate in a special recreational program either before school, at noon or after school. No one is turned away from the intramural program, but neither is it required of all children.

The physical education program is the total program including all three areas, *i.e.* athletics, intramurals and physical education. The important fact to consider is that the basic instructional program is the essential part of the program and is provided for *all* children. The physical education program is the foundation for other programs. The total physical education program

FIG. 2-1 *The Pyramid of Emphasis.*

BOX 2-1. INTERSCHOOL ATHLETICS FOR ELEMENTARY SCHOOL CHILDREN

Purpose. The purposes of this paper were twofold: (1) To analyze and evaluate the place of interschool athletics in the elementary school program and (2) to suggest replacement programs which will meet the same objectives in a more desirable or beneficial manner.

Procedure. The study includes a review of the pertinent research and a theoretical discussion of the merits and inadequacies of interschool athletic programs at the elementary school level.

Major Points of Discussion

1. Athletics at the proper grade level in the proper setting, when directed toward worthwhile objectives, are desirable.
2. Major educational groups stand united against the interschool athletic program for elementary school children.
3. Seminars and group study conferences conducted by professional groups indicate that interschool competition is undesirable before the ninth grade.
4. Physicians and educators suggest that this age group is the "vulnerable age group" in terms of possible physiological predisposition to injury and poor posture.
5. Leadership, which is vital to any athletic program, is often inadequate at the elementary school level.
6. Too much, too soon of any sport seems to breed a dislike for physical activity.
7. Sound basic programs of physical education in the school can develop the same objectives as those claimed by proponents of athletics without the disadvantages of the athletic type programs.

Conclusions. "While certain values of interschool athletics in the elementary school are recognized, their inclusion in the program is inferior to what could be offered. Their disadvantages far outweigh the advantages and assets."

"Sound programs of physical education should be established in the elementary school to develop those objectives commonly held to be developed by the athletic program in the elementary school."

Brinley, Eldon D.: Interschool Athletics for Elementary School Youngsters, *Journal of School Health,* 23:209–215, September, 1964.

might be diagrammed as a pyramid, with physical education as the foundation, illustrating the need for physical education for all children before other programs are added (Figure 2-1). Intramural and athletic programs are added when provisions are made for the more important foundations programs. The program diagram for the secondary school should be represented in the same way. However, the pyramid is often tipped upside down in actual school practice. This can best be illustrated in schools where the only provision is boys athletic teams.

Physical Education is More Than Physical Fitness!

Although physical fitness is a major objective of physical education, it is not the entire program. Fitness is a desirable objective, and certainly much time in physical education is devoted to improving the fitness level of children. It must be pointed out that fitness is only one of the objectives of physical education. Programs of physical training, including calisthenics and other similar "basic training" activities, can not fully meet the needs of children or accomplish the objectives of the sound physical education program.

Physical Education is a Part of the Total Educational Program!

As one phase of the curriculum, physical education makes a contribution to the total development of the end aim of education, the development of the fully functioning healthy individual. Even the most severe of educational critics recognize physical education's role in attaining this end.

"Physical Education is essential."[3] This statement was voiced by Admiral Hyman Rickover, a critic and leader in the fight for more science and math in our schools.

Dr. Conant, former president of Harvard and author of many recent books on education states, . . . "I am also convinced that ideally a period of physical education should be required to all pupils in grades 1 through 12 every day . . ."[4]

Wilhelm Raab, M.D., stated in a popular American sports magazine that, . . . "very much more emphasis should be placed on the rigidly disciplined physical training in the school."[5]

The central objective of education today is said to be "helping to give each child the opportunity to fulfill his potential." Inasmuch as educators agree that the development of the "whole" child is the desirable aim of educational programs, the place of physical education is obvious. Physical education is and should be an integral part of the total educational program.

↓ A Definition of Physical Education

Physical Education is that essential component of education which consists of purposefully selected and planned movement experiences. These motor and physical activities provide a means for growth and development of *all* boys and girls according to their readiness, needs, and interests. Although organic and neuromuscular development are the primary and unique objectives, physical education contributes to the complete education of the individual through associated knowledges, attitudes, and appreciations of physical education, health and physical fitness. Physical education provides special programs for those children possessing special remedial or unremedial defects.

A Physically Educated Person

The ultimate outcome of physical education, as described above, is the physically educated person. This physically educated person could be described as follows:

One who moves effectively within his environment. He possesses efficient movement skills, including a reasonable proficiency in a variety of dance, games, sports, and other physical activities. He possesses buoyant health and physical fitness. Retention of these qualities is insured by a knowledge of and a desirable attitude toward physical activity and related areas. A physically educated person with disability would use his body effectively within his capabilities.

Physical Education Does Not Just Happen!

Assuming that the physically educated person, as described in the previous section, is the product of physical education programs, it would seem necessary to take a look to see if this goal can ever be achieved. Certainly some guided program must be established if the product of excellence is to be attained. However, many parents and other interested people are of the opinion that such a "physically educated" person will evolve merely by "letting the kids play".

Stan Musial,[6] former director of the President's Council for Physical Fitness, suggests:

Parents cannot just assume that their children will learn to play and enjoy sports on their own. Good instruction, in an atmosphere where good sportsmanship and real concern for the child's welfare are the rule, is important. Children who are properly taught derive more good and more enjoyment from sports, and they are more likely to become active and healthy adults

Musial, as other former council directors, has stressed the research evidence which indicates American children to be considerably below European children in physical fitness level.

Our children are not active to the extent deemed desirable for adequate development of desirable levels of fitness. Fitness is not the only objective that suffers as a result of inadequate programs of physical education. It is, however, the objective of physical education most likely to be recognized as unfulfilled because of the dramatic nature of the lack of physical fitness in our youth.

Schramm has a bit of insight into why the physical fitness needs of our children have changed in recent years. "The average child spends on television in his first 16 years as much time as he spends in school."[7]

There are those educators and parents who suggest recess or play before and after school is all children need. Again we know that this is not true.

BOX 2-2. VALUES OF ELEMENTARY PHYSICAL EDUCATION

Purpose. This investigation was designed to study the effects of elementary school physical education upon certain aspects of physical development, motor fitness, motor educability, body flexibility, explosive power and personality of 12-year-old boys.

Procedures. Eighty-one 12-year-old boys were studied. These boys were matched on chronological age, skeletal age, weight, height and the Wetzel Grid. Only boys having been in this school setting for 3 years were studied. The subjects were divided into two groups; those in schools with good physical education programs and those in schools with little or no programs of physical education. Schools were rated as good or bad on the basis of the LaPorte Program Evaluation Score Card.

Subjects in the two groups were measured on maturational elements and affective elements of fitness. Maturational elements were those not likely to change with activity (height, weight, etc.). The affective elements were those likely to change with activity (strength, power, etc.). Boys were also questioned as to their activities outside school.

Results. There were no maturational element differences between the two groups. Boys in good programs were far superior to the boys in the poor programs in affective elements: total fitness, strength, power, and flexibility. Boys who were active outside school were better in both maturational and affective elements as compared to boys not active outside school. This was true of boys in good and poor programs.

Conclusions. It was concluded that elementary school physical education programs definitely improve the physical fitness levels of children.

Whittle H. Douglas: Effects of Elementary School Physical Education Upon Aspects of Physical Fitness, Motor Fitness, Motor Educability and Personality Development, *Research Quarterly, 32:*249, May, 1961.

BOX 2-3. MEETING A SPECIFIC OBJECTIVE

Purpose. The purpose of this study was to discover differences in physical fitness development between groups of fourth grade children having calisthenics designed specifically to meet a physical fitness objective, in addition to regular physical education activities, as opposed to those only having regular physical education activities.

Procedures. One hundred sixty-two fourth grade boys and girls were divided into two groups:

1. normal physical education—some calisthenics
2. normal physical education—extra calisthenics

The experimental groups exercised for 3 minutes and 9 seconds in addition to the normal physical education program. These exercises were designed to develop specific aspects of fitness.

The Oregon Motor Fitness Test was the measure of physical fitness used. The groups were tested at the beginning and end of the school year.

Results. The experimental group had significantly higher levels of physical fitness after re-test than did the group taking the normal program. Both groups improved in physical fitness.

Conclusions. Extra exercises and calisthenics devoted to specific objective fulfillment (physical fitness) improve the fitness levels of children. The extra time is minimal and worth the time in terms of benefits derived.

Fabricuis, Helen: Effect of Added Calisthenics on the Physical Fitness of Fourth Grade Boys and Girls, *Research Quarterly, 35:*135–140, May, 1964.

Nearly 100% of the schools in the country have recess and certainly children are "allowed" to participate before and after school in physical activity. Yet for years we have been assuming magical benefits of recess only to find that current research indicates gross inadequacies in the ability of such programs to develop physical vitality. Recess as a program of physical education is like free reading periods instead of reading instruction. Yes, free reading and free play are desirable, but neither is a substitute for a good instructional program in the area. Some children will read on their own and others will develop the desired outcomes of physical education on their own. But the great majority will not. Even those who do will suffer the hardship of not having been exposed to all of the values of a good program. Recent research investigations have shown the values of physical education programs in elementary schools (Box 2-2).

What about the schools where physical education programs exist but failures still occur on tests of physical fitness? Research evidence supports the notion that "adequate" physical education programs will do the job, especially when the activities are specifically directed at achieving the preconceived objectives of the program. As the educator recognizes the need for physical education, he must then recognize the good teaching process as the method for fulfilling educational objectives of this sound aspect of education.

When an objective such as physical fitness is held to be important and activities or other programs are incorporated to develop this objective, there is little doubt that physical education contributes to the total education of the child (Box 2-3).

Physical Education and Academic Achievement

Since Sputnik, educators have been most concerned with upgrading the elementary school curriculum. As a result considerable time, money, and effort has been spent in attempt to improve the school's program for learners especially in the areas of math, science and reading. New programs in these areas resulted in considerable competition for time in the school day. Some areas of the curriculum, namely music, art, and physical education were labeled as "non academic" or "frills" and were considered, by some, not to be essential as part of the total school program. It is only fair to point out that, like math, science and reading; art, music and physical education were also in need of curricular improvements during this period of educational scrutiny.

Physical education held its own through this period largely on the contributions of the program to the development of physical fitness. The justification of physical education on the basis of physical fitness alone suggests an antiquated mind-body separation. Recent research indicates the need for the development of the "total" child through programs in all curricular areas, including physical education.

The school program offering broad curricular experiences in physical education, music, and art as well as the other vital educational experiences, is likely to make the greatest contribution to the development of the fully functioning healthy individual.

Kephart has conducted considerable research indicating the relationship between ability to perform perceptual-motor skills and success in the classroom. He emphasizes the diagnosis of deficiency in performance of motor skills basic to reading and then prescribes physical education activities to develop these basic competencies.[8]

Clinical evidence presented by Delacato, a researcher for the Institute of Achievement of Human Potential, has suggested similar theories indicating physical education activities to be valuable in remediating and devel-

DEVELOPMENT OF THE "WHOLE" CHILD IS IMPORTANT

BOX 2-4. PHYSICAL EDUCATION AND ACADEMIC ACHIEVEMENT

Purpose. The purpose of the special program in Washington, D.C. elementary schools was to "combat drop-out problems," to solve "fitness problems," and to "improve attitudes and motivation." The program at Bundy Elementary School was one of several such programs.

Procedure. More than 40 elementary school boys were bussed to Bundy Elementary School at 7 a.m. every morning. These boys met for $1\frac{1}{2}$ hours before school. They first participated in physical activity, took showers and then were served breakfast at school. The project was financed by the Department of Urban Service and the Eugene Meyer Foundation. Physical Education majors from nearby universities were used as instructors.

Results. All boys improved in attendance. Teachers indicate boys were more alert. Boys seemed to have better learning skills and fitness. Classroom attitudes improved and thus performance in the academic framework improved.

Conclusions. These special programs benefited the "whole" child in many ways including academic performances. The only disappointment was that "all of the boys couldn't be accommodated."

Breakfast at Bundy's, *The Instructor*, 75:44, September, 1965.

---

oping basic "academic skills." Delacato indicates that such elements as laterality, visual perceptive skills, and proprioceptive skills must be learned before the child is ready to read. These skills could be developed in fundamental physical education classes and activities, especially for children known to be deficient in specific academic skills.[9]

Recent research has been reported indicating that caution should be used in generalizing the contributions of physical education to achievement in the classroom, especially the clinical findings that are based largely on study of the retarded child.[10] However, enough evidence does exist to indicate that physical activity in an objective oriented physical education program does contribute to improved learning in all areas of the curriculum.[11-13] The evidence tends to dispel old wives' tales indicating that one must possess either brains or brawn but cannot possess both. Studies such as Terman's "Study of Genius" lend evidence to the idea that those with brains tend also to be physically superior, while physical efficiency is necessary for optimal mental efficiency.[14]

This information further supports the need for physical education in the elementary school.

BOX 2-5. MOTOR THERAPY AND SCHOOL ACHIEVEMENT

Purpose. The purpose of this study was to investigate the beneficial effects of a special program of gross motor activities as therapy in facilitating academic school achievement.

Procedures. Elementary school pupils who experienced school difficulties in one or more subjects, particularly reading, participated in loosely structured problem solving movement activities for a 2-hour period once a week. These students were compared in academic achievement after a period of one to five semesters, with a matched group of students who did not participate in these special physical education activities.

Results. Scholastic achievement test scores for the experimental (physical activity) group increased for all subjects well beyond what had previously been accomplished or what had been expected. School grades increased in the majority of the cases by one letter grade and in some cases by two letter grades.

None of the matched non-participating cases showed comparable results or improvements. In fact, scores went down in subjects in this group and all have since been referred for motor therapy.

Conclusions. Although groups were small the evidence definitely suggests that motor therapy programs are contributors to the academic improvement among elementary school children. Parents, teachers, and principals involved supported the program enthusiastically with such comments as "marvelous," "remarkable," and "a fine job." The investigator concluded ". . . that physical education has a contribution to make also to academic achievement in the elementary school."

Godfrey, Barbara B.: Motor Therapy and School Achievement, *JOHPER, 35:*22, May, 1964.

A Total Point of View

Current educational philosophies emphasize the importance of the development of the "whole" child through sound educational programs. Considering physical education to be an important contributor to the education of the "whole" child, the educator must clarify his own beliefs concerning physical education. These beliefs form the cornerstone for the development of a point of view which will serve as a basis for the "teaching process" in physical education. The beginnings of the development of a point of view of physical education can be centered around some of the beliefs suggested in this chapter. Through these and other readings, the educator becomes ready to take action formulating his own point of view.

It is on the basis of one's point of view, with an awareness of teaching-learning guidelines and understanding of the learner that program objectives are based. For this reason considerations of personal beliefs are of great importance to the teacher of physical education.

References

1. Lounan, C. L.: The Vulnerable Age, *Journal of Health and Physical Education, 18:*635, 1947.
2. Hale, Creighton J.: What Research Says About Athletics for Pre High School Age Children, *Journal of Health, Physical Education and Recreation, 30:*19, December, 1959.
3. Rickover, Admiral Hyman, U.S.N.: Statement made on Meet the Press, National Television Show, January 20, 1960.
4. Conant, J. B.: From a speech made to the AASA National Convention, Atlantic City, N.J., February, 1960.
5. Raab, Wilhelm: as quoted by Dorothy Stull, A Fit Week for a Second Look, *Sports Illustrated. 8:*45, May 26, 1958.
6. A statement by Stan Musial from *Teaching Lifetime Sports Skills.* Produced by The President's Council for Physical Fitness, Washington: U.S. Government Printing Office, 1968.
7. Schramm, William: An Anecdote, *Phi Delta Kappan, 42:*407, June, 1961.
8. Kephart, Newell: *The Slow Learner in the Classroom,* Columbus, Charles E. Merrill Inc., 1960.
9. Delacato, Carl H.: *Diagnosis and Treatment of Speech and Reading Problems,* Springfield, Charles C Thomas, 1963.
10. Williams, H. G.: Learning, *Journal of Health, Physical Education, and Recreation, 39:*28–31, 1968.
11. Clarke, H. Harrison and Jarman, Boyd O.: Scholastic Achievement of Boys 9, 12, and 15 Years of Age as Related to Various Strength and Growth Measures, *Research Quarterly, 32:*155–162, 1961.
12. Hart, Marcia E. and Shay, Clayton T.: Relationship Between Physical Fitness and Academic Success, *Research Quarterly, 32:*443–445, 1964.
13. Oliver, James N.: The Effect of Physical Conditioning Exercises and Activities on the Mental Characteristics of Educationally Sub-Normal Boys, *British J. Educ. Psych. 28:*155–165, June, 1958.
14. Terman, Lewis M. (Ed.): *Genetic Studies of Genius: Mental and Physical Traits of a Thousand Gifted Children,* Stanford, Stanford University Press, 1925.

Bibliography

PERIODICALS

Abernathy, Ruth: Implications for Physical Education in the Current Re-Examination of American Education, *JOHPER, 32:*19, Jan., 1961.

Almond, Eugenia B.: You've Got to Crawl Before You Can Read, *Scholastic Teacher,* Dec. 11, 1964.

Bechtel, P. C.: Health and Physical Education: What's the Score? *Ohio Schools, 42:*21, Dec., 1964.

Beck, Viola: The Classroom Teacher is the Key, *JOHPER, 34:*23, November–December, 1963.

Bucher, Charles A.: Health, Physical Education and Academic Achievement, *NEA Journal,* May, 1965, 38–40.

Emery, Don: Desirable Directions and Trends in Elementary Physical Education, *School Activities, 31:*225, May, 1960.

Farley, William and Slutz, Don: We Must Work Together to Improve Elementary Physical Education, *Illinois Education, 53:*161–169, Dec., 1964.

Frank, James: Elementary School Not too Early for Interschool Sports, *Physical Educator, 22:*9, March, 1965.

Hall, V. L.: Physical Education: Why Children Need It, *National Elementary Principals. 39:*8–11, April, 1960.

Hutchinson, Doris: Tailored to Fit the Child, *NEA Journal, 52:*27–29, Feb., 1963.

Levin, Phyllis Lee: Putting Muscle Into Marks, *New York Times Magazine,* Nov. 28, 1965.

Luby, Robert R.: Why Physical Education in the Elementary School, *Grade Teacher, 82:*80, Dec., 1964.

Marm, Lillian: Why Physical Education in the Elementary School? *Catholic School Journal, 62:*23, Jan., 1962.

Misner, David E.: Physical Activity and the 3 R's, *Scholastic Teacher,* May 6, 1965, p. 6.

Pennington, G.: Homework in Physical Education to Improve Fitness, *Physical Educator, 21:*73, May, 1964.

Smith, Paul: Physical Education in the Elementary School, *Educational Leadership, 20:*376, March, 1963.

Young, Jean M.: Individualized Physical Activity, *NEA Journal, 54:*22, Dec., 1965.

Your Child's Health and Fitness, *NEA Journal, 51:*33, Feb., 1962.

Leave Your Little Leaguer Alone, *Parents Magazine, 36:*40, June, 1961.

Kids and Athletics, *Changing Times, 15:*22–24, Oct., 1961.

BOOKS

Andrews, Gladys, Saurborn, Jeanette and Schneider, Elsa: *Physical Education for Today's Boys and Girls,* Boston, Allyn & Bacon Inc., 1960.

Bucher, Charles A.: *Foundations of Physical Education,* St. Louis, C. V. Mosby Co., 1964.

Bucher, Charles and Reade, Evelyn: *Physical Education and Health in the Elementary School,* New York, The Macmillan Co., 1964.

Cassidy, Rosalind and Brown, Camille: *Theory in Physical Education,* Philadelphia, Lea & Febiger, 1963.

Davis, E. C. and Miller, D. M.: *The Philosophic Process in Physical Education,* 2nd Ed., Philadelphia, Lea & Febiger, 1967.

Halsey, Elizabeth, Porter, Lorena: *Physical Education for Children,* New York, Holt, Rinehart & Winston, 1963, Chapter 1.

Humphrey, James J., and Jones, Edwina and Haversticks, Martha J. (eds.): *Readings in Physical Education,* Palo Alto, National Press, 1960.

Oberteuffer, Delbert and Ulrich, Celeste: *Physical Education,* New York, Harper & Row, 1962.

Vannier, Maryhelen and Foster, Mildred: *Teaching Physical Education in Elementary Schools,* Philadelphia, W.B. Saunders Co., 1963, Chapter 1.

Webster, Randolph W.: *Philosophy of Physical Education,* Dubuque, Wm C. Brown Co., 1965.

3

Guidelines for Teaching and Learning

Before the teacher can build program objectives, some consideration must be given to the scientific information yielded by researchers in health and physical education. The following section of this book discusses some guidelines for teaching and learning in physical education. These guidelines are based on scientific research and empirical evidence. The intent of these guidelines is to present information which will be of value in most efficiently promoting learning and sound teaching in programs of physical education in the elementary school. These guidelines, together with a founded point of view and an understanding of the learner, will help provide a basis for the development of program objectives.

Guidelines for Developing Physical Fitness

Research has produced considerable scientific evidence which is of value in helping children in developing physical fitness. The following, scientifically based, guidelines are presented to aid the teacher in helping the teacher in more effectively developing physical fitness among children.

1. *"Overload" is necessary for physical fitness development.* Sometimes referred to as the overload principle or the law of use and disuse, the above stated guideline is of great importance in developing physical fitness. The improvement of any aspect of physical fitness is the result of using that aspect more than it is normally used (Box 3-1). If arm strength

19

BOX 3-1. PHYSICAL FITNESS

Definition: Physical fitness is composed of many different aspects including health related physical fitness aspects and motor fitness (skill) related aspects. To function effectively in our society without undue fatigue and to have reserve energy to enjoy leisure time requires adequate development of both the health related and skill related aspects of physical fitness. The important aspects of physical fitness are listed below:

HEALTH RELATED ASPECTS

Endurance. The ability to persist in numerous repetitions of an activity. Specifically, this aspect involves development of the respiratory and circulatory systems of the body.

Flexibility. The ability to move joints through a full range of motion.

Strength. The ability to exert force such as lifting a weight or lifting your own body.

Muscular Endurance. The ability to persist in numerous repetitions of an activity involving strength.

COMBINED ASPECT

Explosive Power. The ability to display strength explosively or with speed.

MOTOR FITNESS ASPECTS

Agility. The ability to change directions quickly and to control body movements (total body).

Reaction Time. The ability to perceive a stimulus, begin movement and finally complete a response.

Balance. The ability to maintain body position and equilibrium both in movement and in stationary body positions.

Coordination. The ability to perform hand-eye and foot-eye tasks such as kicking, throwing, striking, etc.

Speed. The ability to move from one place to another in the shortest possible time.

Implications: School programs should be concerned with developing all aspects of physical fitness. However, the health related aspects are most important to the health and well being of the individual. The motor aspects are desirable but relate mostly to one's ability to perform a specific skill task rather than to one's state of health.

is desired, the muscles of the arm must be "overloaded". If flexibility is the objective, the muscles must be stretched more than normal. Whatever the aspect of physical fitness, development only occurs if "overload" is present. The teacher's concern is to provide a program for children which "overloads" the children or allows them to do more than they would normally do.

2. *Overload is specific.* There are many aspects of physical fitness (Box 3-1). The techniques for developing different aspects are specific to the aspect of physical fitness to be developed. If you want to develop strength, overload specifically for strength. Whatever the type fitness to be developed, the overload should be designed *specifically* to build that aspect of physical fitness. Also of importance is physical fitness of the various body parts. It is possible to overload specifically for arm development or for the development of any specific body part. The type of exercise used for development should be selected specifically to overload the part of the body one wishes to develop.

3. *Normal existence does not produce overload.* The average child or adult does not encounter situations in the course of daily living that provide physiological overload. Those who need to develop fitness the most are often the ones least likely to overload in daily routines.

4. *Overload is best when progressive.* Optimal effects of overload occur when the overload exceeds normal but is within the capacity of the individual. Excessive overload may result in soreness and discomfort with overload.

5. *Proper diet is necessary for physiological development.* Without proper diet any or all of the beneficial effects of activity and exercise may be negated.

6. *Rest and relaxation are necessary to physiological development.* Overload through movement and exercise results in physiological development. Periodic rest and relaxation are essential to recuperation of the organism. Without such rest and relaxation overload is rendered ineffective and even dangerous.

7. *Individuals develop physically at different rates.* All individuals differ widely in terms of total development. Likewise, physical development is highly unique to each organism.

8. *Weight control is a result of proper balance in calories consumed and calories expended.* The great majority of overweight and underweight problems are a result of either lack of sufficient calorie expenditure or excessive caloric intake. Balance between caloric intake and caloric expenditure is essential for weight control. Thus the "easy" methods of weight control not contributing to the intake-expenditure balance are ineffective.

9. *Barring injury, a healthy child cannot physiologically injure his heart perma-*

nently through physical exercise. Contrary to popular opinion, vigorous exercise does not cause permanent damage to the elementary school child. The "wives' tale" that vigorous exercise by children would result in failure of the heart because of inproportionate development of the heart and arteries, is but one belief that has been perpetuated in books of child growth and development. As the "athlete's heart" fallacy was negated indicating that exercise does not cause deterioration of the heart but rather hypertrophy, so has the "child's heart" phenomenon been squelched.

Beneke[1] in 1879 observed the decreased proportional size of arteries as compared to heart size as the child grows older. As a result he indicated that in early stages of childhood the lack of blood carrying capacity of the artery indicated grave danger to the exercising child particularly around the age of 7 to 9. This conclusion seemed logical and for years children of this age were discouraged from performing physical activity. In some instances they still are.

In 1937, Karpovich re-evaluated this hypothesis and noted the obvious "simple" error in Beneke's theory. Although the size of the artery was smaller in proportion to the heart at age 7, the blood carrying capacity was proportional to heart development. The error was a mathematical one. "If, for instance, the circumference of an artery increases twice, the volume of the blood going through it will increase not twice but *four times,* or in proportion to the square of the radius or diameter; in other words, in proportion to the area of the cross-section and *not* the circumference" (Box 3-2).

The young child's heart, if healthy, cannot be permanently damaged through exercise. This does not mean that his potential for exercise is as great as is an adult's however. As stated above, overload is best when progressive. Even though the child is capable of considerably more exertion than previously thought possible, his capacity for exercise is less than an older individual. Therefore, the overload should progress according to his ability to handle the load, and not with adult imposed standards. Although the work load may be less for the child, the ultimate product of our programs, through progressive overload, will be capable of endurance feats previously thought impossible for children.

Guidelines for Skill Teaching and Learning

Since many of the activities of the physical education class involve skill learning, it is important to consider guidelines for effective teaching and learning of skill. The following guidelines are designed to aid the teacher and learner in working to this end.

BOX 3-2. TEXTBOOK FALLACIES REGARDING THE CHILD'S HEART

Purpose. The purpose of this study was to trace the origin of the idea that has been perpetuated in books that childhood is a time of special vulnerability to heart failure because of the small size of the heart in relation to the size of blood vessels, and to prove its fallacy.

Procedures. The investigator traces the literature to locate early reports of this fallacy.

Before 1900 Beneke pointed out "an apparent discrepancy" between the growth of the heart and the aorta and pulmonary artery.

Lesshaft and Quetelet both investigated and supported Beneke's findings. Early books by Schmudt and Young pointed out that this discrepancy begins at age 7 and continues to grow worse with age thus predisposing the young child to hypertension and suggested reduced vigor in the child. They suggested permanent damage could be done to the child's heart through exercise unless this fact was recognized.

At any rate, several investigators and authors perpetuated the idea that the heart of children could:

1. Pump more blood than blood vessels can handle causing high blood pressure.
2. "At this age (7) the heart, which has been relatively larger than the blood vessels, begins to be relatively smaller and this factor with others mentioned diminishes the child's vigor at this period (Young).

The investigator in this study recalculated Beneke's figures noting that the area of the cross section, not the circumference, should be taken into consideration in calculating the capacity of the child's vessels to carry the blood pumped by the heart. The experimenter then calculated ratios of heart function to vessel cross section areas.

Results. The results indicate no discrepancy in development of heart or blood vessels. Both heart volume and blood carrying capacity increase progressively and proportionally with increase in age.

Conclusions. There is no decreased function of heart or blood vessel at any age in childhood. Warnings still mocked today concerning lag in "heart size" or "vessel size" with certain age children are fallacies. "Hygienic warnings based upon erroneous interpretations should be disregarded." "There is no doubt that a heart weakened by some disease may be injured by unsuitable exertion, but if the heart be sound, according to observations made by leading German sport physicians, the danger is remote if possible at all."

Karpovich, Peter V.: Textbook Fallacies Regarding the Development of the Child's Heart, *Research Quarterly*, 8:33, October, 1937.

1. *Most neuromuscular skills are learned early in life.* Childhood is the period of play. Nash[2] indicates that the majority of recreational skills used in adult leisure time are learned in the first 12 years of life (Box 3-3).
2. *Learning is best when the learner is motivated.* Motivation is vital to any learning. A child who is interested in learning or sees the value of learning is most likely benefited from learning situations. Although ultimate motivation must come from within the individual, effective teaching can help the child become motivated to learn.
3. *Learning is best when the objectives of learning are understood by the learner.* Learning is unitary and not a fragmentary process. As the individual sees the total picture of the desired learning he is likely to be motivated to learn the parts or mechanics of that total learning. The "why" of the learning is vital to the ultimate learning that will occur.
4. *Learning is best where practice is distributed.* Learning is more effective when the individual is exposed to many learning periods of moder-

---

BOX 3-3. THE SKILL LEARNING YEARS

Purpose. The purpose of this investigation was to test the concept that recreational patterns of American adults are founded in the skill development activities of childhood.

Procedures. One thousand people with the average age of 35 were asked what they would do if they had one extra day a week, one extra hour a day or a complete year to do as they pleased. These people were asked to take plenty of time to make this decision concerning their principal recreational interest.

Subjects then conducted a personal case history to determine where (*i.e.* in the home, school, etc) and when (*i.e.* at what age?) was this "principal interest" developed. In some cases these interests were traced to an exact time.

Results. Results indicated that 85% of the interests were traced to an age below 12 years. Subjects also reported having developed this "principal skill interest" in the home with mother, father, a relative or a neighbor as a teacher. Seventy % of the 1000 subjects indicated that their interest was developed in the home.

Conclusion. The investigator concluded that there is an . . . "all essential crucial, skill learning decade". This decade may exist from . . . "four to fourteen; six to sixteen, or probably more likely two to twelve". Although skills may be learned prior to or after the basic skills learning period, skills are primarily learned at this early age.

Nash, Jay B.: *Philosophy of Recreation and Leisure,* Dubuque, William C. Brown Co., Inc., 1960, Chapter 13.

ate duration as opposed to longer "cramming" periods. Although learning can occur in "cramming" periods, more effective learning in terms of time spent, information retained, and total learning results from shorter spaced learning periods.

5. *Learning is best when the learner is ready.* The Law of Readiness has long been recognized as a basic concern to the learning process. Some educators have suggested that children cannot learn until they have reached a basic maturation level that is prerequisite to learning. Currently the feeling is that persons *can* learn earlier than previously thought possible. The significant variable is that learning is best or more efficient when the child has attained the proper maturational level. Attempts at teaching skills prior to this time may indicate learning but may also create future learning blocks or create emotional difficulties.

6. *Learning in one activity will contribute to learning another if the activities are closely related.* Transfer of learning will take place if the task to be learned is highly related and the elements of the new task are similar to the elements of the previously learned task. In instances where the elements are highly related but involve some dissimilar elements future learning may be inhibited by previous learning.

7. *Learning is best when reinforced.* Learning seems to occur more rapidly and to be retained longer when some form of positive "feedback" accompanies the learning experience. Feedback (*i.e.* immediate information concerning the quality of an individual's previous performance) or other rewards tend to reinforce the learning experience.

8. *Motor skills should be "overlearned".* Motor skills, as other learning behaviors, should be executed and learned to the point that the skill behavior pattern becomes automatic. Excellent skill performance involves more than mere performance of the task; it involves the development of the skill until the skill pattern becomes automatic.

9. *Learning is specific.* Like overload, learning is highly specific. To learn one skill is not to insure the learning of another. In order to obtain optimal learning in all areas an individual must expose himself to learning experiences in the areas of desired learning. Optimal learning will most likely occur in situations designed to develop a specific learning objective.

Guidelines for Personality Development and Social Learning

If physical educators are to be concerned with social-emotional objectives, some consideration must be given to the scientific findings which suggest to us the most effective ways of accomplishing social-emotional objectives. The following guidelines present information concerning the development of the personality and the accomplishment of social learning in physical education.

1. *The elementary school years are a period of importance in play learning and personality development.* The elementary school years, as well as the preschool years, are a time when play is life and play is the primary mechanism through which personality adjustments are made.

2. *Play is essential to proper personality development.* As discussed in Chapter 5, peer relationships are highly important to personality development. Since play is the primary method of social interaction among children, it logically follows that play is an important mechanism in personality development. Brightbill[3] indicates that "physical skills and the social skills have a direct bearing upon the acceptance of the youngster by their playmates. And this, in turn, is a strong root of personality development." Cratty[4] indicates that, "The need to play seems as fundamental in humans as the seeking of food."

3. *Skill mastery, resulting from physical activity and play, is one effective method of fulfilling man's need to achieve.* Man has a basic need to achieve. Learning and mastering skill, especially among children, contributes to the fullfillment of this need.

4. *Physical prowess (athletic physique and skill in sports activities) relates positively to sound personality.* The possession of physical fitness of all types, as well as ability in activities held to be important by peers, are important to personality development. Studies[5-7] indicate that physically successful boys are outgoing, less anxious, more confident and have enhanced self esteem. Early maturing boys are more skillful and are less likely to experience personality problems than are late maturing boys.

5. *Success is a key element in personality development.* Thorndike's[8] law of effect indicated that a learner will acquire and remember those things which lead to satisfying after effects. Children will tend to retain a response that is praised as opposed to one that is not. Likewise, personality and self image are favorably influenced by successful experiences.

   "Failure to perform well is crushing to a child's ego, while success at play has positive effects upon the child's concept of himself as a person valued by others."[9]

6. *Physical exercise and play are sources of emotional release.* "Play, like sleep, washes away the fatigues and tension that result from the service occupations of life, all the forms of labor which produce the goods of subsistence and all the leisure activities which produce the goods of civilization. Play and sleep, as Aristotle pointed out, are for the sake of these services and socially useful occupations. Since the activ-

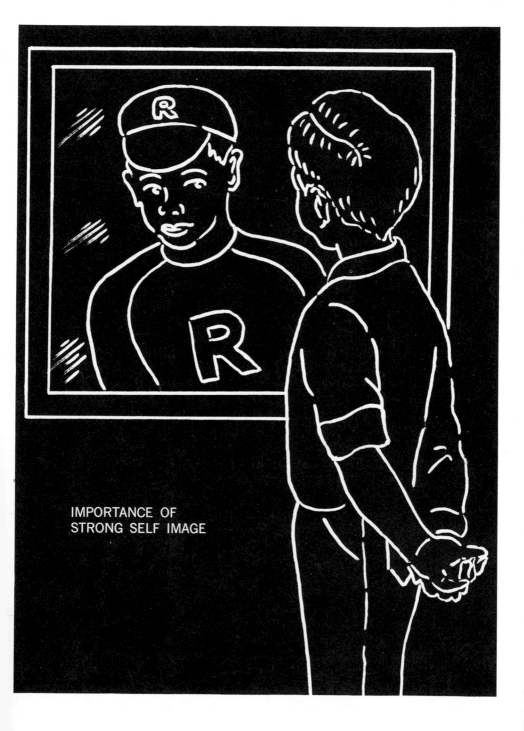

IMPORTANCE OF
STRONG SELF IMAGE

ities of leisure can be as exacting and tiring as the activities of toil, some form of relaxation, whether sleep or play or both, is required by those who work productively."[10]

7. *A child's Self image is important to his personality development.* The way a child sees himself, as well as the child's concept of himself as he thinks others see him, is important in the development of his personality. Through play and physical activity the child can improve his self image and more accurately define his personal assets and liabilities.

8. *A child's "peer rating" is determined to a large extent by his choice of play activities and his success in these activities.* Research[11] indicates that children characterize their playmates, not only by their success in activity, but also by the play activities they select. Children need to learn many forms of socially acceptable play.

9. *Social attitudes and behavior are best established in activities with specific social objectives.* Leadership, citizenship, sportsmanship are not things which automatically happen. Experience in these areas will help to contribute to these specific outcomes, especially when these experiences are social situations involving first hand contact with the desired leadership, citizenship or sportsmanship.

10. *Physical activities provide a setting for the elimination of social prejudices.* Much evidence has been accumulated to indicate that play and physical activity are areas in which social prejudices break down allowing more meaningful interactions between people. Professional sports illustrate the point, since this is an area where individuals are rated on their ability to perform regardless of their race, creed, or color. The fact that this carries over to elementary school game situations was illustrated in a study by Morgan and Nussel (Box 5-3).

11. *Social approval is affected by physical prowess.* "Children judge each other primarily upon the basis of what they can do. . . . A child who cannot or is unwilling to engage in gross physical output is not generally accorded as high a place in the status hierarchy as a child who participates vigorously in the available games and activities."[12]

12. *Children can learn socially desirable cooperative and competitive behavior through play.* Cooperation is a social necessity. It is through cooperation that effective game situations evolve. By the same token, competition is an aspect of society that encourages initiative in societal endeavors. It has been suggested that competition and cooperation are both normal human activities. These aspects of human behavior cannot be suppressed without destroying social structure and individuality. Both cooperation and competition, in the proper perspective, are essential and desirable aspects of life, play, and social situations. Physical activity provides a setting for development of desirable behavior in these areas.

Some General Guidelines

Several guidelines for teaching and learning cannot be classified with the preceding guidelines but are none the less important. The following is a list of guidelines for general consideration by the teacher of physical education.

1. *Physical education is for all children.* Education has a basic purpose the development of the whole child. This whole child is to be provided the opportunity to achieve his full potential in all areas of learning. Physical education is a necessary and integral part of that educational program for every child.
2. *No two children are alike.* Each child is an individual. He is unique. Growth, development, learning, and environment all are involved in the evolution of this being. Teachers must recognize this principle and teach each child accordingly.
3. *All behavior involves the "whole" organism.* All experience involves the integration of total being. Physical activity is not physical only, but involves the mental, emotional, and all human processes. Learning is a result of all experiences. Regardless of the nature of the experience the "whole" individual is involved.
4. *Children emmulate the behavior of teachers.* Children, particularly in the elementary school years, identify with adult ideals, frequently the teacher, the parent or an athletic hero. When the identification is to an individual establishing a good example, the child is likely to manifest the type behavior that is the objective of educational programs.
5. *Children need both "self regulation" and proper supervision.* Although self regulation is important to effective learning for children, proper supervision is also important. Children must be exposed to the right combination of the two if learning is to be most effective. Too much supervision may result in dependence while too little supervision may result in a breakdown of "self regulation".

References

1. Beneke, F. W.: Uber das Volumen dez Herzens and die Weite der Arteria pulmonalis and Aorta ascendeus. Marburg, V. Theodor Kay, 1879.
2. Nash, J. B.: *Philosophy of Recreation and Leisure,* Wm. C. Brown Co., Inc., Dubuque, 1960, Chapter 13.
3. Brightbill, Charles K.: *Man and Leisure,* Englewood Cliffs, N.J., Prentice-Hall, Inc., 1961, p. 163.
4. Cratty, Bryant J.: *Psychology and Physical Activity,* Englewood Cliffs, N.J., Prentice-Hall, Inc., 1968, p. 91
5. Greenberg, Pearl: Competition in Children; An Experimental Study, *American Journal of Psychology.* 44:221–248, 1932.

6. Jones, Mary E. and Bayley, Nancy: Physical Maturing Among Boys as Related to Behavior, *Journal of Educational Psychology. 41:*129–148, 1950.
7. Schoenfeld, William A.: Inadequate Masculine Physiques as a Factor in Personality Development, *Psychosomatic Medicine. 12:*49–54, 1950.
8. Thorndike, E. L.: *The Fundamentals of Learning,* New York, Teacher's College, Columbia University, 1932.
9. Cratty, Bryant J.: *Psychology and Physical Activity,* Englewood Cliffs, N.J., Prentice-Hall, Inc., 1968.
10. Kelso, Louis O. and Adler, Mortimer: *The Capitalist Manifesto,* New York, Random House, 1958, p. 17–18.
11. Sutton-Smith, B. and Robert, J. M.: "Rubrics of Competitive Behavior, *34:*119–126, 1964.
12. Cratty, Bryant J.: *Psychology and Physical Activity,* Englewood Cliffs, N.J., Prentice-Hall, Inc., 1967, p. 52.

Bibliography

PERIODICALS

Erickson, Kenneth A.: The Principal's Physical Education Principles, *The Bulletin of The National Association of Secondary School Principals, 44:*13–16, May, 1960.

Foster, Frank P.: Warming Against Physical Fitness Mania, *New York Times Magazine,* Feb. 9, 1964.

Harrison, Clarke H.: Physical Fitness Benefit: A Summary of Research, *Education, 78:*460, April, 1958.

Hilssendager, Donald: Comparison of a Calisthenic and Non-Calisthenic Physical Education Program, *Research Quarterly, 37:*148, March, 1966.

Irving, Robert N., Jr.: Why All the Fuss About Fitness? *Educational Leadership, 20:*376, March, 1963.

Riordan, Ray: Fitness Through Elementary School Physical Education, *Physical Educator, 22:*22, March, 1964.

The Contributions of Physical Activity to Growth, *Research Quarterly, 31:* May, 1960 (Entire issue).

Editorial Staff, Our Unfit Youth, *Good Housekeeping,* Jan. 1962, pp. 123–125.

BOOKS

Comwell, Charles C. and France, Wellman L.: *Philosophy and Principles of Physical Education,* Englewood Cliffs, N.J., Prentice-Hall, Inc., 1963.

Irwin, Leslie W. and Humphrey, James H.: *Principles and Techniques of Supervision In Physical Education,* Dubuque, Wm C. Brown, Inc., 1954.

Williams, Jesse F.: *The Principles of Physical Education,* 8th ed., Philadelphia, W. B. Saunders Co., 1964.

4

The Learner

Perhaps the most important area of concern to the teacher, in developing programs, is understanding the learner. Guidelines and a founded point of view contribute to the teacher's ability to construct sound programs by contributing to the understanding of the foundations of physical education. Both an understanding of scientific guidelines and a founded point of view are vital to the teacher's ultimate success, but they contribute little to the understanding of the most vital element in the sound education program, namely the learner.

The learner or group of learners that the teacher must deal with in the school situation is a highly specific concern of the teacher. Learners are different from country to country, state to state, city to city, school to school, classroom to classroom, and individual to individual. Therefore, the study of the learner must be highly specific to the learning situation. For most effective assessment of the learner, each teacher must individually measure and evaluate the characteristics, needs, and abilities of the group for which he is responsible.

Because this text does not deal specifically with one tangible group of learners (*i.e.,* third graders in Jones Elementary School, Woodville, California), it is impossible to make a concrete assessment of the nature of any single learner or single specific group of learners. The text can, however, discuss generally accepted characteristics, needs, and interests of children in the age groups common to the elementary school. This chapter is an attempt to create a picture of the typical learner at each level of the elementary school. The teacher can use this as a guide in identifying characteristics, needs, and interests likely to be noticeable in a specific individual or a specific classroom of children. Many children will be above or below the "normal" levels of growth and development suggested for each grade level. However, the picture created by this general information may provide the sketch for the final portrait of the children for whom the learning program is provided.

Growth of the Learner

HEIGHT AND WEIGHT

Physical growth is by no means uniform. Individual growth differences occur at all ages as indicated by an exceptionally tall girl in the sixth grade or the extremely short boy in the third grade. These differences must be considered in developing objectives and programs in physical education. However, it should be recognized that children are more alike in their growth patterns than they are different. Assuming proper nutrition, freedom from disease and a reasonably good environment, all children will grow at a relatively constant rate during the elementary school years. The growth differences that do occur will be controlled by the hereditary background of the child but may be modified by environmental conditions. It is known that children with exceptional hereditary endowments, in terms of physical size, still follow relatively normal patterns in terms of the *rate* of growth. Figure 4-1 illustrates the height, weight, age and percentage of adult growth attained by the typical learner at any grade level. The special symbols ♂ and ♀ represent males and females respectively. By observing the symbols at each grade level the reader can determine the relative size of boys as compared to girls at any grade level.

That growth is quite steady is seen in the increase in size of the figures representing children at each grade level. Growth spurts do occur prior to the entrance to elementary school in the early years of childhood, and at the beginning of puberty. Neither of these growth spurts is represented to any great extent in Figure 4-1 because the early spurt normally occurs before entrance to elementary school and the adolescent spurt does not occur until the late elementary school years or until entrance into junior high school. However the fact that girls exceed boys in height and weight at age 11 for the first time does reflect the beginning of puberty for girls. Figure 4-2 illustrates the fact that puberty normally begins at approximately 13 years of age among boys and at approximately 11 years of age among girls. Each stick figure in the diagram represents 10% of the sample measured. Close observation of Figure 4-2 shows wide variation in the age at which physical maturity is attained for members of the same sex as well as showing wide variation between sexes. However, it is still worth mentioning that most elementary school children are pre-pubescent and thus growing at a relatively constant rate. Those children who have begun to mature in the ele-

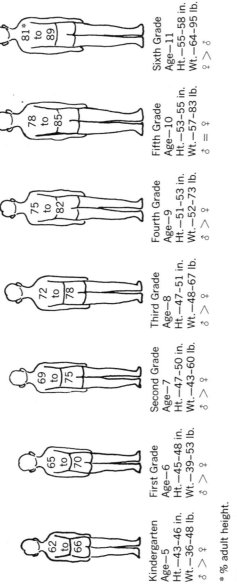

Kindergarten	First Grade	Second Grade	Third Grade	Fourth Grade	Fifth Grade	Sixth Grade
62 to 66	65 to 70	69 to 75	72 to 78	75 to 82	78 to 85	81* to 89
Age—5	Age—6	Age—7	Age—8	Age—9	Age—10	Age—11
Ht.—43–46 in.	Ht.—45–48 in.	Ht.—47–50 in.	Ht.—47–51 in.	Ht.—51–53 in.	Ht.—53–55 in.	Ht.—55–58 in.
Wt.—36–48 lb.	Wt.—39–53 lb.	Wt.—43–60 lb.	Wt.—48–67 lb.	Wt.—52–73 lb.	Wt.—57–83 lb.	Wt.—64–95 lb.
♂ > ♀	♂ > ♀	♂ > ♀	♂ > ♀	♂ > ♀	♂ = ♀	♀ > ♂

* % adult height.

FIG. 4-1 Normal Physiological Characteristics of Elementary School Children. (Based on information from How We Grow by Bayley, Nancy: The Encyclopedia of Child Care and Guidance, New York, Double-Day & Co., Inc., 1963.)

*adult height

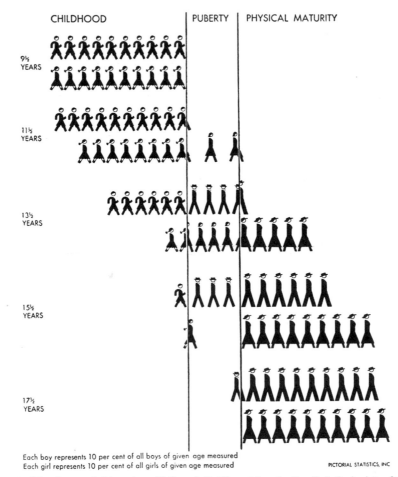

Each boy represents 10 per cent of all boys of given age measured
Each girl represents 10 per cent of all girls of given age measured

PICTORIAL STATISTICS, INC

FIG. 4-2 *When boys and girls mature. (Keliher, A. V.: Life and Growth. New York, D. Appleton-Century Co., 1941.)*

mentary school are likely to be more different than their peers than are expectional pre-pubescent children.

One environmental factor which may effect growth in addition to diet, sleep, and freedom of disease is exercise.[1] There is little doubt that there is a minimal amount of exercise which is prerequisite for supporting normal growth. Although this minimal level has not been adequately defined, it is clear that exercise does play a role in the normal growth of children.

BONES

During early childhood the bones are not completely calsified or ossified. The bones are much like cartilage, consisting of greater amounts of water and smaller amounts of mineral. As one gets older there is a gain of nearly

60% in the mineral content of the bones. Thus one measure of true physical age of a child, as contrasted with chronological age, is the amount of mineralization of the bones. A common measure of physical age consists of an x-ray picture of the small bones of the wrist to determine the ossification of these bones.

The mineralization of the bones is more rapid in girls than boys and this advanced bone growth is especially pronounced at the upper elementary school level because of the earlier maturation age of girls.

Figure 4-3 illustrates the basic changes in body proportions as the child grows older. The very young child has different proportions than does the older child or adult. Close observation of the figure would indicate considerable differences in the ultimate sizes of the different body parts at different age levels. For example, the head is approximately half full size at birth, while the legs grow to four or five times their birth length by the time the child becomes an adult. Thus it is the long levers of the body which are undergoing the largest growth rate during the school years.

CHANGES IN BODY PROPORTIONS FROM BIRTH TO MATURITY

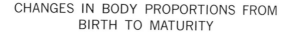
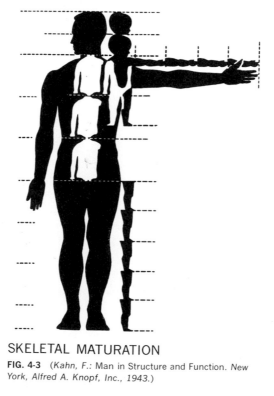

SKELETAL MATURATION

FIG. 4-3 (Kahn, F.: Man in Structure and Function. New York, Alfred A. Knopf, Inc., 1943.)

Exercise does appear to be a significant factor in affecting the growth of the skeletal system. Scientific evidence indicates exercise to stimulate greater growth in bone diameter, although it does not appear to effect the length of bone growth.

MUSCLES

As seen in Figure 4-1, the child may attain nearly 90% of his adult height by the age of 12 (sixth grade). Proportionally, the child's weight may not be as advanced as the height by this age. This is a result of the relatively slow development of the muscle tissue prior to puberty. Even in cases where weight increase is proportional to growth in height, a great amount of the body weight is likely to be fatty tissue in the pre-adolescent child.

At puberty, hormones are secreted which promote muscular development in girls as well as boys.[2] The male sex hormone as well as the adrenal hormones stimulate an increase in the weight of muscle tissue and enlarged muscle fibers. However, the female hormone tends to inhibit the development of excessive muscular growth. Thus the development of basic sex differences in muscle development after puberty. The increased muscle mass stimulated by the hormone changes results in a proportional decrease in percentage of body fat as compared with muscle mass after the beginning of puberty. Because of the sex differences in muscle build up after pubescence, the percentage of fatty tissues is greater among girls than among boys.

Exercise, specifically an overload in work intensity, causes increased muscle development, resulting in firmer, stronger, and more supple muscles. Exercise seems to promote the protein building power of the body causing great muscle growth in much the same way as the hormones stimulate muscle growth during puberty.[3]

HEART

As discussed in Chapter 3, the growth of the heart muscle is proportional to the blood carrying capacity of the blood vessel. The heart size is also roughly proportional to body size, but during the elementary school years the body growth may be slightly greater than the growth rate of the heart. Nevertheless, there is no evidence to indicate that a healthy heart can be injured through physical exercise. A number of safeguards are built into the body to prevent over strain such as: shortness of breath, pain in the side, and muscle cramps.[4]

Like any other muscle, the heart reacts to overload. Thus exercise stimulates heart growth both in size and in function.

HEALTH RELATED FITNESS

Of particular concern to the teacher is the development of health related fitness such as strength and endurance. These aspects of fitness are important because of their contribution to the prevention of such conditions as heart disease, low back pain, and other common medical complaints.

At some time in the life of every individual a level of fitness is attained which represents his life time maximum. At this time he will be fitter than at any other time in his life. It seems that the average individual reaches this maximal level some time during his school years. Except in the case of trained professional athletes and active physical laborers, the exercise and activities of the school days may not be equalled after graduation from high school or college. Figure 4-4 which is based on national performance physical fitness norms, would indicate that physical fitness curves are still increasing in boys at 17 or near high school graduation. The graph indicates a nearly linear increase in physical fitness as the young boy grows older. There does appear to be a slight lull in physical fitness performance in many boys around the age of 11 or 12. Observation of Figure 4-4 would indicate a potential increased strength and endurance among boys after high school since the curve has not reached its peak during the high school years. At any rate this graph gives a picture of the typical fitness development of an American boy but does not necessarily reflect "what should be" in terms of improved performance in strength and endurance.

Figure 4-5 illustrates patterns of development that indicate considerable

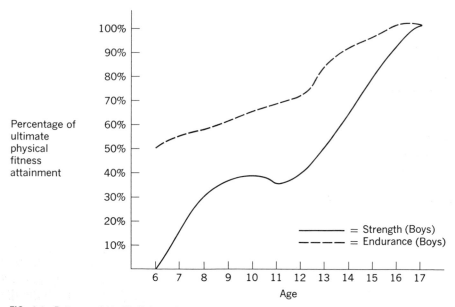

FIG. 4-4 *Patterns of Health Related Fitness Development of American Boys. (Based in part on the results of the AAHPER Youth Fitness Test, Youth Fitness Test Manual, Washington, D.C.: NEA Press, 1965.)*

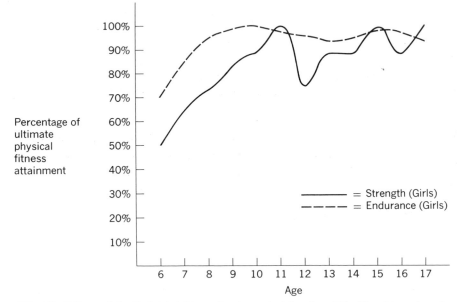

FIG. 4-5 *Patterns of Health Related Fitness Development of American Girls. (Based in part on the results of the AAHPER Youth Fitness Test, Youth Fitness Test Manual, Washington, D.C.: NEA Press, 1965.)*

differences between boys and girls. Unlike the boys, the linear relationship (*i.e.,* the older you are, the greater your performance) does not exist for girls. Maximal performance in feats of strength and endurance are accomplished, in many cases, at around 14 or 15 years of age and are never again to be equaled, even after the age of 16 or 17. As illustrated in Figure 4-5, near maximal performances occur frequently at age 10 or 11. These performances may never again be equaled for some individuals.

In reading Figures 4-4 and 4-5, it is important to recognize that 100% of fitness attainment merely represents that point in time when the maximal amount of fitness is attained in the lifetime of an average individual. This 100% might be a low level of performance but still be the best the individual ever attains in physical fitness performance. It would seem reasonable that the level of fitness attained at the lifetime peak could be improved for almost all individuals. However, it is the intention of this discussion to point out at what age maximal fitness occurs in most individuals, disregarding the actual amount of fitness attained at that lifetime peak.

Figure 4-6 illustrates the "drop off" characteristic of strength and endurance performances among American girls. Much discussion has occurred concerning the reason for this physical fitness drop at such an early age. Many have suggested that the drop in performance may be a result, at least in part, of sociological expectations and that this drop could be eliminated or corrected if proper attitudes prevailed among girls concerning the cosmetic value of exercise. If this were true, their performance should get better as these girls grow older. Figure 4-6 illustrates what such a possible "fitness attainment curve" might look like if this were true. The suggestion is that American girls are expected to discontinue physical performance in order to concentrate on the social graces when they reach high school.

There is little doubt that biological changes in puberty, as characterized by hormone changes, effect the strength and endurance potential of girls. These biological changes might account for the lull in performance in the age groups of 9, 10, and 11. However, this one fact can hardly account for the dramatic loss of performance at post pubescent ages as indicated in Figure 4-6, especially since muscle growth is stimulated after puberty in girls as well as boys although to a lesser extent. Current evidence would indicate that both biological and sociological factors are involved in this decreased performance. The lack of motivation to perform well in testing situations might account for some of the drop off. It is my opinion that no single factor can completely account for the drop in performance but that increased understanding and emphasis on the values of physical fitness could modify this drop off in performance. Since attitudes are developed early, it might be hypothesized that proper programs in the elementary school might help overcome social variables which might stymie physical fitness performance in later life.

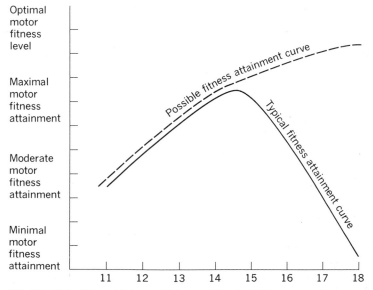

FIG. 4-6 *Motor Fitness Attainment Patterns of American Girls.*

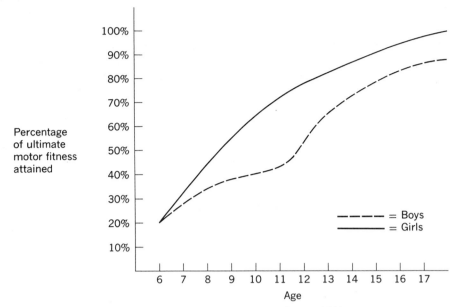

FIG. 4-7 *Patterns of Motor Fitness Development of American Boys and Girls.*

MOTOR FITNESS

Other variables commonly considered to be physical fitness variables include such aspects as: power, speed, and agility. Although these are not specifically health related, they are important as outcomes of physical education programs. For this reason it is important to consider growth patterns in relation to these particular variables.

Figure 4-7 indicates improved performance in these aspects with increased age for both boys and girls. The more rapidly elevating curve for girls does not indicate greater performance for girls in these variables, rather it indicates that the amount of ultimate attainment for girls is attained earlier and more steadily than is the maximal attainment for boys. Boys appear to level off slightly prior to puberty and then have a spurt in development of these aspects at the onset of puberty. The boys attain their maximal level of performance at a later age than do the girls. In terms of absolute performance, American boys exceed American girls in performance at all age levels.

GENERAL MOTOR ABILITY

Closely associated with motor fitness is general motor ability. This skill variable involving the ability of the individual to manage his own body in various skill situations, is frequently evaluated by means of the Brace Test (Figure 4-8). As an intelligence test is supposed to measure intellectual ability or potential, the Brace test is frequently referred to as a measure of skill potential. Certainly this variable relates to physical fitness, especially motor fitness but it is purported to measure independent variables associated with basic skill potential. Figure 4-8 presents patterns of development of boys and girls in this measure of potential skill ability. As in the other measures of physical performance, the performance of boys increases with age, with maximal performance being achieved at the later adolescent ages. However, the drop off in the performance of girls is evidenced in much the same way as it was with physical fitness measures. The maximal performances of girls is attained between the ages of 12 and 15 with a drop off occurring after these ages.

It should be pointed out that, like intelligence, general motor ability is an elusive quality. Since many specific skill capabilities make up skill potential, a true general motor ability probably does not exist. Just as intelligence is a combination of many factors, so is general motor ability. The Brace Test, although not a true measure of skill potential, is a test which gives an

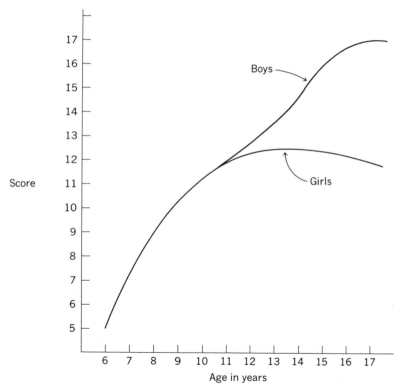

FIG. 4-8 *General Motor Ability (Brace Test). (Brace, D. K. Measuring Motor Ability, Courtesy of A. S. Barnes.)*

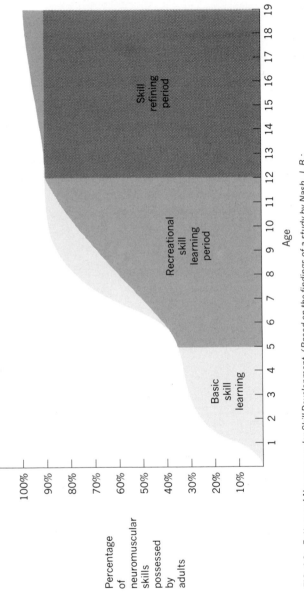

FIG. 4-9 Patterns of Neuromuscular Skill Development. (Based on the findings of a study by Nash, J. B.: Philosophy of Recreation and Leisure, Dubuque, William C. Brown Co., Inc., 1960.)

indication of current skill levels resulting from basic skill potential as well as from previous skill learning.

THE SKILL LEARNING YEARS

Figure 4-9 indicates that many of the basic motor skills learned during a lifetime of the individual are attained during the first 5 years of life. As suggested earlier in the text, approximately 85 to 90% of the recreational skills learned by the average individual are learned prior to the age of 12. The period after the age of 12 is considered as the skill refining period because this is the time when the individual is improving performance in skills but is not learning many new basic skills. It is also pointed out in Figure 4-9 that the learning characteristic of a particular age group may be carried over into the next but the pattern is most likely to occur as illustrated. Thus a person may learn new skills later in life, but more likely he will concentrate on improving those skills which he already knows.

INTELLECTUAL GROWTH

Figure 4-10 represents individual intelligence curves for five boys and five girls. The curves plotted over a 25-year period aptly illustrate the differences in the rate of intellectural maturation in individuals of varying intellectual capability. As would be expected, all of the children increase in score as they mature. However, it is especially interesting to note that differences in intellectual capacity tend to become more apparent as the

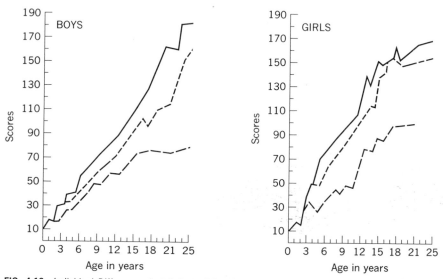

FIG. 4-10 *Individual Differences in Intellectual Development.* (*Courtesy of Bayley, Nancy:* American Psychol., 10:805–818, 1955.)

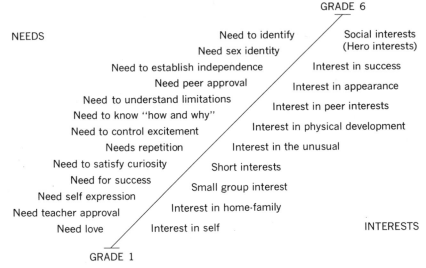

GRADE 6

NEEDS

Need to identify
Need sex identity
Need to establish independence
Need peer approval
Need to understand limitations
Need to know "how and why"
Need to control excitement
Needs repetition
Need to satisfy curiosity
Need for success
Need self expression
Need teacher approval
Need love

Social interests
(Hero interests)
Interest in success
Interest in appearance
Interest in peer interests
Interest in physical development
Interest in the unusual
Short interests
Small group interest
Interest in home-family
Interest in self

INTERESTS

GRADE 1

FIG. 4-11   *Social and Emotional Growth.*

individual's age increases. Fluctuation in intelligence curves for a given individual may be a result of any number of factors such as physical health on test days, motivation to score well, and the like.

SOCIAL-EMOTIONAL GROWTH

If such objectives as sportsmanship and leadership are to be concerns of physical education, it is essential that the growth and development in social-emotional areas be understood. Figure 4-11 illustrates some of the growth patterns in these areas by suggesting some of the social-emotional needs and interests of children at various age levels in the elementary school. Most noticable is the shift from the self interest of the child to the more social characteristics of the intermediate grade child.

References

1. Rarick, G. Lawrence: Exercise and Growth During the Growing Years, *Journal of Health, Physical Education and Recreation*, 39:37–38, 1968.
2. Korenchevsky, V., Hall, K., Burbank, R. C., and Cohen, J.: Hepatotrophic and Cardiotrophic Properties of Sex Hormones, *British Medical Journal*, 1:396–399, 1941.
3. Rarick, G. Lawrence: Exercise and Growth, in *Science and Medicine of Exercise and Sport.* Edited by Warren R. Johnson, New York, Harper and Row, 1966, p. 440.
4. Espenschade, Anne: Organic and Neuromuscular Development, *Children In Focus*, A Yearbook of The AAHPER, Washington, NEA Press, 1954, p. 56.

Bibliography

PERIODICALS

Espenschade, Anna: Motor Performance in Adolescence, Including the Study of Relationship with Measures of Physical Growth and Maturity, Monograph, *Society for Research in Child Development,* Volume 5, Serial 24, #1.

Glease, G. T. and Klausmier, H. J.: Relationship Between Variability in Physical Growth and Academic Achievement Among Third and Fifth Grade Children, *Journal of Educational Research,* March 1958, p. 521.

Havighurst, Robert J.: Physical Education and the Tasks of the Body, *Anthology of Contemporary Readings,* Edited by Slusher and Lockhart, Dubuque, Wm. C. Brown & Co., 1966.

Sutton-Smith, B., Rosenburg B. G. and Morgan, E. F.: Development of Sex Differences in Play Choices of Adolescents, *Child Development, 34:*119–126, 1963.

BOOKS

English, H. B.: *Dynamics of Child Development.* New York, Holt, Rinehart & Winston, 1961.

Gesell, Arnold L.: *The Child From 5 to 10.* New York, Harper & Brothers, 1948.

Harlock, Elizabeth B.: *Child Development.* New York, McGraw-Hill Book Co., 1950.

Jenkins, G. G., Shacter, H. S. and Bauer, W. W.: *These Are Your Children.* 3rd ed., Chicago, Scott, Foresman & Co., 1966.

Olson, Willard C.: *Child Development.* Boston, D. C. Heath & Co., 1949.

United States Department of Health, Education and Welfare, Office of Education. *Basic Body Measurements of School Age Children.* Washington, June 1957.

Aahper Yearbook, *Children in Focus.* Washington, D.C., NEA Press, 1954.

Johnson, Warren (Ed.): *Science and Medicine of Exercise and Sports.* New York, Harper & Row, 1966.

Clarke, H. H. and Haar, F. B.: *Health & Physical Education for the Elementary School Classroom Teacher.* Englewood Cliffs, N.J., Prentice-Hall, Inc., 1964.

5

Objectives

On the basis of a founded point of view, a knowledge of basic guidelines, and a knowledge of the learner, the teacher is challenged with determining the objectives of physical education. What is the responsibility of physical education in helping the child become a fully functioning healthy individual? Perhaps the best way to begin to answer this question is to determine the general objectives of the physical education program disregarding the grade or age level of the children. Certain purposes of physical education are general enough and of enough magnitude that they require the efforts of physical educators at all grade levels. Once these general objectives have been defined, the teacher can determine the needs of specific children so as to outline the specific objectives for children at any grade or ability level.

The Physical-Fitness Objective

One of the major contributions made by the physical education program to the total education of the child is the development and understanding of physical fitness. It has often been said that physical fitness is the unique objective of physical education in that physical education is the only area of the total curriculum which has physical fitness as its specific educational concern.[1]

A physical fitness report originally appearing in the *New York State Journal of Medicine* in the late 1950's was serious enough in its implications to later be called the "Report that Shocked the President."[2] This report, pointing out the serious deficiencies in the physical fitness levels of American youth, included the results of considerable research and was ultimately

46

responsible for the founding of the President's Council on Youth Fitness by President Eisenhower. This council, now called the President's Council on Physical Fitness, is charged with initiating action to improve the physical fitness level of *all* American citizens. One immediate concern was the improvement of physical education programs.

The original report that "Shocked the President" included test results indicating exceptionally low levels of physical fitness among our youth. These reports were especially shocking because of the implication that American children were less fit than children in other parts of the world. Most of these studies used the Kraus-Weber test as a basis for measuring the level of fitness in children. The most notable of these studies is the one reported by Kraus and Hirschland (Box 5-1). Other studies indicated children in the United States to be less fit than children in Japan,[3] and Denmark.[4] One study indicated that British girls were more fit than American boys.[5]

The late President Kennedy reinforced the need for physical education programs, specifically when he said:

> In a sense, physical fitness is the basis of all activity of our society . . . For physical fitness is not only one of the most important keys to a healthy body, it is a basis of dynamic and creative intellectual activity . . . For the physical vigor of our country is one of America's most precious resources. If we waste and neglect this resource, if we allow it to dwindle and grow soft, then we will destroy much of our ability to meet great and vital challenges which confront our people. We will be unable to realize our potential as a nation.[6]

Kennedy also suggested the importance of physical fitness in the following statement:

> But the harsh fact of the matter is that there is also an increasingly large number of young Americans who are neglecting their bodies —whose physical fitness is not what it should be—who are getting soft. And such softness on the part of individual citizens can help to strip and destroy the vitality of a nation.[6]

The efforts of Presidents Eisenhower, Kennedy and the Council on Physical Fitness seem to be paying dividends if recent reports are accurate. In a recent educational report, President Johnson reported the following information:

> In every corner of our nation more boys and girls are spending more time each day in healthful exercises and games.[7]

President Johnson, also a supporter of the need for physical education programs, went on to report that two-thirds of schools have strengthened their physical education programs since the original report to President

BOX 5-1. THE PHYSICAL VITALITY OF OUR YOUTH

Purpose. This investigation was designed to determine the fitness of American youth as measured by a minimal test of muscular strength and to compare these levels of fitness in American youth (6 to 16) to the levels of fitness possessed by European children. This study was conducted in response to repeated treatment of problems of poor posture and poor musculature in children treated in an American medical clinic.

Procedure. Children were tested on the Kraus-Weber test in the following numbers: 4000 Americans, 2000 Italians and Austrians, and 1150 Swiss. Children were selected for testing from cities of similar sizes in all countries. The Kraus-Weber test was used as the test of minimal fitness. This test includes six items administered on a pass or fail basis. The items test strength and flexibility of the large muscle groups of the body. Only children classified as "well" were tested.

Results.

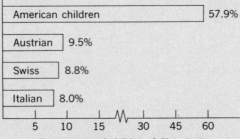

Percentage of children failing test

Conclusions. American children are not as fit as European children. At no age level do the American children approach the fitness levels of European children. American children seem to be the product of a "highly mechanized society," while European children must still walk everywhere they go. American children do not get sufficient exercise. American physical education programs need expansion, especially on the elementary and pre-school levels.

Kraus, Hans and Hirschland, Ruth P.: Minimum Muscular Fitness Tests in School Children, *Research Quarterly, 25*:178–187, 1954.

Eisenhower. Seventeen states have increased school physical education requirements, and teaching positions in health and physical education have increased 27%, while the increase in school enrollment has increased only 11%. Indications are that many more children are now passing physical fitness tests since the inception of the new programs. A most recent study by Hunsicker indicates that considerable improvement has taken place in the fitness of our youth since 1958 (Box 5-2).

However, many are quick to point out that recent improvements in the fitness of our youth do not mean that all needs are being met. As early as 1963, President Kennedy reported progress in the drive to improve the fitness level of our youth but he was quick to point out the need for continuing efforts in this area.[8] President Johnson pointed out that 14% of our children are still not exercising at all in the schools. Another 27% join in physical activity only 1 or 2 days a week. Johnson urges "Building the Great Society is a task which will test our strength and staying power, and we must see to it that the rising generation of Americans are equal to the task.[7]

The Social-Emotional Objective

Many claims have been made for sports and physical education concerning the social and emotional benefits of these activities. Sports are alleged to build sportsmanship, leadership, character and other social and personality variables. In as much as free play and physical education periods are situations during the school day when children can interact socially, it seems logical to assume some accomplishment of these desired outcomes. The key to the development of these social-emotional values seems to be an organized effort directed specifically toward the development of these values. The scientific evidence tends to support this concept:

> Supervised recreation, or sport seems to act as a deterrent to juvenile delinquency, but unsupervised recreation and certain forms of commercial recreation apparently have deleterious effects.[9]

Bucher states:

> Education plays an important part in solving social problems. Physical education, as part of the total educational process, can contribute to this goal. Physical education is a social experience. Through physical activities great strides can be made in achieving social progress and more satisfaction in living. Juvenile delinquency, race prejudice, intolerance and discrimination can be alleviated and progress can be made toward their elimination from democratic society.[10]

The concept that sports have been one area where race differences are forgotten is often generalized to physical education, with the suggestion that children learn to forget prejudices best in a physical education setting. A recent study by Morgan and Nussell tends to substantiate the idea suggesting physical education class to be a place where children can truly develop social values (Box 5-3).

BOX 5-2. IMPROVEMENT IN YOUTH PHYSICAL FITNESS

Purpose. This study was conducted to establish norms for the AAHPER physical fitness test, to determine current levels of physical fitness among American children and to compare the levels of fitness of children in 1965 with the levels of youth fitness in 1958.

Procedures. As in a study conducted in 1958 by the same authors, a representative sample of boys and girls in the United States were tested on the seven items of the AAHPER physical fitness test. The sample included 500 boys and 500 girls in each grade level, grades 5 to 12. 100% of the schools sampled responded.

Computers established percentile scores for each sex, grade level and fitness item. Scores on the test items were compared with the scores of the similar study done in 1958.

Results. The results indicated that scores on physical fitness measures among American children were greater in 1965 than in 1958. In most tests these improvements were statistically significant. The following figures illustrate the physical fitness increases:

COMPARISON OF FITNESS DATA, 1958–1965

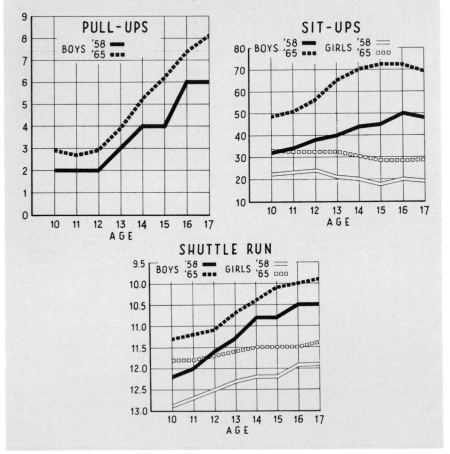

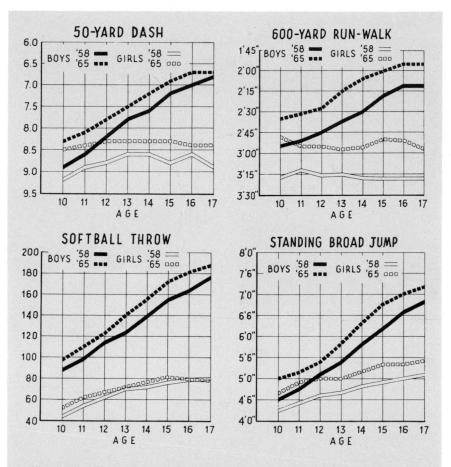

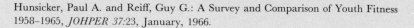

Conclusions. The results indicate that ". . . the physical fitness level of public school children, grades 5 to 12, in 1965 was above that in 1958."

Hunsicker, Paul A. and Reiff, Guy G.: A Survey and Comparison of Youth Fitness 1958–1965, *JOHPER 37:*23, January, 1966.

Physical education and play are also considered to contribute to the social development of the individual through aiding personality development. Cavanaugh[11] and others indicate that individuals who play, recreate and participate in games, dance, and other physical education activities tend to be better adjusted than those who do not participate.

Henry Harlow, the famous student of primate behavior, has done considerable research with monkeys and with children which suggests "play is essential to personality development." Harlow states, "Of course research

BOX 5-3. PLAY AND SOCIAL INTERACTION

Purpose. The purpose of this study was to compare the relationships of play preference to play behavior and to investigate other variables of social interaction among third grade children of different racial and social groups.

Procedure. Thirty-nine third grade boys and girls were studied to determine social interactions among Negro children, orphan Caucasian children and non-orphan Caucasian children. Sociograms were constructed to determine boy-girl social interactions and to determine interactions between the three sub-groups studied.

Sociograms were constructed according to the following: seating choices, work with choices, and play choices. Children were then observed in actual play situations to determine choices in tag type games. Actual game choices were compared to suggested play choices. Other choice comparisons were made.

Results. Although popular students and isolates tended to remain popular or isolates in the game situations, the suggested play choices were not the actual play choices. Significant deviations occurred from suggested choices to actual choices. Many intergroup choices occurred in the play situations.

Conclusions. "There are apparently factors operating in the dynamic play situation which alter expected behavior as based on play preference." Play may be a variable which aids in the break down of social barriers.

Nussell, Edward and Morgan, William: Play Preference and Play Behavior in a Group of Third Grade Children, A paper presented to the research section of the Ohio Association of Health, Physical Education and Recreation, 1965.

on non-human animals, even monkeys, will never resolve the baffling complex roles of various kinds of early experiences in the development of the human personality. It is clear, however, that important theoretical and practical questions in this realm can be resolved by the use of monkeys." He further suggests a "close behavioral resemblence of disturbed monkies to disturbed children." A classical study by Harlow illustrates the extreme social importance of peer play in the development of the personality (Box 5-4).

There is no doubt that social experiences are vital to the development of the child. Observation of the behavior of elementary school children would illustrate the importance of social acceptance to the child. That the social relationships of the children are related to physical prowess is observed in the "fad" patterns in wearing apparel. Parents soon become aware of the social values of wearing sneakers or gym shoes to school. Other sports apparel

BOX 5-4. IMPORTANCE OF PEER PLAY RELATIONSHIPS

Purpose. Originally the purpose of this study was to obtain sturdy mother monkeys for research purposes. When monkeys were isolated, they developed social and sexual abnormalities. This study was conducted to determine the importance of peer relationships in the prevention of these abnormalities.

Procedures. Young Rhesus monkeys were studied under several experimental situations. The young monkeys were raised in the following environments:

1. With wire surrogate mothers
2. With terry cloth surrogate mothers
3. With real mothers
4. With peers and no mothers.

Monkeys were raised in combination situations, that is, with peers and surrogate or real mothers also. Surrogate mothers fed the young monkeys through nipples. Behavior of the monkeys raised in these different environments were then studied to determine the importance of peer play and mother-baby relationships in social development.

Results. Monkeys raised with peers and artificial mothers were superior in play, sex behavior and self-defense ability when compared to monkeys raised with real mothers and no peer play. Monkeys having no peer play experience, having been raised only with mother-baby relationships, displayed abnormal self-aggressive behavior, compulsive habits and other abnormal behaviors. Monkeys raised with peers and artificial mothers did not display these characteristics.

Conclusions. Peer play relationships are essential to personality development among young monkeys. "It is clear that important theoretical and practical questions can be resolved by the study of monkeys."

Harlow, Henry F.: and Harlow, Margaret K.: Social Deprivation in Monkeys, *Scientific American, 207*:138, November, 1962.

are extremely popular among children, such as shirts bearing numerals resembling team uniforms.

Noting this phenomenon, investigators have currently been concerned with understanding the importance of physical prowess as a variable in the developing self image of the child. Schoenfeld indicated that boys who lack adequate physical development tend to have personality problems.[12] Findings of a number of studies indicate that physical prowess is an important factor in social development as well as in developing a desirable self image.[13-15]

However, all situations in physical education do not necessarily develop desired social-emotional outcomes. When asked to write on the topic, "What does physical education mean to me?", a 10-year-old girl responded:

I hate to go to gym, I do,
Tho' I like soccer and baseball, too;
But the kids are unkind just the same,
That's what I don't like about the game.

When I do something wrong they boo,
And I have done it wrong, tis true,
But if they wouldn't boo at me,
Why I'd a better player be.

I'm shaky for fear they will boo;
And I'm terribly nervous, too,
When I missed the ball the other team won,
That is why gym is no fun.[16]

It might be suggested that an improvement could occur in this youngsters reaction if social objectives had been considered and activities were planned to help children meet personal potentials. Perhaps the girl's concept of physical education might change to read:

I like to go to gym, I do,
We do lots of things there, some old and some new.
The kids are oh! so kind to me,
For that's part of the game too, you see.

When I do something wrong they say—
Oh you'll do better another day.
They help me try to do better each time
And when I do, up a tree I could climb.

Now I never get nervous when I'm in Phys. Ed.
And when I do wrong, there nothing is said.
For everyone knows that mistakes are made
And improvement takes place with a little aid.[17]

Rarick and McKee after studying third grade children suggest, "As children grow older, proficiency in gross motor activity assumes greater importance as evidenced by the prestige value placed on skillful performance by the child's peers."[18]

There seems to be little doubt that physical education has a signifiant contribution to make in the area of social and personality development, especially when programs are designed with these outcomes in mind.

The Skill Objective

The learning of motor skills is a means as well as an end. Not only do we wish for children to develop skill so that they may function fully in child-

SKILL LEARNING
IS IMPORTANT
AT ALL STAGES
OF DEVELOPMENT

FIG. 5-1

hood, but it is also essential that we develop skill as a means toward accomplishing other physical education objectives.

Nash[19] pointed out the importance of skill learning as a means to developing physical education objectives in the following statement:

> Skills lay the foundation for at least three phases of development: a) organic power, b) thinking and problem solving, and c) emotional adjustment. It is during the first few years of life, certainly before the age of twelve, that the child lays down an organic basis upon which he must build for life.

Just as reading is a skill which must be learned as a means to further learning, so is motor skill a means to other ends in learning. However, skill is and should also be an end in itself. With the ever increasing amounts of leisure time available to American citizens, skill becomes a way of effectively using leisure. Teaching children skills that can be used during free time becomes a worthy end in itself. As discussed in Chapter 3, people do things at which they are successful. As part of the goal of developing the fully functioning individual, it is important to provide learners with enough skill for them to be able to succeed in the leisure activities of their choice.

Part of the skill objective is to provide each learner with a wide variety of skill in those activities which will help him in performing the skills of normal day living as well as the skills normally used during the leisure time. Thus, the teacher is concerned with promoting fundamental skill learning such as walking, running, falling, jumping, and swimming. By the same token such leisure time skills as tennis, badminton, seasonal sports and others are important as part of the general skill objective.

The Weight-Control Objective

Of major concern to many American citizens is the problem of obesity or overweightness. Although much of the concern is among teen aged and adult women, for cosmetic reasons, it is becoming clearer every day that obesity is a real problem among children. Recent studies indicate that 15 to 20% of American and British children are obese.[20-22]

Even more startling than these findings are those of Stunkard and Burt who report that childhood obesity is likely to develop into adult obesity.[23] Analysis of data collected on 2000 individuals over an extended period of time indicates the chances of an obese child becoming a normal weight adult to be 1 in 4. Further, the chances of becoming a normal adult, if this excess weight is not lost in adolescence, are 1 in 28. Thus the idea that "baby fat" is a sign of health or that children will outgrow this condition is unfounded.

That a balance between caloric intake and caloric expenditure is necessary for weight control was reported in Chapter 3. However, it is of interest to note the findings of investigators concerning the best way to maintain this balance. Recent findings indicate inactivity (lack of energy expenditure) to be as serious as overeating in the development of childhood obesity (Box 5-5). Studies of girls in camp situations indicate obese girls eat less than non-obese girls and are considerably less active than their non-obese counterparts.[24] There is little doubt that both overeating and lack of physical activity are culprits in the development and maintenance of obesity. Regulating physical activity is of particular concern in teaching physical education.

Two misconceptions have been particularly damaging to the idea that exercise or activity can be a significant factor in weight control. First, the idea that long periods of exercise are necessary if the activity is to be an effective contributor to weight loss. Although this is true, exercise need not be performed all at one time for maximal benefits in controlling weight. Short periods of exercise performed daily in addition to normal routine can be effective in weight reduction. For example, all other things being equal, a secretary changing from a manual to an electric typewriter will gain 5

BOX 5-5. DIET AND ACTIVITY OF ELEMENTARY SCHOOL CHILDREN

Purpose. To determine the relative contributions of diet and physical inactivity in the development of childhood obesity.

Procedures. Diet records of 50 fifth grade children were collected over a 7-day period. During this week the children were filmed during regular physical education classes. The film was analyzed and an activity score was determined for each child. The children were assigned to one of four groups on the basis of body fatness (determined by skinfold measurement). The four groups were compared on diet and physical activity levels.

Results. Obese children ate no more than non obese children nor did they consume more or less amounts of protein, fat or carbohydrate. The obese children were significantly less active in all activity situations than were their non obese peers.

Conclusions. The relative inactivity of the obese children and the relatively similar diets of all children regardless of body fat, tended to support the contention that inactivity may be as important or more important than excessive caloric intake in the development and maintenance of childhood obesity.

Corbin, Charles B., and Pletcher, Phillip: The Diet and Physical Patterns of Obese and Non Obese Elementary School Children, A paper presented to the research section of the American Association of Health, Physical Education and Recreation Convention, Las Vegas, 1967.

ACTIVITY IS AN
IMPORTANT
FACTOR IN WEIGHT
CONTROL

FIG. 5-2

pounds over the course of one year—just because of the decrease in energy expenditure. Thus, one can visualize the accumulative effects of exercise and activity in controlling weight.

A second misconception is that exercise increases appetite. Although this may be true at high levels of activity, it is not true for short bouts of exercise normally used as measures of weight control.[24]

The physical educator's responsibility is to help individuals realize balance between caloric intake and expenditure. In the case of those wishing to lose weight, the objective is to provide an imbalance in favor of greater expenditure in relation to caloric intake. The converse is true for those wishing to gain weight.

The Cognitive-Affective Objective

It is the obligation of schools to help children learn to learn. Although many objectives of the physical education program are directed toward this goal, it is through the development of cognitive-affective objectives that children learn to learn as opposed to learning information only.

The Cognitive-Affective objective is accomplished in two basic ways: (*a*) concept forming and (*b*) concept using. Conceptual knowledge (concept forming) is more than verbal knowledge or attitudes (overt expression). Conceptual knowledge implies the meaning and interpretation of some event or fact. Concept using is the ultimate goal to be accomplished. Naturally, concept using requires prerequisite concept formation. Thus concept forming provides a basis for thought and action (concept using).

In physical education it is becoming increasingly clearer that understanding and the formation and use of concepts about exercise and movement must be developed early if adults are going to make intelligent decisions about exercise and movement in later life. Intelligent decision making is *not* an automatic occurrence, it depends on the ability to think. "Thinking is the process of organizing and storing concepts . . ."[25]

An Ultimate Purpose—The Carry Over Objective

In helping a child achieve his potential in terms of the above-stated objectives, the teacher is most often concerned with the current performances of the children. Is the child physically fit enough? Is he skillful within his own limitations? Certainly these questions and others are important, but of ultimate concern to the educator is whether these values of physical education will be "carried over" or applied to the adult living situation.

The concern is not merely with today but with the individual's ability to continue to function fully as an adult in our society. This idea could be applied to each of the above listed objectives.

1. Does the individual remain physically fit as an adult?
2. Does the individual continue to perform skillfully and to reap the benefits of such skillful performance?
3. Does the individual function as a socially-emotionally efficient adult?
4. Does the individual maintain desirable weight as an adult?
5. Do desirable attitudes and appreciations persist in adulthood?
6. Are understandings of physical education applied to adult daily life situations?

This "carry over" objective is one which is part of all other objectives but is also the ultimate measure of success of an effective physical education program.

Developing Operational Objectives

Once the teacher understands the basic objectives of physical education, he can begin to determine the specific purposes for any particular grade level. What should the teacher expect to help children accomplish as part of helping them become fully functioning individuals? In answering this question the teacher establishes the specific objectives for his group of learners.

Since all teachers will be concerned with accomplishing the previously listed general objectives, regardless of the grade level, it then becomes their task to define specific operational objectives within each of the general objectives of physical education. These operational objectives must be stated in such a way as to be practical and reasonable as far as their accomplishment by students. These statements of objectives are the blueprints on which the programs of physical education are based. Like blueprints, they must outline what is to be done in such a way that the proper action can be taken in an unambiguous way. Certainly it is worth pointing out that objectives or blueprints are merely the basic plans which are designed to provide the accomplishment of predetermined basic needs. Ultimately many things may be done that are not outlined in objectives or blueprints and it would be foolish to be limited to these basic statements. However, because certain basic requirements must be accomplished as prerequisites which are necessary for things to be accomplished later, the statement of objectives is one type of insurance for providing for these basic prerequisites. It is necessary to state specific objectives as the most important essential outcomes of a particular program. A variety of experiences may provide many concomitant outcomes but the essential outcomes must be emphasized.

A practical plan for determining these specific operational outcomes is outlined in Figure 5-3.

The general objectives are the outgrowth of ones point of view and the guidelines basic to physical education. Each teacher then designs specific objectives based on his own point of view, the guidelines of physical educa-

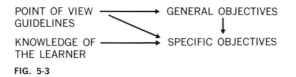

FIG. 5-3

tion and guided by the general objectives of physical education. After evaluating the characteristics, needs and interests of his specific learners, the teacher designs a number of specific objectives within each of the general objectives which have already been established as consistent with the foundation areas of physical education.

The teacher outlines a number of specific objectives within each general objective but as related to learners of a particular age group. Some examples of specific operational objectives within general objective headings for various grade levels are listed below:

Physical Fitness   (Grade 1)
1. Development of large muscle strength, specifically the muscles of the trunk and around the large joints of the body. (Behavioral Expectation: Pass all of the items of the Kraus-Weber Test.)
2. Development of simple dynamic and static balance. (Behavioral Expectation: Perform simple stunts such as stork stand, one foot hop, etc.)
3. Development of simple agility and ability to change body position. (Behavioral Expectation: Perform zig-zag run around obstacles.)

Skill   (Grade 2)
1. Development of fundamental skills of catching, throwing, skipping, striking and kicking.
2. Maintenance of fundamental skill ability in walking, running, leaping, and hopping. (developed in earlier grade)
3. Development of skill in a variety of games involving fundamental skills.
4. Development of basic skills of walking and galloping to music.
5. Developing an understanding of force, space, time, and other movement elements.

Weight Control   (Grade 3)
1. Expending energy through sustained physical performance.
2. Developing an understanding of the value of exercise in weight control.

Social Emotional   (Grade 5)
1. Provide experience for self evaluation to help the child understand his self limitations. (Behavioral Expectations: Perform and improve on selected self testing stunts.)

2. Provide situations where all students can achieve.
3. Development of social responsibility in group situations. (Behavioral Expectation: Controls temper, helps enforce and obeys both moral and game rules.)
4. Development of independence through providing for situations involving making choices and decisions.
5. Provide for opportunities to record personal improvements in physical performance.

Cognitive-Affective (Grade 6)
1. Development of an understanding of exercise and its relation to the development of the heart and circulatory system.
2. Development of an understanding of overload as a factor in developing strength.
3. Development of an understanding of the rules of seasonal cultural activities.
4. Development of an understanding of the value of specific exercise in developing physical fitness.
5. Development of an understanding of courtesies of seasonal cultural activities.

It is important to note that the above listed specific operational objectives are only hypothetical examples of the type of objective which would be practical in building elementary school physical education programs. The actual objectives for any particular program would ultimately depend on the specific group of students for which the program is designed. However, the above listed objectives would be the type that each teacher would develop as the blueprints for the program.

Guidelines for Developing Specific Operational Objectives

The following points should be considered in preparing the specific objectives for a specific group of learners.

1. Consider the specific characteristics, needs, and interests of the learners in your class.
2. List only the most important objectives within each of the general objectives.
3. Be brief. If too many objectives are listed they become bulky and unmanageable.
4. Try to list objectives which can be evaluated.
5. Be specific. All physical education objectives cannot be accomplished in one year. Try to accomplish *something* rather than a whole lot of nothing.
6. Do not limit student experiences to specific objectives, but do strive to accomplish the specific objectives.

References

1. Kaufman, Raymond, Our Unique Contribution, *JOHPER, 31:*26+ , September 1960.
2. Boyle, Robert H.: The Report That Shocked The President, *Sports Illustrated, 3:*30, August 15, 1955.
3. JOHPER Staff, Are Japanese Youth More Fit than American Youth?, *JOHPER, 31:*61, February, 1960.
4. Knuttgen, Howard G.: Comparison of Fitness of Danish and American School Children, *Research Quarterly, 32:*190–196, May, 1961.
5. Pohndorf, Richard H.: British Youth Takes a Fitness Test, *JOHPER, 32:*75, January, 1961.
6. Kennedy, John F.: The Soft American, *Sports Illustrated, 13:*15, Dec. 26, 1960.
7. President Johnson as quoted by Theodore Shuchat, "Educational Scene," *Grade Teacher, 82:*6, 1965.
8. Kennedy, John F.: Physical Fitness: A Progress Report, *Look, 27:*82–83, Aug. 13, 1963.
9. Neumeyer, M. H.: *Juvenile Delinquency in Modern Society,* Princeton, N.J., Van Norstrand, 1961, p. 228
10. Bucher, Charles A.: *Foundations of Physical Education,* St. Louis, C. V. Mosby Co., 1960, p. 328.
11. Cavanaugh, Jean: Recreation in Relation to Personality Adjustment, *Journal of Social Psychology, 15:*63–74, 1942.
12. William A. Schonfeld. "Inadequate Masculine Physique as a Factor in Personality Development of Adolescent Boys," *Psychosomatic Medicine, 12:*49–54, 1950.
13. Dennis Wayne. "A Cross Cultural Study of the Reinforcement of Child Behavior," *Child Development. 28:*431–38, December 1957.
14. Glenn R. Hawkes. "A study of the Personal Values of Elementary School Children," *Educational and Psychological Measurement, 12:*645–63, Winter, 1952.
15. Percival Symonds. "Education for the Development of Personality," *Teacher's College Record. 50:*163–69, December, 1948.
16. Current Trends and Practices in Physical Education, *Clearing House,* December, 1964.
17. Debth, Judy: a paper submitted in partial requirement of a course in Elementary School Physical Education, 1966.
18. Rarick, Lawrence and McKee, Robert: A Study of Twenty Third-Grade Children Exhibiting Extreme Levels of Achievement on Tests of Motor Fitness, *Research Quarterly. 20:*142–52, May, 1949.
19. Nash, Jay B.: The Skill Learning Years, *Children in Focus.* Washington, D.C.: NEA Press, 1954, p. 71.
20. Tanner, J. M. and Whitehouse, R. H.: Standards for Subcutaneous Fat in British Children, *British Medical Journal, 155:*446–450, 1962.
21. Mayer, J.: Some Aspects of The Problem of Regulation of Food Intake and Obesity, *New England Journal of Medicine, 274:*610–616, 1966.
22. Johnson, M. L., Burke, B. S. and Mayer, J.: The Prevalence and Incidence of Obesity in a Cross Section of Elementary and Secondary School Children, *Am. J. Clin. Nutr., 1:*37–44, 1956.

23. Stunkard, A. J. and Burt, V.: A report given to the sixth multidiscipine research forum of the American Medical Association, 1966.

24. Johnson, M. L., Burke, B. S. and Mayer, J.: Relative Importance of Inactivity and Overeating in Energy Balance of Obese High School Girls. *Amer. Journal Clinical Nutrition, 4:*33–44, 1956.

25. Ryans, David G.: The Use of Concepts in Teaching and Learning. *The Journal of Teacher Education., 15:*81–99, March, 1964.

Bibliography

PERIODICALS

Anderson, K. N.: Inactivity Complicates the Fat Child's Problem. *Today's Health, 41:*78, 1963.

Nicholas, W. H.: Our Flabby Youngsters, *Good Housekeeping,* 1962, p. 12.

Jones, R. M.: The Too Plump Child May Need Your Help, *Family Circle,* 1961, p. 43.

Lester, David: The Fat Child Can be Helped, *Good Housekeeping,* Feb., 1962, p. 53+.

Blair, T. J.: Physical Fitness—Major Objective? *Educational Leadership, 20:*379, March, 1963.

Steinhaus, A. H.: Significant Experiences—A Challenge to Physical Education, Physical Educator, *19:*5, March, 1962.

Wilkinson, Charles: How a Top Coach Would Run Your Program, *School Management, 9:*35–39, Aug, 1965.

6

Planning the Program

Programs are provided as a means to accomplishing objectives. These are the action phases of the teaching-learning process. Although understanding of foundation areas and the statement of objectives is an essential prerequisite to building programs, the program phase of the teaching-learning process is the action phase. It is here that the teacher implements his knowledge. It is in programs of physical education that children are to work toward the goal of becoming physically educated.

The activities and experiences included in the physical education program could be likened to the tools of any profession. First, the teacher selects the best possible tool (an activity or experience) for the accomplishment of the objectives. For example, if the objective were to dig a hole, he would define what kind of a hole he wished to dig. Knowing this specific objective, one would then select the best tool available for the job. If the objective were to dig a very large hole, one might select a steam shovel, but if he wished to dig a small hole, the selection might be a spade. If no shovel were available, he would have to dig the hole with his hands. But it could be done. The teacher defines what is to be done in the physical education program. Next, he determines what tool or tools would best accomplish the task at hand. If swimming is best for meeting a specific objective, it should be used. However, if no pool is available or if the instructor knows nothing about swimming, a different tool would be selected.

When one tool is not available for some reason, the next best tool for meeting that objective should be selected. In this manner the teacher selects the best possible tool available to accomplish the specific objectives outlined for the learner.

The Tools

It is essential that a teacher of physical education be aware of the tools available for the accomplishment of specific objectives. The following is a list of tools which are commonly available to the elementary school teacher as a means to the accomplishment of specific objectives.

Fundamental Skills. These activities are specifically designed to help students develop ability in the basic skills of walking, running, jumping, leaping, galloping, striking, catching, kicking, skipping, and the like. This tool area includes drills and small group activities as well as some game-type activities.

Movement Exploration. These are relatively unstructured activities designed to allow children to solve problems through movement and to investigate the movement elements such as time, space, and force.

Rhythmic Activities. Included in this tool area are basic folk, social, and square dances as well as the basic skills of moving to music. Also included are selected rhythmical and singing games.

Low Organized Games. Games which involve few rules and a minimum of instruction are included in this tool area. Such games range from highly active to relatively inactive and are conducted with a variety of implements and may be used with large groups.

Highly Organized Games (Sports and Athletic Games). The sports and recreational games of our culture are classified in this tool area. Softball, football, soccer, basketball, volleyball, and modifications (lead up) of these games are examples of highly organized games. Also included are games involving considerable knowledge of rules and strategy such as four square, tetherball, and bombardment. These games are applicable to recreational situations after school and during the noon hour.

Relays. These include activities involving participation in squads or small groups as teams in many different types of basic activity. Relays commonly pit one squad or group against another in a competitive situation, although relays need not necessarily be of a competitive nature. Relays may include ball handling, running, and other basic skills.

Gymnastics and Tumbling. Gymnastics and tumbling include participation in basic activities of body relocation and agility on the mats, as well as activities on the balance beam, the tumbling table, the trampoline, the overhead ladder, the horizontal bar and other pieces of apparatus.

Physical Fitness Activities. These activities include calesthenics, exercises to music, basic vigorous games, circuit training, interval training, stunts, and the obstacle course.

Classroom Discussions and Experiments. These experiences include investigation of the benefits of exercise through discussion of various facts and results of simple experiments conducted in class. Also included are discussions of rules, strategies, and courtesies of various activities.

Each of these tool areas is discussed in detail in the second section of this text.

Determining What to Teach

Of prime importance in developing programs of physical education is the decision involving what is to be taught. Because the teacher of physical education is concerned with meeting a wide variety of objectives, it is evident that a wide variety of experiences would be included in the program. A discussion of the merits of some different types of activities follows:

STRUCTURED VS. UNSTRUCTURED ACTIVITIES

In the evolution of current programs of physical education in the United States, many types of activities have been considered as "the" experiences which will best meet the needs of children. Early programs, as influenced by European "physical culture", emphasized highly formal activities such as gymnastics and group calesthenics. Later the Americans, largely influenced by the British, emphasized the less formal, but often highly structured programs of sports and games. More recently, emphasis in the elementary schools and in the high schools to some extent, has been in the area of the minimally structured movement exploration type of program. At all stages of the development of American physical education, the debate has continued as to which type of activity is more valuable to the learner, the structured or the unstructured.

Steinhaus[1] has suggested a theory of activity which would be consistent with the views expounded in this text. He suggests. . . . "that formal activities were formed activities, shaped by others, and dictated to performers who learned them by imitation. Informal activities on the other hand were unformed activities directed from within and created anew each time by the performer. With this idea each activity could now be placed on the diagram (Figure 6-1). Corrective exercises, obviously to serve their purpose, must be completely formed from without and belong to the extreme left. Modern dance and perhaps even more so, the twist, jitterbug, wattusi, and what have you, especially when men and women are mutually involved, belong on the extreme right, a new creation each time they are danced."

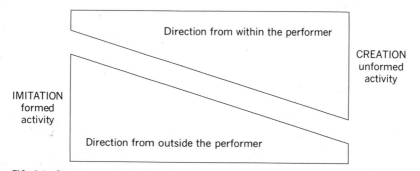

Direction from within the performer

CREATION
unformed
activity

IMITATION
formed
activity

Direction from outside the performer

FIG. 6-1 Structure vs. Unstructure Activity.

One can see that activities range in type and can be placed at many points on this diagram. However, objectives are also divergent. One objective may require an informal activity if it is to be fulfilled, while another may require a formal activity. The debate as to which is more valuable is then resolved and it can be seen that all types of activity are valuable depending on which objective is to be met.

ACTIVE VS. PASSIVE ACTIVITY

Another topic of concern in selecting physical education activities deals with the value of active as contrasted with passive activities. Steinhaus[1] has the following comments on this subject:

> The present physical fitness movement rightly stresses the importance of more and more activity for the average American. 'Off your seat and on your feet' is still a good slogan. But this is not enough! We as physical educators must recognize also, the values of reducing neuromuscular activity from the amount common in ordinary sitting to a state of as near zero activity as possible. The average business man who is burdened by the stresses of today's high pressure existence may well get more relief for his insomnia, rising blood pressure, or building ulcer by 'cooling down' his overactive central and autonomic nervous systems with well spaced 30 second snatches of relaxation at his desk, than he can get from an occasional afternoon or weekend on the golf course or from isometrics in his office.

Again the answer appears to be related to the objectives of the program. Certainly active experiences are necessary if physical fitness is an objective of physical education. But if we are concerned with other objectives, such as those suggested by Steinhaus, it is clear that nonactive or passive experiences may play an important role in the physical education program. The issue is not whether we include active or passive experiences but how much of each will be best for the accomplishment of selected specific objectives.

Determining Priorities

The determination of priority of objectives is important in deciding what to teach. The teacher's objectives are the determiner of program priority. As the teacher develops objectives, he is describing the resultant product of his program of physical education. In determing educational priorities, the teacher must accomplish two things: (1) weigh the importance of each objective, and (2) convert objectives to programs.

One method of weighing the importance of objectives is to list major objectives in rank order. Once the objectives have been ranked, they can be assigned a numerical value in terms of their relative importance (Figure 6-2). For example, if the teacher has identified five major objectives, the total

Objectives	Weight of Objective	Gym and Tumb.	Rhythms and Dance	Move. Explor.	Fund Skills	Relays	Low Organ. Games	Physical Fitness Activity	Sports	Class Room
1. Social-Emotional	(44)									
a. Provide for self expression in physical activity.	10		5	5						
b. Development of creativity through provision for outlet of curiosity.	10		5	5						
c. Provide for successful experiences.	10			10						
d. Develop ability to share and take turns.	7						7			
e. Develop ability to work in small group situations.	7		2				5			
2. Physical Fitness	(20)									
a. Development of large muscle strength specifically in the muscles of the trunk and around the large joints of the body.	10	5						5		
b. Development of simple and dynamic balance.	5	3						2		
c. Development of simple agility and ability to change body position.	5	3						2		
3. Skill	(18)									
a. Development of fundamental skills of: walking, running, leaping, galloping, and hopping.	10				10					
b. Development of ability to use the above listed skills in game situations.	5						5			
c. Understanding the use of space in playing games.	3			3						
4. Cognitive-Affective	(15)									
a. Development of understanding of safety rules of playground equipment.	3			3						
b. Development of understanding of basic behavior necessary in playing simple games.	3						3			
c. Understanding how simple exercises work to make you strong.	3							3		
d. Understanding why you should be fit and what fitness means.	2									2
e. Understanding why you should play.	2									2
f. Understanding good posture.										2
5. Weight Control	(3)									
a. Provide for energy expenditure.	3							3		
TOTALS	100	11	12	26	10	0	20	15	0	6

FIG. 6-2 Weighting Physical Education Objectives.

value of the five objectives might be given a value of 100. Thus each of the five objectives now has a weighting indicative of its relative importance compared to the other four objectives. Priority has been established in terms of the greater weighting of certain objectives as compared to others. Note in the example in Figure 6-2, the five major objectives have weightings ranging from 45 for the social-emotional objective to 3 for the weight-control objective. It is important to note that Figure 6-2 is an example. The determination of priorities in this example depends on the beliefs of the individual establishing the priorities, and perhaps more importantly on the needs, interests, and characteristics of the learners for whom these priorities are being established.

Once priority of general objectives has been made (weightings), the same thing can be done for specific objectives. Each of the specific objectives within a general classification (*a, b, c, d,* and *e* under item 1, Figure 6-2) can then be given a weighting or a priority. When this is done, the teacher has established the priority of each of the objectives to be accomplished by children. It is important to note that the total of the weightings of all specific objectives would equal 100. The total weighting of specific objectives within a general objective heading should equal the weighting of that general objective (example: *a, b, c, d,* and *e* weightings should equal the total for objective 1).

Once priorities have been established the teacher will want to determine

GYMNASTICS & TUMBLING	11
RHYTHMS & DANCE	12
MOVEMENT EXPLORATION	26
FUNDAMENTAL SKILLS	10
RELAYS	0
LOW ORGANIZATION GAMES	20
PHYSICAL FITNESS ACTIVITIES	15
SPORTS	0
CLASSROOM ACTIVITIES	6
TOTAL	100

FIG. 6-3 *Program Priorities.*

which activities or tools will best meet the program's objectives. This conversion of objectives can be done as outlined in Figure 6-2. First the specific objectives are listed with their relative weightings. Also listed (across the top of chart) are the tools available to the teacher of physical education. The teacher reads down the list of objectives placing the weighting value of each objective under the activity area which will best meet that objective. For example, the development of simple and dynamic balance is given a weight of 5. Since both gymnastics and physical fitness activities develop that objective, 3 weighting points are assigned under gymnastics and 2 under physical fitness activities. After all values are assigned, the weightings under each activity are added up. The objectives are now roughly converted to program areas and the teacher will have some idea about the priorities for the program.

Figure 6-3 illustrates the weightings of program areas resulting from the conversion process diagrammed in Figure 6-2. These values will give the teacher some idea of where to place program priority in order to meet his objectives.

Selecting Content

In determining program content, the basic question to be answered is, "How much time should be spent in each area?" In answering this question, program priorities, as discussed above, are of major importance. However, other considerations are important. Some basic considerations in determining the time to be spent in each activity are listed below:

1. Activities with high priority weighting will likely require more time than low priority activities.
2. Some activities require more time because of organizational problems such as putting up equipment in gymnastics.
3. Some activities are more easily taught than others and therefore require less time.
4. Some activities meet many objectives, and therefore may be overemphasized in the conversion of objectives to programs.

Since program priorities are the basic concern in selecting content, the teacher will lean heavily on the priorities listed in Figure 6-3 as the program is developed. However, the other factors listed above will also be considered in selecting content. The teacher would then start with the program priorities and make adjustments as they are necessary (Figure 6-5).

For example, in Figure 6-5, the program priorities are modified and the content is ultimately selected. In this example physical fitness activities are reduced from 15 points to 10 points because of the fact that many areas of the program develop this aspect, and it was possible that less time was necessary in this area. However, time was needed for evaluation, and this was

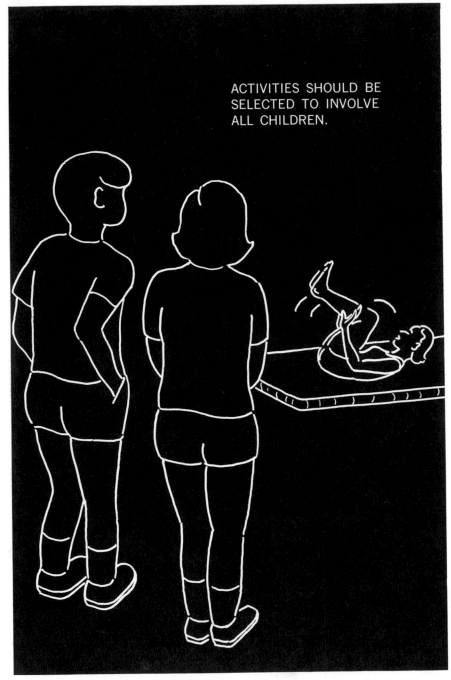

ACTIVITIES SHOULD BE SELECTED TO INVOLVE ALL CHILDREN.

FIG. 6-4

PROGRAM PRIORITIES

	Gym Tumb.	Rhythms Dance	Movement Educ.	Fund. Skills	Phys. Fitn.	Class Room	Low Games	Eval.
	11	12	26	10	15	6	20	0

ULTIMATE CONTENT SELECTED

	Gym Tumb.	Rhythms Dance	Movement Explor.	Fund. Skill	Phys. Fitn.	Class Room	Low Org. Games	Eval.
	10	10	25	10	10	5	20	10

FIG. 6-5 *Content Selection.*

accomplished by assigning points from other areas. The resultant values in the lower half of Figure 6-5 would represent tentative time allotments for each of the activities in the physical education program.

Planning for Efficient Teaching and Learning

Once the decision has been made, at least tentatively, concerning what to teach, the teacher must concentrate on planning for efficient teaching and learning. This can be done most effectively by first planning the general or yearly program, and then proceeding to the specific or daily and unit plans.

The Yearly Plan

In preparing the yearly plan, the teacher is, in effect, scheduling the activities that were established in the previous process of selecting content (Figure 6-5). Since a certain percentage of times was established for teaching each activity in Figure 6-5, the immediate problem is to convert percentages of time to actual school days.

It is assumed that physical education would be taught every day or 180 days a year. If less time is available in a particular situation, merely figure the number of days by multiplying the percentage of time alloted for one activity by the total number of days available. In this example, gymnastics and tumbling is scheduled for 10% of 180 days or 18 days.

Assign each tool or activity to a particular time period. For example,

	Gym and Tumb.	Rhythms and Dance	Movement Explor.	Fund. Skills	Low Organ. Games	Physical Fitness Activity	Class Room	Eval.	Total Days
First Six Weeks				18	6	3*		3	30
Second Six Weeks			18		6	3*		3	30
Third Six Weeks	18		6			3*		3	30
Fourth Six Weeks		18	3			3*	3	3	30
Fifth Six Weeks			9		12	3*	3	3	30
Sixth Six Weeks			9		12	3*	3	3	30
Total Days	18	18	44	18	36	18	9	18	180

FIG. 6-6 *Example Yearly Schedule.*

* Physical fitness activities may be a small part of each day's class.

10% or 18 days are alloted for fundamental skills, thus 18 days are assigned to some time in the school year. In this case during the first 6 weeks (Figure 6-6). Continue this procedure until *all* tools are assigned to a particular time in the yearly schedule. This gives the teacher a general idea of what will be taught and when.

Guidelines for Yearly Planning

1. *Consider the Weather.* Certain activities are best taught out of doors, and are best scheduled in the early fall or late spring.
2. *Consider the Facilities.* All facilities and equipment are not available at all times. Those facilities and pieces of equipment which are limited in their availability should be scheduled for maximum use when they are available.
3. *Consider the Instructional Progression.* Some activities require pre-requisite learning. These activities should be scheduled later in the year, after the pre-requisites have been taught. Also it is important to schedule the pre-requisite activities early.
4. *Consider the Activity Type.* Some activities are best taught in large blocks of time, while others are best taught in smaller distributed blocks. There are three basic scheduling patterns:
   a. Block: All time assigned to a particular activity or experience is massed so that several consecutive days will be devoted to the same activity. (Example: Fundamental Skills in Figure 6-6)

     b. Distributed: Periods of time devoted to a particular activity are distributed to allow for several successive days scheduled at different times during the year in this scheduling pattern. (Example: Movement Exploration in Figure 6-6)

     c. Daily: Time allotments for one particular tool area is distributed so that a certain amount of the physical education is devoted to that activity each day. (Example: Physical Fitness in Figure 6-6)

  5. *Consider Student Interests.* The interest of students must be considered if teaching and learning in physical education is to be most efficient.

Unit Planning

Once the teacher has developed a yearly schedule, the next step is to plan for specific blocks of time. This is often called unit planning because an attempt is made to plan for all activities in one specific area, the unit.

Figure 6-7 is one example of how a unit may be planned. The planning is accomplished by filling in the areas designated. The following discussion details the procedure for unit planning.

Lesson Objectives. The objectives should be easy to identify since they were the basis for the selection of the activity to be included in the unit in the first place.

Merely, return to Figure 6-2 and locate the column for the particular tool area for which you are planning the unit. Determine which objectives were the basis for the selection of this tool area by noting which objectives have weightings assigned in this tool area column. Example: In rhythms the objectives 2-A, 2-B, and 2-C were the reason why rhythms were selected as part of the program. Thus these objectives are carried over to the unit plan so that we can plan for their accomplishment. Place these objectives on the unit plan outline (Figure 6-7).

Learning Experiences. The learning experience should be selected specifically to meet the objectives as stated in Step A. Many experiences are available within each tool area, but only the best tool for meeting these particular objectives should be listed. List these activities on the unit plan outline.

Materials Needed. Under this heading on the unit plan, list what ever materials, equipment, or supplies that will be necessary during the entire unit. Prior to the beginning of the unit the teacher will locate all equipment, etc., so that it will be available when needed.

Class Organization. Included under this heading on the unit plan should be such things as: changing shoes, taking showers, special events such as films, etc., which are not part of the normal routine.

Evaluation. Evaluation includes any experience which will be provided to help the teacher estimate progress of students toward meeting the objectives of the unit. Such special experiences should be listed on the unit plan.

Teaching Unit_____ Grade_____ Dates_____ No. of Periods_____

Ⓐ Lesson Objectives	Ⓑ Learning Experiences Review: New:

Ⓒ Materials Needed	Ⓕ Comments
Ⓓ Class Organization	
Ⓔ Evaluation	

FIG. 6-7 *Unit Plan Outline.*

After the completion of each unit, the teacher should record comments as to the success or failure of the unit in promoting desired outcomes among children. In future planning the teacher can refer to these comments as a means toward improving the program.

Guidelines for Unit Planning

1. When possible, a variety of activities should be included in the program. In selecting the specific activities within a unit, if two activities meet an objective equally well, select the new or different one.
2. Select activities and experiences which involve all children and *not* the few outstanding performers.
3. One unit plan should be prepared for each tool area.

Daily Planning

Once the more general unit plan is prepared, the teacher will want to focus on daily planning. The daily plan emphasizes "what am I going to do today to promote efficient learning in physical education". Daily planning could be done on a planning sheet such as Figure 6-8.

First, list the specific objectives to be accomplished on the day for which you are planning. These will be taken from the unit plan. However, the daily lesson will probably concentrate on one or two, rather than all of the unit objectives. These daily objectives may be defined in greater detail than in the unit plan (Figure 6-8).

The schedule of learning experiences section includes a list of all activities to be taught as well as the time and techniques necessary for the teaching of these activities.

List materials and equipment to be used for the daily lesson plan in the appropriate space on the lesson plan sheet.

List specific evaluation experiences to be used on the day of the planned lesson.

Provide a space on the daily lesson plan to be filled in after the lesson to aid in future planning.

Provisions for Program Improvement

After the teacher has decided what to teach and has developed plans for effective teaching, he must make other considerations. Two of these considerations that are of great importance are *program flexibility and program changes for improvement.*

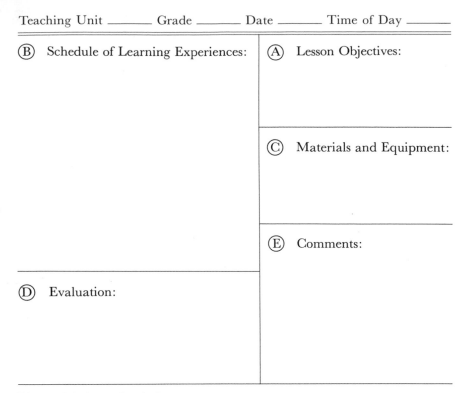

Teaching Unit _____ Grade _____ Date _____ Time of Day _____

Ⓑ Schedule of Learning Experiences:

Ⓐ Lesson Objectives:

Ⓒ Materials and Equipment:

Ⓔ Comments:

Ⓓ Evaluation:

FIG. 6-8 *Daily Lesson Plan Outline.*

PROGRAM FLEXIBILITY

It must be recognized that the planning of programs through yearly planning, unit planning, and daily planning is done to aid the teacher in helping children learn to learn. If and when planning becomes so restrictive that it detracts from the learning, the teacher's purpose has been defeated. It is important to emphasize that *planning is for the benefit of the teacher.* For this reason, plans should be flexible. If a unit takes longer than expected, take the time necessary. When an adaptation in planning is needed, make it. However, one must be concerned, at all times, with the overall objectives and modifications should be made only after considering most efficient learning for children.

PROGRAM CHANGES FOR IMPROVEMENT

One basic reason for planning is to give the child the best possible program of physical education. As the child grows and learns, his needs change. As our society changes, our point of view may change. For the above reasons, changes may be necessary from day to day, month to month, or year to year. If changes are needed to *improve* the learning experiences of children, make the changes. However, if changes are made for the sake of change, the overall effectiveness of the teacher-learning process will be reduced. Changes should only be made for program improvement.

The Total Program Plan

After planning the program, the teacher will have a reasonably good idea of what he is going to teach. The yearly schedule which is the result of considerable planning is done to make sure that the most effective learning experiences are included in the program when and where they will be most effective. If no such schedule were developed prior to the beginning of the school year, the chances of using each learning experience effectively would be limited. For this reason it is essential that the yearly schedule be completed prior to the beginning of the school year. If circumstances are altered so that the schedule requires change, then only it should be changed. However, the changes should be made after considering the ultimate value of the change in terms of meeting the outlined objectives for the program.

The unit plan need not be completed prior to the beginning of the school year but should be completed prior to the beginning of each unit. The daily lesson plans within each unit should be planned before the beginning of the unit but should be flexible enough so that changes can be made when necessary.

In some cases a unit may be distributed over an entire year. For example, physical fitness as planned in the example yearly schedule (Figure 6-6) is taught for a few minutes each day but nevertheless all activities taught for physical fitness may be considered as a unit. In such cases it is advisable to complete the unit plan prior to the beginning of the school year but to complete the daily lesson plans as needed with some prepared in advance.

If a planning process is followed so that the teacher has a yearly schedule, unit plans for each tool area, and daily lesson plans for each class period in physical education, the teacher would then compile these plans and place them in a loose leaf notebook. He would then have the best justification possible for the inclusion of physical education in the program. He would be able to say, "This is what I expect to accomplish, this is how I expect to do it, and here is when it is going to be done."

Each year the process of planning would be reconsidered and redone. Since children change from year to year, the programs would also change from year to year. Also the things which did not work last year would be eliminated from the program or modified in order to help students better meet objectives. The comments made on unit and daily plans would be taken into consideration in developing new plans. However, much of the program could be retained without change. If certain plans worked well in accomplishing an objective and that objective is again considered to be important, the same plan could be used again. Through this process the teacher improves from year to year. What was good and still is applicable is retained. The not so good is altered. Thus each year the program becomes more and more effective in helping students become fully functioning healthy individuals.

Special Considerations in Program Planning

The following suggestions should be considered in planning and conducting programs as outlined in this chapter:

1. Meet your objectives first—programs are planned to meet specific objectives but objectives are not intended to limit program outcomes. First consideration should be directed toward meeting the objectives which the teacher has established. However, any other benefits resulting from the program which help the individual become healthy and fully functioning should be encouraged.
2. The planned program *insures* nothing in terms of meeting objectives for the learner. It is possible that the best program in the world would fail if proper teaching techniques, motivational considerations, etc., were not considered. The planned program does increase the chances that the objectives of the learner will be accomplished.
3. As children change so changes the program. Program adjustments should be made in accordance with such changes.
4. After planning through a detailed process, the resulting program for the learner may seem quite fixed. It is easy to say, "I planned it by the method suggested so that is the way it will be done." *Do not* bind yourself to the planned program. Keep in mind the objectives and needs of the learner and if you can better accomplish this with a modification—then make the change.

Summary

It is most important that the reader be aware of the fact that the information presented in this chapter is of a hypothetical nature. The examples suggested are just that, examples. In actual planning, the teacher might classify learning experiences considerably differently from those listed here. The important point is not that the teacher do exactly as outlined in this chapter, but rather that he have an idea of how he can develop programs for effective teaching and learning.

Reference

1. Steinhaus, Arthur H.: Some New Theories of Exercise, *The Physical Educator,* 22:21–22, March, 1965.

7

Movement Exploration

Movement is the basis of activities of man. Man copes with his environment through movement. The young child learns to understand his environment through physical contact with his environment and through movement. Survival requires that man walk, talk, lift, push and pull, all of which are movement. Recent investigations indicate that even sedentary human experiences involve movement. Thinking of an activity actually involves active stimulation of the muscle fibers involved in the "mental activity". Most recently, scientists have indicated that thinking of speaking involves slight movements of the tongue.

Perhaps of greatest significance is the fact that human control of the environment is a result of movement. Seeking shelter, preparing food, and even the simplist modern day house work involves movement. These movements are man's means of adapting to the environment. Efficient movement is of great concern in the education of man. Movements are learned as a means of accomplishing purposes in life but the joy of movement can also be an end in itself.

Physical education, as part of the school curriculum, is uniquely concerned with movement as an educational dimension. As previously discussed, movement in the form of skilled behavior, is a major objective of physical education. By the same token, movement is the means through which objectives of physical education are accomplished.

What is Movement?

It is impossible to see what man is thinking. Man's potential for performance is almost as difficult to observe. Although the physical appearance of an individual may give an indication of his potential, it is only through his movement that we really see what he can do.

Movement involves changes in body position from the simple to the most complex. Movement may involve a single body part or a change in position of the entire body. Movement includes the ability of an individual to perform relatively passive movements of single body parts or it may involve dynamic bursts of energy involving the entire body. Daily living may require many types of movement including the need to perform simple movement or even highly complex movement skills such as batting a ball or dribbling a basketball.

Movement is Unique to Each Individual

Although many similar movement functions are performed each day, each individual has his own "movement style". Millions of people walk each day but no two people walk the same way. The activity may be the same, but the movement complex is different. Purposes in moving may be similar, but again, the movement is different. It is in helping each individual develop his *own* efficient life "movement style" that physical education contributes to one's movement education.

The English Movement Education

Physical education in the English elementary school is centered around a movement education experience. This concept developed more than two decades ago, emphasizes the importance of each individual. The basic premise is that children learn best when they solve their own movement problems. The student is given a movement problem from which he develops unique learning experience. It is in solving problems in his self-created learning experience that movement education becomes a reality.

Investigation of different types of movement is encouraged as children move within the limitations of the movement problem. In the beginning, students are encouraged to investigate many possibilities of solving a problem such as, "In how many different ways can you support the body on two different parts?" As the student seeks a problem solution, the teacher may give directions to aid children in improving the quality of movement patterns. Included among the English movement education experiences may be activities on gymnastics apparatus and activities with a variety of sports type implements.

Such movement exploration emphasizes consideration of creative experience. Although experiences are original and individual in nature, without specific "how to do it" instruction, the programs do have highly specific objectives.

The success of "movement education", as evidenced by the high degree of movement skill and physical fitness of children graduating from movement programs, has resulted in the use of this educational approach in the secondary schools of England. The successful programs have been the stimulus for "movement exploration" currently utilized as an effective means of accomplishing some of the physical education objectives in the schools of the United States.

Movement Exploration—A Problem Solving Approach

In discussing movement exploration, Hunt suggests that ". . . the body has all the 'know how' to move well without being taught—our prime job is to provide selected experiences and to emphasize man's active part in the process of discovery and refinement."

This discovery and refinement process in movement exploration is designed to meet the needs of individuals. Like any other tool area in physical education the child is considered before programs are prepared. However, the nature of movement exploration offers the child an opportunity to solve problems within the limits of his own ability and for this reason movement exploration experiences can be considered as truly individual experiences. In addition to effectiveness in meeting many physical education objectives such as skill and fitness development, movement exploration provides children a unique opportunity for creative development (Box 7-1). The word "exploration" implies freedom of experience and expression in developing levels of creativity among children.

Movement exploration is and should be true problem solving for children. It is the child's unique solution to a movement problem that makes the movement experience true exploration. It is also through the problem solving process that the program becomes an individual experience. The child is encouraged to explore movement through the following problem solving steps:

1. *The teacher poses the movement problem*—Example: In how many different directions can you move your body? Forward, backward, to the side, etc. (See chapter 12 for movement exploration suggestions.)
2. *The child explores the problem.* Each child works independently to solve the problem through movement.
3. *Various movement solutions may be demonstrated.* The children may be asked to show how they have solved the problem.
4. *Specific instruction may follow.* The teacher may direct students to a specific desired solution.
5. *Students are encouraged to find a solution.* In some cases a *best* solution may be determined *by the student* while in other cases a variety of final solutions may be encouraged.

BOX 7-1. CREATIVITY THROUGH PHYSICAL EDUCATION

Purpose. This report based on 7 years of investigating methods for developing creativity and critical thinking, points out the important role which physical education can play in developing these desirable attributes in children of all ages.

Contents. Torrance suggests 7 guides to the development of creativity:

1. *Do Not leave creative development to chance.* The teacher should plan deliberate methods of problem solving if creative objectives are to be developed.
2. *Encourage Curiosity and Other Creative Characteristics.* In physical education the teacher should encourage questions about simple body functions. (These are often discouraged.)
3. *Be respectful of Questions and Unusual Ideas.* "Research indicates that one of the simplest and most powerful ways of encouraging creative growth is to respect the questions that children ask, respect the ideas they present. . . ."
4. *Recognize Original and Creative Behavior.* Point out creative and unusual movements and movement achievements in physical education.
5. *Ask Questions that Require Thinking.* Analysis of questions asked in the classroom and on examinations indicate that about 90% of such questions deal only with the recognition or reproduction of textbook information.
6. *Build the Learning Skills that Your Pupils Have.* When children enter school they have already developed a variety of skills—use them.
7. *Give Opportunities for Learning in Creative Ways.* Research indicates that man can learn more efficiently and economically if he is allowed to explore, question, experiment, test and modify.

Some Results. First and second grade students who participated in special movement exploration programs conducted by Baker scored exceedingly well in creativity. Torrance indicated that almost 50% of these students exceeded mean scores for fifth graders on tests of creativity.

A special group of third grade students were tested before and after a 4-month movement exploration program. Results indicated significant improvement in all but one aspect of creativity. These students improved significantly in the creative aspects of fluency, flexibility, and originality.

Conclusions. "The incidents, although few, in which I have specifically studied the development of creative thinking abilities through health education, physical education and recreation have convinced me that these fields can make important contributions to the general freeing and development of the creative thinking abilities in schools."

Torrance, E. Paul: Seven Guides to Creativity, *JOHPER.* 36:27, April, 1965.

Meeting Physical Education Objectives
Through Movement Exploration

In contributing to the development of the fully functioning healthy individual, movement exploration makes a significant contribution to the general objectives as discussed in Chapter 5. Movement exploration is particularly effective in contributing to the following physical education objectives:

1. *Helping children learn to move.* This includes helping children in developing the ability to move efficiently and includes developing certain specific motor skills.
2. *Helping children understand their movement limitations.* Through exploring movement, children progress at their own rate in accordance with their own abilities and are encouraged to understand their own strengths and limitations.
3. *Helping children understand the utility of movement.* As children learn how to move, the value of this movement becomes apparent. An understanding of the use of movement for leisure time recreation and for effective daily living can be developed.
4. *Helping children learn to enjoy movement.* Of particular concern to the physical educator is that movement be an enjoyable experience. People do those things they enjoy. By helping children experience success at their own individual rate, we encourage enjoyment of movement.
5. *Helping children learn the techniques of discovery.* Problem solving experience in a movement exploration activity aids in the development of this objective.
6. *Helping children retain and develop creativity.* As an aspect of the fully functioning healthy individual, creativity is most important. Movement exploration is an effective tool in helping children retain and develop their creativity.
7. *Helping children develop a movement vocabulary.* The child learns the meaning of various movements terms so that he can organize many combinations of movement in efficiently responding to a posed movement problem.

The Dimensions of Movement

In developing an understanding of movement it is important to understand that there are different dimensions of movement. Although most movements may involve more than one dimension, each dimension is discussed separated mainly for the development of an understanding of total movement. For the sake of this discussion, movement is classified in four dimensions: movement of the body parts, locomotor movements, moving implements, and objects, and moving with others.

MOVEMENT OF BODY PARTS

Movement in this dimension involves movement of the various body parts, while the total body remains static. Body parts include the head, the arms, the legs and the trunk. The following elements define various movements of body parts. All movement elements exist along a continuum (Figure 7-1).

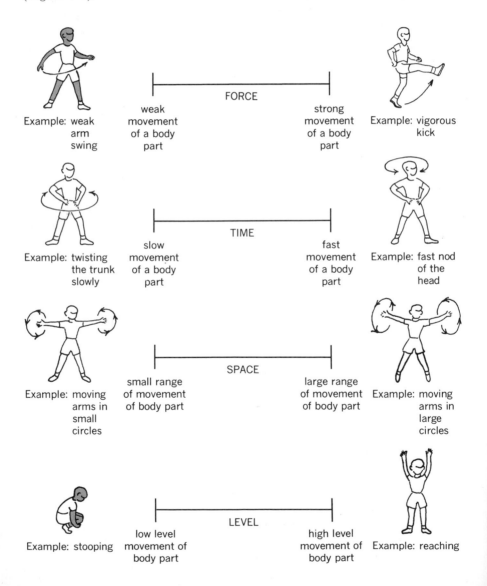

| | | FORCE | | |
| Example: weak arm swing | weak movement of a body part | | strong movement of a body part | Example: vigorous kick |

| | | TIME | | |
| Example: twisting the trunk slowly | slow movement of a body part | | fast movement of a body part | Example: fast nod of the head |

| | | SPACE | | |
| Example: moving arms in small circles | small range of movement of body part | | large range of movement of body part | Example: moving arms in large circles |

| | | LEVEL | | |
| Example: stooping | low level movement of body part | | high level movement of body part | Example: reaching |

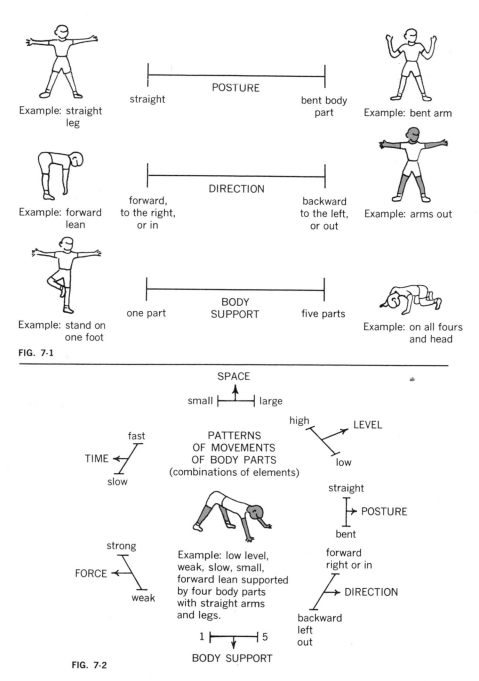

Example: straight
leg

POSTURE

straight   bent body
part

Example: bent arm

Example: forward
lean

DIRECTION

forward,
to the right,
or in

backward
to the left,
or out

Example: arms out

Example: stand on
one foot

BODY
SUPPORT

one part   five parts

Example: on all fours
and head

FIG. 7-1

SPACE

small ⊢—⊣ large

TIME

fast

slow

PATTERNS
OF MOVEMENTS
OF BODY PARTS
(combinations of elements)

high

LEVEL

low

straight

POSTURE

bent

FORCE

strong

weak

Example: low level,
weak, slow, small,
forward lean supported
by four body parts
with straight arms
and legs.

1 ⊢—⊣ 5

forward
right or in

DIRECTION

backward
left
out

BODY SUPPORT

FIG. 7-2

When several movement elements are combined, the combined movement is called a pattern of movement. Figure 7-2 points out how several elements of movement can result in a movement pattern.

LOCOMOTOR MOVEMENTS

Movement in this dimension includes self engaged movement of the entire body through space. Walking is a locomotor movement. Like movement of the body parts, the various elements of the locomotor movement dimension exist along a continuum. Figure 7-3 shows the elements of locomotor movement.

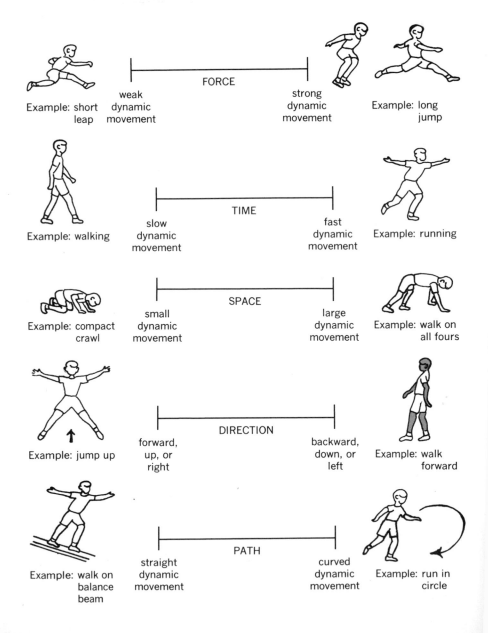

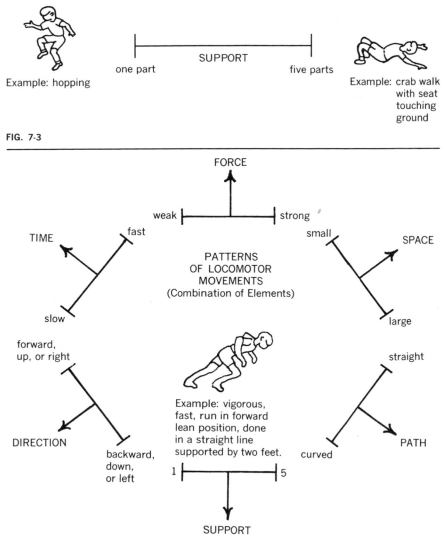

FIG. 7-3

FIG. 7-4

As previously discussed under the dimension, "movement of body parts", a movement involving several movement elements is considered a movement pattern. Figure 7-4 points out how several elements of movement can result in a movement pattern.

MOVING IMPLEMENTS AND OBJECTS

The third movement dimension involves similar elements to the other two dimensions (*i.e.*, force, time, space, etc.) but as these elements contribute to imparting movement to implements or objects.

7

1. *The Implement.* The implement may be used to extend the space range of a body part or to improve the amount of force which the body can impart to an object. The use of a baseball bat or tennis racket improves the bodies movement function in both of the methods above mentioned. Like other movement dimensions, the control of the use of all or any of the movement elements in using an implement is the essence of efficient movement.

2. *The Object.* In imparting force to an object, such as throwing a ball or striking a ball, all elements of movement of body parts and loco-motor movement are involved. In striking or kicking another element is involved, namely accuracy. The direction element of locomotor movement is similar but it is the accuracy element of imparting movement to an object which is of greatest importance in such movements.

Moving With Others. The fourth and final dimension of movement involves all of the previously mentioned dimensions in a social setting. Although movement can and should be a highly individual experience, many times movement involves interaction with others. In these instances the previously discussed dimensions must be controlled. Control of movement is essential if the mutual benefit of all persons involved is to be considered. For example, although an individual can impart tremendous force to an object, it might be dangerous to throw or strike a ball with great force when playing with a person of limited movement potential. For this reason, movement in the social dimension must be controlled.

Integrating the Movement Dimensions

The four dimensions of movement (movement of body parts, locomotor movement, moving implements and objects, and moving with others) can be combined in integrating movement. For example, in running, the body parts are involved in many elements of dynamic locomotor movement. Body parts, the arms and legs, are alternately bent and straightened, the trunk has a forward lean, etc. As the individual runs he may dribble a ball, thus imparting movement to an object. This involves integration of three of the movement dimensions. Since this movement may be performed in a social setting such as a game of basketball, the fourth movement is integrated with the other three. It is evident that all movement involves a combination of the various elements and dimensions of movement.

A Child's Potential for Movement

The real determination of a child's potential for movement can be made after evaluating the child's ability to perform along the continuum of each element of movement within each movement dimension. The wider the range of ability along the continuum for each element of movement, the greater the child's potential for movement in that element. For example, if the child can perform strong movements as well as weak movements, he has good potential on the force element. However, if his musculature limits the strength of his movement, he is limited in his movement on the force continuum. If the child is highly flexible, he can move through a large range of movement but if not, he is limited in movement in the space continuum. So it is with all of the movement elements, the greater the range of movement along the continuum for each element, the greater the child's potential for movement.

The ultimate goal of movement exploration is to help each child achieve the greatest range on each movement continuum. Further, it is the goal of physical education to help each child use his ability in combination with other movement elements and dimensions.

Guidelines for Developing Movement Experiences

The following are suggestions for teaching effective movement exploration:

1. Do *not* over define the problem—make sure many responses are possible.
2. The problem can be further defined as children begin to move—to help children in discovering movements.
3. Make sure all elements and dimensions of movement are considered in posing problems for children.
4. Progress from single elements to combinations of elements.
5. Progress from single movement dimensions to combinations of dimensions.
6. Use all senses (sight, hearing, touch) in exploring space boundaries and environment.
7. Use rhythms in exploring various movement dimensions.
8. Emphasize movement *quality* rather than quantity.
9. Teach fundamental skills when necessary.
10. Avoid demonstrations which may limit student responses and stymie creative movement.
11. Use praise for creative movement responses.
12. Keep children active.
13. Make children aware of the need to listen closely to the statement of the movement problem.
14. Since movement is an individual experience, the teacher should attempt to observe individual performances.

BOX 7-2. A DEMONSTRATION LESSON IN MOVEMENT EXPLORATION

T: Teacher's questions, remarks, and suggestions
C: Children's responses, answers
_____: Action
T: If we said how tall could you be, what would you do?
C: I'm stretching with my neck. Stretch _____.
T: If we said how small could you be, what would you do? Let's see?
C: Roll up: squeeze up: shrink _____.
T: How wide can you be? _____. Make yourself even wider _____.
T: Now shall we put ourselves in a box—a nice, tall, skinny box. (Children pulled various parts of them in _____.) And now let's break ourselves out of the box and see how much space we can use; let's change the range of out movements as we break out. (Some started head first, others started stretching feet first _____.)
T: Let's put ourselves back in a little box and then make it go up like a tall box of flowers, like a gladiola box.
T: How do we get to go higher? (This was the first question that elicited verbal response from the majority of children: most of the other responses had been motor responses up to this point.)
KAREN: We could jump.
T: What could we put with a jump?
CLARK: We could hop and jump.
T: Why don't we try this? Hop-jump, hop-jump. (The children went up and down and sideways, circling.) What does it say? Can you clap it?
GEORGE: "One foot, two feet" is what it says.
T: Shall we try it? (Music followed the group, and was used for the first time.) Why don't you really let go? See how much space you can cover. Let's clap it again while you catch your breath _____. Shall we do it narrow and then wide? _____ Think of being back in that box and then springing out _____. See if we can go farther out if we use the upper parts of our bodies, too _____.
T: What would help to remind us to jump and hop?
DAVE: We can say to ourselves as we do it, "Jump and hop," or, "Two feet and then one foot."
T: That's a good suggestion. Let's try _____. Some of us aren't quite doing it. What do you suppose is wrong?
CLARK: It's because we are jumping too far to the side.
SHERAN: Maybe we are forgetting to hop and just jumping all the time.
GEORGE: Yes, but do we want to move just up and down or out to the side?
T: Maybe we should try both—jump and hop in place, and then in space out to the side, and then in place again. Now let's move out every time we hop _____. That's it, jump where you are and then move out on your hops _____. Maybe if we say what we are doing, it will help _____.
GEORGE: Golly, I didn't hop because my jump carried me too far. I kept forgetting to hop. Suppose we watch George and all say "Jump, hop," while he does it _____.

T: Is he covering space?

C: Oh yes, just look at him go. Whee!

T: Suppose we think of another way to cover space, using first a little kind of movement and then a big one, changing out range as we move. While you are resting think of ways, and then we shall try them.

T: Could we work on different levels? What levels are we now?

C: Low and medium.

T: How long can you get? Now let's see if we can move our head: our feet: our hands. Now let's go way up tall. Now can you move some way in-betweenish? Now as high as you can go. Is this _____ high or low level?

C: High, high.

T: What else can we do?

JOYCE: We could bounce. We could bounce our heads and our fingers, too.

T: Can you bounce sideward?

C: Sure.

T: This time try a little bounce with a small part of you, and then a big bounce with a large part of you _____. Good. Now let's see if you can change your levels while you keep on bouncing _____.

T: Suppose we all get into three's, or not more than four's. Let's watch this group of three for a minute. Jackie, suppose you be the pivot and establish a level you want to start from _____. Now the other two take another level so that we see three levels. Good _____. We said that there were three levels, and now we can see those three levels. Now, do you think that you could change your levels so that we would continue to see three different levels? Let's make a game out of it.

JOEL: Can we do it: One can be high. One can be low, and I'll be in between.

T: Shall we all work now at the same time, and see if we can continually change our levels within each group? Use any movements which seem good to you. And be careful to stay close enough together so that you can watch each other and we can tell that you are a group changing your levels. Let's see the pivot person _____. Now the others in relation to your center of pivot _____.

PETER: This like statues.

T: For just a second, let us watch Peter's group, working out their pattern of levels _____.

PETER'S GROUP: One jumping and turning (high level)
Another hopping, all bent over (medium level)
Another slithering around on his tummy (low level)

T: Now let's see if you can change your levels, moving slowly from one to the other.

T: Let's all try. You have to concentrate and keep your eyes on the rest of your group. Try moving a little slower. When we say "stop" everyone stop right where he is, but move all of the time in between. Stop. Hold your different levels. What is another way we could call "stop"?

BARB: We could freeze.

T: O.K. Let's move, changing levels until we hear the call "freeze." Freeze.

T: This time, suppose that we watch Penny's group _____.

PENNY'S GROUP: Jumping and reaching with alternate hands (high level)
Slow and fast shakes (in between level)
Bending and stretching down low and sidewards (low level)
C: Jack looks like a cat; he looks like a shaggy dog to me moving close to the ground.
T: What level is Jack?
C: Low
T: George's group was doing something very interesting. They have quite a level's pattern started. Let's watch them _____.
GEORGE'S GROUP: (Moving in and out and up and down progressively, they turned in toward the center as they changed levels.)
T: Let's all try changing levels once more, using another kind of movement and making it a jerky quality. We shall go on with this another day.
T: It's choice time. What will the activity be today?
C: Duck and Dive: more Freeze: Levels again: Hokie Kokie (and so on).
T: The Hokie Kokies seem to be in the majority. Suppose we turn to the person nearest us for a partner and start singing and clapping to the chorus part. This time on the chorus part, ". . . and we do the Hokie Kokie and we do it Okie Dokie . . . ," partners figure out something to do together. Let's try them out.
BOBBY AND PARTNER: (Jumping in opposition to each other, away from and toward the group circle.)
PETER AND PARTNER: (Swinging up and down in opposition.)
DANNY AND PARTNER: (Nonplussed Terry by saying, "Can you do the Mexican Jump?" and then proceeded showing. Both were soon doing it.)
JOEL AND PARTNER: (Jumping in opposition to partner—up and down.)

Andrews, Gladys. *Creative Rhythmic Movement for Children.* Englewood Cliffs, N.J.: Prentice-Hall, Inc., 1954, pp. 41–43.

Movement Exploration: An Effective Tool

Movement exploration is one tool for meeting educational objectives. Since movement is the only means by which man can cope with his environment, physical education has a unique opportunity for contributing to the achievement of man's potential. As movement is explored and objectives are met through movement experiences, the ultimate objective of education is achieved, the development of the fully functioning healthy individual.

Bibliography

PERIODICALS

Torrance, E. Paul: Seven Guides to Creativity, *JOHPER, 36:*27, April, 1965.
Howard, Shirley: The Movement Education Approach to Teaching is English Elementary School, *JOHPER, 38:*31, January, 1967.

Boyd, B., Cox, G., Gheus, C. and Williams, S.: What Ever Happened to Basic Movement Skills, *JOHPER, 37:*21, May, 1966.

Locke, L. F.: The Movement Movement, *JOHPER, 37:*26, January, 1966.

Allenbaugh, Naomi: Learning About Movement, *NEA Journal, 38:*48, March, 1967.

College Physical Education Association, The Art and Science of Human Movement, *Quest,* A monograph. No. II, Spring, 1964.

BOOKS

Andrews, G.: *Creative Rhythmic Movement for Children,* Englewood Cliffs, N.J., Prentice-Hall, Inc., 1954.

Andrews, G., Sanborn, J. and Schneider, E.: *Physical Education for Today's Boys and Girls,* Boston, Allyn & Bacon, 1960.

Brown, C. and Cassidy, R.: *Theory in Physical Education,* Philadelphia; Lea & Febiger, 1963.

8

Helping Children Understand Physical Education

The basic premise of physical education in the elementary school in recent decades seems to be: "If an individual learns to play successfully, he will continue to play." Physical education teachers have concentrated their efforts on teaching skill as the major part, if not the whole of physical education. The teaching of these skills is and has been to help the child in becoming successful in play. Since one of the basic objectives of physical education is to "carry over" into later life that which is learned in the physical education class, the skills approach was deemed desirable and successful.

Modern educators have come to question the validity of the "skills only" physical education program. Although there is some scientific support for the contention that people will continue to do those things in which they are successful, it is evident that there are exceptions to the rule. Perhaps the basic premise would be stated better as: "If an individual learns to play successfully, it is more likely that he will continue to play." While the idea that an individual with good skill in tennis is more likely to spend an afternoon on the tennis court than one with less skill is generally acceptable, there is little doubt that many people with much skill in sports *do not* use their skill in actual participation.

Skill development is an important objective of physical education and it is important that programs meet this objective. However, if the true objective of physical education is to help each individual achieve his potential, to become fully functioning, and to carry over what is learned into later life, then a more important concern becomes apparent to the teacher of physical education. How do we help a person become totally physically educated, and perhaps most important, how do we help an individual maintain physical fitness, and to play effectively throughout life.

The development and use of skill is one means to this end. Those persons who possess skill and participate in sports and other movement experiences may well make use of their physical education. However, for physical education to make its greatest contribution, the individual must possess skill, but further, he must understand and appreciate the value of physical activity, exercise, and movement as a means of becoming totally physically educated. In other words, he must understand *why* he should participate in sports or continue exercise during and after his school years. This is part of the cognitive-affective objective as discussed in Chapter 5.

If physical education is to contribute to developing the fully functioning healthy individual, and an understanding of the *why* of exercise is important to the development of this objective, specific planning must be undertaken to insure the attainment of this objective. It is not adequate to say that health education will take care of it, or that the information will be covered in science. It is physical education's responsibility to develop these understandings and appreciations in children.

Some Aspects of Knowing and Understanding

Although this chapter is greatly concerned with the *why of exercise* there are other parts of the cognitive-affective objective that are of concern in teaching physical education. The following is a list of some of the aspects of knowing and understanding which should be developed in the elementary school.

1. *Learning How to Move.* Children can learn to move in many physical education activities including movement exploration. Developing skill is part of understanding how to move. However, the developing of the understanding of the best ways to move, including understanding why certain ways of movement are better, cannot be developed in activity classes alone. For this reason there is value in studying such things as stability, momentum and other concepts in the classroom.

2. *Understanding Personal Movement Capabilities.* Understanding ones movement capabilities is vital to the "carry-over" of physical education to later life. As the individual understands that all persons are unique in their movement capabilities, he begins to understand his own movement limitations and strengths. Again this can be taught in the activity class but certain aspects of understanding movement capabilities could be better handled in a classroom type atmosphere. Such

things as understanding about the body, its changes, as well as understanding limitations imposed by certain body types are examples of topics for classroom discussion.

3. *The Health Benefits of Movement.* For an individual to make an intelligent choice concerning whether to continue to exercise or participate in physical activity, or not to participate, he must develop an understanding of the benefits of such exercise or activity. When he fully realizes the value of exercise, he is in a better position to make a choice as to activity or inactivity as a life's pattern.

4. *Making Movement Decisions.* Once the individual has learned the value of physical exercise, he is in a position to choose the type of movement experience in which he will participate, if any. Of considerable importance is the development of an understanding and an appreciation of the value of each type of exercise and movement as a technique of keeping fit and healthy.

5. *Value of Efficient Movement.* Understanding the value of efficient movement is important if the individual is to understand fully the reasons for practicing to improve his skill performance. Included are values such as the recreational value of efficient movement and efficient movement as a means of preventing fatigue.

6. *First Aid.* Every physically educated individual needs to understand fully and to appreciate the techniques of first aid as a means of operating efficiently in society.

7. *Safety.* Children need to develop an understanding and appreciation of such things as use of playground equipment, traffic safety, and bicycle safety.

8. *Rules and Strategy.* If sports and games are to be of value in maintaining health or in helping one live a life of a fully functioning healthy individual, understanding the rules and strategies of these sports and games is essential.

Techniques for Helping Children Understand Physical Education Concepts

There are many ways of teaching that might be effective for an understanding of physical education. The following is a list of some of these techniques:

1. *Teacher Presentations.* Certain types of information, as in other subject matter areas, can be presented in the normal teaching type presentation. In cases where factual recall is essential, this technique is quite effective. The teacher of physical education would best use this technique in presenting materials such as first aid procedures. Although

	Learning How To Move	Understanding One's movement Limitations Capabilities	Health benefit of movement	Making proper movement decisions	The value of efficient movement	First aid	Safety	Rules and strategy
Grade 1	Basic skills-walk, run. Understanding movement terms.	Learning about normal growth.	The importance of play.	Choice of play.	Utility of movement.	Keeping cuts and scratches clean.	Playground safety. To and from school safety. Unsafe strangers.	Simple games. Group cooperation.
Grade 2	Understanding movement Posture, basic skills.	Learning about normal growth.	Exercise and the ability to do work. Exercise and fatigue.	Learning the value of many movement activities.	Prevention of fatigue.	Sun burn, simple cuts and abrasions. Who to call in case of accident.	Safe use of ropes, bats, etc. Bicycle safety.	Simple game rules. How to watch game.
Grade 3	How to lift, carry, push, pull. Posture basic skills.	Self testing of movement ability.	Exercise and diet. Exercise, rest, sleep.	Learning the how and why of relaxation. Learning the value of fitness.	Economy of efficient movement.	Simple first aid procedure. (What not to do)	Unsafe dares, water safety, fire drills, safety signs.	Relay rules and strategy.
Grade 4	Principles of movement and their application. Stability, gravity.	Understanding weight control, amounts of body fat, and body type.	Exercise and wt. control. Exercise and strength, overload, low back pain.	Learning values of exercise.	Beauty of efficient movement.	Emergency first aid procedures. What to do at an accident, bleeding, poisoning.	Unsafe play, knife safety.	Rules and strategy of
Grade 5	Principles of movement and their application. Inertia, force.	Understanding one's own skill, capacity? Relation of time, agility, balance, speed.	Exercise and disease. Exercise and respiration.	Learning the value of exercise. Learning about stress.	Prevention of fatigue.	Mouth to mouth artificial respiration. Others.	Medicines, rough play falls.	Sports and
Grade 6	Principles of movement and their application. Friction, acceleration, others.	Understanding one's own level of physical fitness endurance, strength, flexibility.	Exercise and heart. Exercise and other body systems.	Learning the value of exercise. Efficient use of exercise.	Recreational use of efficient movement.	Artificial circulation. Review emergency first aid and artificial respiration.	Vacation safety. Pedestrian safety. Use of tools. Acts of God. Alcohol and smoking safety.	Games

class discussion should be encouraged, specific "best" methods have been developed by researchers and the information should be presented in a straight forward manner. For example, mouth to mouth artificial respiration should be taught according to techniques prescribed as most effective. Children may ask questions and discuss the techniques to gain greater understanding, but the actual information should be clearly presented either by the teacher, a film, or in some other effective way. Presentation of specific game rules, safety techniques, and other concepts could be presented effectively in this lecture manner.

2. *Class Discussions.* As pointed out in chapter 4, learning is best when the learner is a participant in the learning situation. The class discussion is an effective technique for involving students, especially in promoting learning of certain physical education concepts such as: the value of efficient movement, and making proper movement decisions. Students can draw from their own experience in these discussions and with direction from the teacher, they can develop understanding and appreciation for these concepts.

3. *Activity Classes.* Certain of the concepts of physical education can be best learned in the movement setting. The teacher can make the learning of strategies more meaningful if students are taught while involved in the actual game in which the strategy is used. Rules of safety can also be learned effectively in the actual movement situation. A child may best learn the safety rules of trampoline if he learns the rules in the actual gymnastics class.

4. *Experiments in Problem Solving.* As pointed out by Torrance in chapter 7, learning can be highly efficient and meaningful if the child is involved in creative problem solving experiences. Just as movement exploration problems can be planned to help children develop skillful performance, so can problem solving experiences be posed in the classroom to help children understand some of the concepts of physical education. For example, a problem such as: "What happens to the heart during and after exercise?", could be posed during a laboratory physical education session. The children could collect data, including their heart rate, before and after exercises of various intensity. They might then try to determine what happened to the heart during this exercise. With the direction of the teacher, such problem solving experiments could be of great value in helping children understand the value of exercise (For specific problem solving experiments, see chapter 13).

The steps for planning problem solving experiments for children in physical education might be as follows:

a. *Present the problem.* The problems should be stated simply so that the children can see pathways for discussion. However, its solution should be such that the children can relate the meaning of the problem to their own behavior.

b. *Discuss what might happen.* If data are going to be collected, the children, with the direction of the teacher, attempt to predict what they will find in collecting these data.

c. *Collect data.* The students collect information on themselves or classmates, which could be of help in solving the problem.

d. *Suggest possible solutions.* Why did the result turn out in this way? What are some of the possible meanings of the results?

e. *The best solution.* With the direction of the teacher, the students select the best solution or pose the best answer to the problem which will have meaning to the children in better understanding physical education.

Organizing for Developing Understanding

The four techniques for helping students develop an understanding of physical education may be included as part of various parts of the school curriculum. In organizing programs for meeting the cognitive-affective objective of physical education, four patterns of planning are possible. These patterns are listed below:

1. *Regular Physical Education Classes.* The teacher presentation technique and the activity class technique lend themselves best to this pattern of organization. During the regular physical education class, specific attention can be directed to the specific concept to be learned. This may be in the form of a talk given to all of the students by the teacher or as specific instructions given to students needing special attention. This is the traditional method of accomplishing the knowledge objective in physical education.

2. *Correlation with other Subject Matter Areas.* In certain instances several subject matter areas may desire to accomplish common objectives. Any or all of the above listed techniques may be used to accomplish these objectives. Correlation, or cooperation in providing educational experiences, might be accomplished with health education in discussing subjects such as weight control or posture, with science in discussing certain exercises and their relationship to the heart, or with social studies on discussing the role of recreation in our modern society.

3. *Laboratory Sessions.* Laboratory sessions may be conducted during physical education class time or at other times during the school day. These sessions are most often devoted to conducting experiments in problem solving. During these periods students collect information and

investigate problems pertaining to various aspects of physical education. This is *not* a new concept in education. Experimental laboratory sessions are quite common in the sciences, even in the elementary school. The use of such laboratory sessions is a new approach in meeting the objectives of physical education (See chapter 13 for example laboratory sessions).

4. *Special Programs.* An understanding and appreciation of physical education can also be accomplished through the use of special total school programs. Examples of these special sessions might be Bicycle Safety Day, a day during which all bicycles are checked for safety and talks and films are given to all students; or *Physical Fitness Day,* a day when physical fitness is tested for all students and talks or films are presented to students.

Suggestions for Helping Children Understand Physical Education

1. Development of knowledge, understanding, and appreciation of physical education is an important objective of physical education. The teacher cannot assume that all parts of this objective will be accomplished in the traditional activity or "skill" oriented physical education program. If children are to understand *all* aspects of physical education, plans must be made to provide for this development. *Don't leave the development of knowledge and understanding to chance.*

2. It is not uncommon in the elementary school to have a number of days during the year when weather or lack of facilities causes the physical education class to be taught inside without proper facilities, perhaps in the regular classroom. Many times physical education is eliminated on these days and in other instances so called "bad weather" or "quiet games" are planned. These games, such as eraser tag, and others are in most instances of little value in accomplishing physical education objectives. It is my opinion that use of such periods for class discussions or laboratory experiments would be more profitable in meeting the objectives of the physical education program. Several experiments or organized class discussions could be planned in advance for use on bad weather days or other days when the children are confined to the regular classroom.

3. In planning for developing an understanding of physical education, determine the specific aspect to be learned, and pick the best tool for helping students learn that aspect. If rules of sports are the specific objective then activity sessions in the particular sport may be best. However, if the specific aspect to be learned is "Why exercise?", then it is possible that laboratory sessions may be the better tool.

10

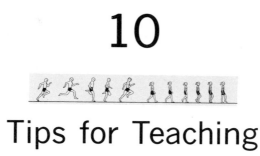

Tips for Teaching

The teacher can meet the objectives in physical education more effectively if he can organize so that the time spent in the physical education class is used efficiently. It is the purpose of this chapter to discuss some ways of efficiently using class time as well as to provide some general practical suggestions for the teaching of physical education.

Organizing Students in Squads

The use of squads in physical education is one technique by which the teacher can successfully save valuable teaching time. Frequently the roll must be called, students may have to be divided into teams, or pre-instruction exercises must be performed before the instruction for the day may begin. Squad organization is one method of reducing the time required to carry out there functions. A squad is a group of students who are assigned to a team or organized group, often at a prescribed location. Squads may be named or numbered to help students identify with their group.

At the beginning of the physical education period, students can be taught to gather with their squad in a prescribed location. Squad leaders can be appointed or elected to perform such functions as calling the roll. If competitive teams are to be selected, one or more squads may perform as teams thus reducing the amount of time necessary for team organization. Exercises or warm-up calisthenics also could be performed in squads. Since students automatically line up in squads when reaching the play area the teacher need not take the time to organize students for activity.

This technique is usually more effective with intermediate rather than primary grade children.

SQUAD SELECTION

Squads can be organized into homogeneous or heterogeneous groups. Homogeneous grouping is desirable for skill learning situations but may not be so desirable for team situations. For this reason either type grouping can be utilized at appropriate times. Homogeneous groups can be selected by the teacher after observing student performance. Random selection such as counting off by numbers, or drawing lots is perhaps the most often used method of selecting heterogeneous groups. However, teacher selection or student choosing can also be used. It is important to recognize that student selections may not be most effective in situations where competition is involved. Frequently the best performers are chosen and the poor performers are left standing until last. For this reason choosing of squads by the children should be done with care.

SOME SUGGESTIONS FOR SQUAD ORGANIZATION

1. Spend some class time early in the year discussing squad organization with the students. Discuss their responsibilities so that "time" requirements for daily routine is minimal.
2. Make squads as small as possible. The squads should be organized according to the unit being taught. For example, if soccer is being taught, squads should be approximately 11 or team size. However, in cases where activities do not demand a specific size, reduce squad size to 5 or 6. The smaller the squad, the greater the student leadership opportunities.
3. Select squad leaders. These squad leaders can call the roll, lead exercises, act as team captains, etc. Periodically (every 2 or 3 weeks) select new squad leaders to give all children an opportunity to lead. As students develop responsibility they may select their own leaders.
4. Assign prescribed locations for squads to meet. For example, lines may be painted on the gym floor, labeled 1, 2, 3, etc. Each squad leader will have his squad line up behind the proper mark at the beginning of each class.
5. Periodically squad leaders or squads should select the activity in which they will participate.
6. Establish signals to be used by the teacher or squad leaders. For example, circling one hand above the head means "return to squads" or holding both hands above the head means quiet.
7. Make it clear to squad leaders exactly what their duties are.

Formations for Teaching

The following are common formations which can be used in teaching. The teacher should spend some time at the beginning of each year acquainting students with these formations. A few minutes spent discussing what to do or what not to do when forming a particular formation may save considerable teaching time later in the year. Students should also become familiar with the names of various formations.

The Circle

Students form in a circle. The easiest method of forming a circle is to have several concentric circles painted on the floor or asphalt in various colors. Students merely stand on the painted line of a particular color to form a circle. (For example: Blue = Big Circle; Red = Medium; and Green = Small Circle). At times it is impossible to paint a circle on the ground. In such cases students should join hands in a group (as small as possible) and begin to walk backward . . . just prior to the time when students arms are taut, the hands should be dropped. Circle size can be regulated by having students all step forward or backward at the same time. Discourage pulling on arms of other students.

Variations
1. Facing Center
2. Facing Clockwise
3. Facing Counter Clockwise
4. Partners Facing

The Double Circle

Again, circles painted on the playing surface is the easiest method. When this is impossible have the inside circle form as discussed above. Then have persons in the outside circle fall in behind someone in the inner circle. If the teacher wants new partners, have one circle stand still while having the outside circle walk.

Variations
1. All Facing Clockwise
2. All Facing Counter Clockwise
3. Facing Center
4. Partners Facing

Straight Line Facing Teacher

Again the best method for formation is to have a line painted on the playing surface. If no line is available use the edge of the grass, or a jump rope which has been stretched on the ground. The teacher should position himself quickly so the students know which way to face. Students should allow an arms distance between each other.

Variations

1. Double Line . . . Same as above with two straight lines one behind the other.

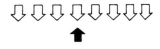

The Single File Line

This formation is one in which all children fall in behind one child who is facing the teacher. The easiest method of organizing a single file line is to have previously organized squads follow their leader and fall in one squad after another to form a single file line when students are not in squads. The teacher should first form students in a straight line facing the teacher. Then have all students make a quarter turn and they are in a single file line. Have students learn to keep an arms distance between them and the person in front of them.

Variations

1. Double File . . . Same as above with two single file line standing side by side.

Counting Off (By The Numbers)

The formation of squads is often done by "Counting Off". To do this students first form a straight line facing the teacher. To count off by two's the student to the far left says "One", the next "Two", the next "One" etc. . . . Until each student is a one or a two. This can also be done by Three's, Four's, etc. All "One's" then become squad or team one, the "Two's" become squad or team two, etc.

Suggestions

1. After counting off have students raise their hand before going to their squad. This shows that they have remembered their number.

2. Make students stay in their original position in the straight line during counting off procedure. This prevents team "Fixing" by students.

Facing Straight Lines

First have all students form a straight line facing the teacher. Have students count off by two's. Have two's fall in behind the ones. The ones then walk forward until they are the desired distance from the two's. The one's then turn around and face the two's.

The Principles of Learning

The reader is encouraged to refer to the discussion of the principles of learning as discussed in Chapter 3. It is in following these principles that the teacher is most effective in helping children learn.

The remainder of this section deals with additional information which would be of value to teachers in helping children learn in physical education.

SKILL LEARNING CURVES

Normally one would expect performance to improve after practice. However, in learning new skills performance may actually drop off before it gets better. This is especially true when the performer has previously established a pattern of skill behavior which is not the same as the skill being taught in physical education.

As seen in Figure 10-7 learning will normally occur gradually and performance will improve with practice until a plateau is achieved. After this plateau is reached performance will not improve significantly with practice. At this time the performer has reached maximal performance in skill (at least with the current technique).

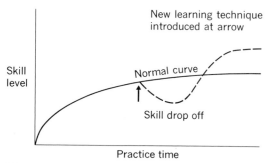

FIG. 10-7 *Skill Learning Curves.*

However, if a new practice technique is introduced (Figure 10-7), the performance may "drop off." This is caused by interference in new learning as a result of old habits. For example, a golfer may learn golf on his own, and with practice improve in score from 120 to 100 where he reaches a plateau and his score does not improve. The golfer then may seek professional instruction. His score may "drop off" to 110 or even, 120. He must forget his old skill pattern which is interfering with the "new" skill pattern. If he continues with the "new" technique (assuming it is a better mechanical method), his performance will gradually begin to improve until it surpassed his previous score perhaps 90 or even 80, where it would level off as did the original learning.

It is important that the teacher and children understand this "drop off" phenomenon, especially in the elementary school. Children are impatient, often expecting immediate results from practice. If the teacher and children are not aware of this phenomenon, the children may abandon the new technique prematurely and revert to the old less effective method of performance.

In teaching new skills the evaluation should be deferred until the learning has overcome the "drop off" in performance. The students should be helped to understand this "drop off" so that they will continue to practice for the ultimate plateau in performance.

FEEDBACK

As mentioned in Chapter 3, learning must be reinforced. It is through auditory, visual, tactile and kinesthetic feedback that performance is reinforced. When a batter hits the ball, he determines his success by the visual observation as to how far the ball traveled. The sound of the "crack" of the bat also provides feedback information. Finally, if it "felt good", the batter is positively reinforced. When all of this feedback information tells the batter "that was good", he will try to produce the same type performance again.

One problem with the learning of skill is that the performer cannot always tell what "feedback" information to choose in an effort to improve his performance. In helping elementary school children, it is the teacher's responsibility to provide feedback information for the pupil. It is the teacher's remark, "that was good", or "try this" which provides the information which will help the children improve their performance. The child cannot see himself, so it becomes the teachers "feedback" of the child's performance which aids the child in performing. The sooner the information is "fedback" to the child, the more efficient the learning. Teachers are cautioned to avoid feeding back too much information at one time. This can result in "paralysis of analysis" which makes the performer ineffective in his performance because he is working so hard on the specific details of the performance that the total performance becomes ineffective. One recent development which aids in effectively "feeding back" information about skill performance is the use of closed circuit television.

TECHNIQUE SHOULD PRECEDE ACCURACY

As the child learns a skill, it is important that technique be learned early. For example, in throwing a softball, the teacher should emphasize the ballistic action of the arm, encouraging children to throw hard. If the emphasis is on accuracy, such as pitching in a game or throwing at a target, the child may begin to place the ball, pushing with the arm rather than throwing.

As technique improves with the emphasis on a ballistic throwing action, the accuracy will improve. However, those who have emphasized accuracy early in their skill learning will be limited in the effectiveness of their skill performance in later years. This is because many sports skills are ballistic in nature. The emphasis on accuracy keeps the performer from developing true ballistic movements.

Some General Suggestions for Teaching

The following are some tips which may be useful in teaching elementary school physical education.

1. If a whistle is to be used in teaching, inform students early as to its meaning. For example, one blast means "assemble" and two blasts means "quiet." Once the use of the whistle is established, use it only as described and use it as little as possible. Excess use will make it ineffective. The whistle may be most useful as a device for promoting safe play rather than a teaching tool.

2. Teachers need not be able to perform skills to teach them. Students can be used to demonstrate skill performance.

3. In teaching skills, the teacher should circulate calling attention to "correct performance" rather than mistakes.

4. Children in primary grades may need to be taught in large groups, while upper level students may benefit more from small group performance.

5. When possible make activities *fun.*

6. Keep all students active.

7. Expect the best from children. Elementary children can accomplish many difficult tasks. Rather than expecting little, give them a chance to be successful.

8. Officiate! Children like to play by the rules. It is when the children are not backed up in their group decisions that rules deteriorate. Help them enforce their own rules.

9. Learn the difference between noise (excitement) and noise (distraction). Certainly children should be quiet when the teacher is giving instructions, but children should make noise in playing games. Often the classroom teacher is so used to enforcing "quiet" that students become afraid to yell. Noise in activity may be desirable.

10. Children will be active in physical education class. When they come to the activity class they will wiggle, squirm, and move in any way possible. This is natural. Perhaps it is advisable to get children in activity early and save new rules or discussions until later in the period.

11. Do not argue with elementary school children, especially about sports. Intermediate grade children are ardent sports fans and frequently what seems unimportant to the teacher may be serious to the child. Remember, you may be wrong and what seems petty to you may be serious to the child. Listen!

12. Students should operate in groups that are as small as practical. For instructional purposes, work with small groups when possible so all children are not inactivated for the instruction of a few.

13. We all make mistakes. Admit it if you are wrong. Children respect honesty and self awareness.

14. When explaining rules, be brief. At first children should be concerned only with essential rules. Promote discussion of more detailed rules after the children have experienced the game situation.

15. Keep your objectives in mind at all times as you teach.

16. Above all *teach!* Do not just stand there, help children accomplish objectives.

Experiences for Meeting Physical Education Objectives

The following nine chapters of this text are included to give the teacher an idea of some of the educational activities which can be included in a program of physical education as tools for helping children accomplish program objectives.

It should be emphasized that these educational activities and experiences are but a representative sample of the types of tools available for helping children to become physically educated. For this reason a reference list is provided at the end of each chapter to help the teacher in locating additional activities.

Emphasis should also be placed on the fact that the following activities are tools for use by the teacher in helping children in becoming physically educated. Like any tool, the use of these activities as tools, requires wise use even if it is the best tool available for helping children meet a specific objective. (The reader is referred to Chapter 10 for suggestions on the effective use of the experiences included in the following chapters.)

11

Fundamental Skills and Fundamental Skill Activities

The activities listed in this chapter are designed to accomplish specific skill objectives. Although other objectives may be met in these skill learning activities, specific skill learning is the objective of each activity. Activities are arranged in a sequence from the most elementary (for primary grades) to the most difficult (for intermediate grades). The exact grade at which any particular skill would be introduced depends on the skill level and past experiences of specific students.

STANDING

Equipment: None.

Instructional Procedures: Usually every child entering the school can stand. However, it is in learning to stand properly that the child overcomes possible future back pain or working inefficiency. Although there is no single best posture for all persons, there are some principles of standing which can be passed on to children.[1] They are:
1. The total body weight is centered squarely above both feet, or inclined slightly forward.
2. The lower limbs, pelvis, trunk, and head are aligned vertically, or inclined very slightly forward from the ankles.

3. The pelvis is centered squarely above the feet and provides firm support for the trunk.
4. The chest is slightly lifted but not in a forward elevation.
5. The head is erect with the profile vertical and the chin level.
6. The feet point forward or slightly outward.
7. The ankles, as seen from the front or back, are straight. There is neither pronation (inward sagging), nor supination (exaggerated cupping or arching.)
8. The total posture is maintained without evidence of strain or tension.

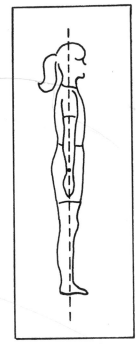

WALKING

Equipment: None.

Instructional Procedures: Poor walking habits developed in childhood can result in abnormal adult walking performance. The teacher should take time, early in the elementary school to teach children the following techniques of proper walking and dynamic posture.

1. Follow the proper walking sequence. See opposite figure.
2. Feet should be placed heel first.
3. Toes should be pointed directly in the line of walking.
4. Feet should be lifted off the ground with each step.
5. Arms should swing alternately in opposition to the forward foot.
6. Extremely slow or fast walking is inefficient.

Activities: One activity useful in teaching proper walking is to walk a line on the floor. In this way the teacher can observe performance which is not directed straight ahead of the walker.

SKIPPING

Equipment: None.

Instructional Procedures: Skipping is actually a step-hop maneuver and should not be introduced until after children have mastered the one foot hop. In teaching the maneuver the step-hop should be taught first. In the step-hop the performer first steps, then hops with the same foot. This is immediately repeated with the opposite foot. This is repeated alternately with each foot. When the step-hop is mastered, the hop is shortened from 8 to 12 inches and the total maneuver is speeded up. This is the skip.

├── Step ──┼── Hop ──┼── Step ──┼── Hop ──┤

BEGINNING SKIPPING

├── Step ──┼── Hop ──┼── Step ──┼── Hop ──┼── Step ──┤

ADVANCED SKIPPING

FALLING

Equipment: Mats.

Instructional Procedures: The following principles should be followed in falling:[2]

1. Sit and roll—lower the center of gravity and distribute the body weight over a large area.
2. Protect boney projections taking fall on fleshy body parts.

3. Extend arms and legs on landing bending as weight is taken on these limbs. Use them as shock absorbers.
4. When landing on the feet, keep the center of gravity over the feet.

Activities: Practice these principles on mats.

LIFTING

Equipment: Objects such as boxes.

Instructional Procedures:
1. Keep the feet flat on the floor at shoulder width.
2. Keep the back straight.
3. Do not turn body while lifting.
4. Keep object close to the body.
5. Lift by straightening legs.

Activities: Practice with empty boxes, etc.

PUSHING

Equipment: Table or big box.

Instructional Procedures:
1. If possible slide heavy objects rather than lifting them.
2. Push in direction of desired movement.
3. Push on a level with the center of gravity if possible.
4. Push by straightening the legs. Keep feet spread apart.

Activities: Practice with box or table.

PULLING

Equipment: Rope.

Instructional Procedures: Follow the principles of pushing.
1. Lean away from object if possible.
2. Be careful not to pull the object on yourself.

Activities: Practice with two or four man tug-o-war.

ROLLING A BALL

Equipment: One ball for every two children.

Instructional Procedures:

1. Place a large playground ball on the floor in front of the children. Two children work together facing each other at a distance of 10 to 15 feet.
2. First, push with both hands behind the ball. The ball should be pushed from between the legs with the hands behind the ball.
3. Second, push with one hand—practice pushing to and from partners first using the right hand then the left.
4. Third, roll the ball with two hands. The procedure is the same as step #2 except the ball is held between the legs with both hands and pushed from there.
5. Finally, roll the ball with one hand. Hold the ball one hand behind the ball (dominant hand) and the other on top and in front of the ball. Bend the knees slightly. Step forward with the opposite foot. Swing dominant arm forward, releasing the hand on top of the ball. Push from behind the ball rolling it forward. Emphasize opposite foot forward.

Activities: Practice rolling between partners in all of above steps.

THROWING AN OBJECT—UNDERHAND (TWO HANDS)

Equipment: One ball or bean bag for every two children.

Instructional Procedures:

1. Stand holding the ball in both hands. With the feet at shoulder width and one foot slightly forward.
2. With the arms held straight, bend the knees bringing the ball down between the knees.

3. Straighten the knees as the arms lift forward. The hands push from under and behind the ball.
4. Release the ball when it reaches belt height. Follow through with the arms.

Activities: Practice throwing the ball or bean bag to a partner. Practice throwing the ball or bean bag into the air and catching it. Teach the two hand arm catch at the same time.

THROWING AN OBJECT—UNDERHAND AND ONE HAND

Equipment: Balls or bean bags.

Instructional Procedures:

1. Begin standing in the starting position used for rolling a ball.
2. Hold the ball with the throwing hand under and behind the ball, the other hand holds over the top of the ball.
3. Bend the knees slightly, swing the throwing arm back.
4. Step forward with the foot opposite the throwing hand.
5. Do not swing the throwing arm forward until the body is well forward.
6. Swing the arm vigorously forward lifting non-throwing hand from the ball.
7. Release the ball at waist height, follow through with the throwing arm.

8. Release the ball from the hand then the fingers.

Activities: Practice throwing to a partner. Practice throwing against a wall. Do not practice for accuracy until skill is well established. After children become more skillful encourage them to throw without the help of the non-throwing hand.

THROWING AN OBJECT—TWO HAND AND OVERHAND

Equipment: Balls.

Instructional Procedures:
1. Face the direction of the throw with the ball held over the shoulder

of the dominant hand. Keep the dominant hand behind the ball with the other hand in front of the ball.

2. Step forward with the opposite foot.
3. When weight has moved on to the opposite foot, move both arms forward from the shoulder.
4. As the ball moves off the shoulder, straighten the elbow then pushing the ball with the hands and fingers.
5. Release the ball slightly above shoulder height.
6. Follow through.

THROWING AN OBJECT—ONE HAND OVERHAND

Equipment: Balls or bean bags.

Instructional Procedures:
1. Thrown similar to two hand overhand except non-dominant hand is not used.
2. Use same procedure as the two hand throw except the non-dominant hand is held extended forward for balance.
3. While holding the ball prior to throwing it, keep the hand under the ball.
4. Support the ball on the fingers and thumbs.
5. Continue step as described for the two hand throw.

Activities: Practice with various size objects. Practice with both dominant and non-dominant hands. Master two hands throw before beginning with one hand.

CATCHING WITH ARMS

Equipment: Large balls.

Instructional Procedures:
1. Stand with feet spread with one foot slightly forward.

2. Hold the arms in front bent at the elbow. Form a "basket" with the forearms and hands.
3. Keep the eye on the ball.
4. Move backward allowing the "basket" made by the arms to "give" as the ball hits.

Activities: Practice catching in combination with throwing. Use large balls. Do not advance to catching with the hands until children have gained confidence with the arms.

CATCHING WITH HANDS

Equipment: Small balls or bean bags.

Instructional Procedures: Same as catching with the arms except the object is caught in spread and relaxed fingers. Elbows and fingers should act as shock absorbers. When catching above the waist, palms should face the ball. When catching below the waist, palms should face up.

STRIKING—ONE HAND UNDERHAND

Equipment: Soft inflated balls.

Instructional Procedures:

1. Hold the ball in one hand standing with the same foot ahead of the other.
2. Hold the striking arm back and slightly bent.
3. Step forward with the opposite foot, at the same time swing the striking arm forward.
4. Straighten the arm just prior to striking the ball.
5. Keep the eye on the ball.
6. Keep the fingers bent into the palm. Strike the ball with the heel of the palm.
7. Strike the ball out of the opposite hand, swinging forward and upward.
8. Follow through.

Activities: Practice striking the ball against a wall. Catch the ball and strike again.

STRIKING—TWO HANDS UNDERHAND

Equipment: Soft inflated balls.

Instructional Procedures:

1. This technique should be used when striking an object which is moving toward the performer below the waist.
2. Stand with feet spread at shoulder width. Grasp one hand inside the other so that the tops of both thumbs are facing upward.
3. Extend the arms to full length.
4. As the ball approaches the performer, it should be allowed to strike both arms between the elbows and the wrists.
5. On vigorously approaching balls, the arms should "give" allowing the ball to bounce off the arm.
6. On softly approaching balls, the arms should swing together in the direction of the ball before hitting.

Activities: Practice hitting back and forth with a partner. First at short, then greater distances.

STRIKING—ONE HAND OVERHAND

Equipment:

Instructional Procedures:

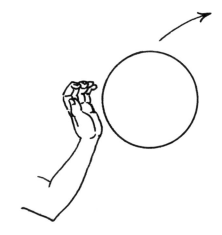

1. The ball is thrown into the air with the non-striking hand.
2. The striking hand is held in the same manner as the underhand strike with ball contact being made with the heel of the hand.
3. After the ball is thrown into the air the striking arm swings toward the ball as in throwing the ball. The ball should be struck at eye level, slightly in front of the body. Do not teach this skill until throwing and underhand striking are mastered.

Activities: Practice striking against a wall.

STRIKING—TWO HANDS OVERHAND

Equipment:

Instructional Procedures:

1. This technique should be used to strike an oncoming ball that approaches above the waist.
2. The hands should be held in front of the face at eye level with the thumbs toward each other. The palms should face outward and slightly upward.
3. Flex the elbows.
4. Get in a position under the on-coming ball. Keep the eyes on the ball.
5. Strike the ball at forehead level or higher with the finger tips. Extend the elbow to strike.
6. Be careful not to carry the ball on the hands, strike it.

Activities: Practice striking to and from a wall or a partner.

STRIKING WITH AN IMPLEMENT—HITTING A STATIONARY OBJECT

Equipment: Ball and bat, wands or paddles.

Instructional Procedures:

1. Place a ball on the ground slightly in front of the body.
2. The feet should be spread at shoulder width, with the foot opposite the strik-ing hand placed forward.
3. With a bat or wand in the dominant hand, swing the arm backward and upward. When the striking hand has reached the shoulder level, start a for-ward swing. Place the body weight on the forward foot.
4. Swing the shoulder forward first, then the upper arm, the lower arm and finally the implement with a snap of the wrist.
5. Strike the ball with the implement.
6. Keep the eyes on the ball. Follow through.
7. If a short implement is used, the knees must be bent prior to striking the ball.

Activities:
1. Practice striking the ball back and forth between partners.
2. When the skill is mastered, place the ball on a tee made of 2-inch rubber hose and practice striking the ball from the tee.
3. Divide the class in half with one group at one end of the gym and the second group at the other end. Give each student an implement and a ball. Have them strike the ball at the other end of the gym. As a ball rolls at them from the other end, strike it toward the other end of the gym. At the end of a certain time, count the number of balls at each end of the gym. The side with the least number of balls is the winner.

STRIKING WITH AN IMPLEMENT—HITTING A MOVING OBJECT

Equipment: Balls and bats or paddles.

Instructional Procedures:
1. Hold the implement in one hand and a ball in the other. Drop the ball in front of the striking hand.
2. Drop the ball allowing it to bounce to waist height.
3. Swing the implement as in striking a stationary object.
4. Keeping the eye on the ball, strike it at waist height. Follow through.
5. As proficiency is developed swing the implement to the side rather than under the shoulder.

Activities:
1. Practice bouncing and striking against a wall.
2. Practice, adding the second hand to the implement before striking.
3. Practice striking a slowly thrown ball.

TWO HAND BOUNCE

Equipment: Large rubber balls.

Instructional Procedures:
1. Drop the ball and catch it with two hands.
2. As proficiency is gained strike the ball downward with both hands after each bounce.
3. Next, practice walking while bouncing and catching the ball with two hands.

4. As proficiency is gained strike the ball downward with both hands while walking. Strike (actually push) with the finger tips.

ONE HAND BOUNCE

Equipment: Medium size balls.

Instructional Procedures:
1. Drop the ball.
2. Strike it downward with one hand after each bounce.
3. Push rather than strike as proficiency is gained.
4. Walk while bouncing the ball.
5. Keep the eyes on the ball at first. As proficiency is gained practice bouncing with out looking.
6. Practice using left as well as the right hand.

INSTEP KICK

Equipment: Rubber balls.

Instructional Procedures:
1. Place the ball on the ground in front of the kicking foot.
2. Step forward first with the non kicking foot. Plant that foot slightly behind and beside the ball, bend the non-kicking leg.
3. Kick through first with the upper part of the kicking leg, then the lower part and finally the foot.
4. With the toe turned slightly out kick the ball on the instep (the shoe strings).
5. Keep the eyes on the ball and follow through.
6. Practice with both feet.

Suggestions:
1. To kick the ball higher into the air place the opposite foot closer to the ball, turn the toe out or kick for a lower spot on the ball.
2. For a low kick, kick straight over the ball (toe in) kick high on the ball and stand further from the ball.

TOE KICK

Equipment: Rubber balls.

Instructional Procedures: The same as the instep kick except the ball is contacted with the toe. Accuracy is sacrificed for possible greater distance.

THE PUNT

Equipment: Medium rubber balls.

Instructional Procedures:

1. Hold the ball in both hands at waist height, with the arms extended.
2. Place the kicking foot slightly in front of the opposite foot.
3. Stride forward with the opposite foot taking the body weight on that foot.
4. Keeping the head down, drop the ball after the step with the opposite foot.
5. Kick the upper leg first with a bent knee, then straighten the knee immediately prior to contacting the ball.
6. Point the toe making contact on the strings of the shoe.
7. Keep the arms extended to help maintain body balance.

CONTROLLING THE BALL—WITH THE FEET

Equipment: Balls.

Instructional Procedures:

1. To control the ball with the feet while running or walking the ball should be kicked alternately with each foot in front of the body so that a full step or two can be taken, but the ball should not be kicked so far that another performer could gain control in a game situation.
2. The ball should be kicked as in the instep kick. However, the toe can be turned inward or outward.
3. In controlling the ball both feet should be used.
4. In moving outside an object the toe should point out when kicking. In moving inside an object the toe should point in when kicking.

JUMPING ROPE—INDIVIDUAL

Equipment: One rope for each child (8 to 10 feet)

Instructional Procedures:

1. Hold both ends of the rope in one hand on the same side of the body.

2. Practice swinging the rope in one hand without jumping. Swing the empty hand as if it were swinging the rope. Practice with each hand.
3. As proficiency is developed practice jumping beside the rope as it is swung in one hand.
4. Grasp the rope in both hands. Throw the rope over the head allowing it to lay on the ground in front of the performer. Step over. Repeat.
5. Practice the above while traveling forward at a walk, then a slow run.
6. When proficiency is developed swing the rope with both hands and jump in place.

Variations:
1. Jump on both feet.
2. Hop on one foot.
3. Jump, hop, jump, hop.
4. Jump without allowing the rope to touch the ground.
5. Jump with a partner standing facing in at you.
6. Hop right, hop left, etc.
7. Jump backward.
8. Click heels in the air after each jump.
9. Cross hands and jump through on every other jump.
10. Skip while moving forward over the rope.
11. Practice various combinations.

JUMPING ROPE—GROUPS OF THREES

Equipment: One rope for every three children, 15 to 20 feet long.

Instructional Procedures:
1. First have two performers be the twirlers and one the jumper (alternate periodically).
2. Practice swinging the rope up 3 feet one direction then 3 feet the other way. Do not turn the rope all of the way over. Jump over the rope each time it swings by.
3. When proficiency is gained have twirlers practice swinging the rope. From a standing position beside the rope jump the rope as it is swung by the twirlers.

4. When proficiency is gained, start outside the swinging rope. Run in just before the rope hits the top of the arc. Jump. Run out immediately after the jump.

Variations:
1. Run in, jump, run out the other side.
2. Run in and out without jumping.
3. Add to the number of jumps taken each time.
4. Jump when rope does not touch the ground.
5. Jump a fast turning rope.
6. Touch the toes between each jump.
7. Touch the ground between each jump.
8. Hop on one foot.
9. Alternate the hopping foot.
10. Practice combinations of the above.
11. Jump two ropes swinging in opposite directions.

CHANTS FOR GROUP JUMPING

Jack be nimble, *Jack* be quick
Jack jump over the candle stick.
Jack jump up, *Jack* jump down
Jack jump out or _____ will frown.
(Use the jumper's name instead of Jack). (Put the new jumper's name in the blank).

Jumper, jumper, how do you do? (Bow while jumping)
Jumper, jumper, touch your shoe,
Jumper, jumper, turn around.
Jumper, jumper, touch the ground.
Jumper, jumper, you are through,
Jumper, _____ skee daddle-do.
(Substitute jumpers name in the blank). (Execute the maneuver as called).

FUNDAMENTAL SKILL DRILLS

Equipment: Mats, balls.

Organization: For each of the following drills students should be divided in squads of three or four in a single file line behind a mat (may be done without the mat)

Drill one:
1. Hop down the mat both feet together keeping the hands on the hips.
2. Repeat #1 but alternately move feet apart then together.

3. Repeat #2 but thrust the hands forward then back to the hips, alternating with each jump.
4. Hop down the mat making a quarter turn with each hop.
5. Repeat #4 with 1st quarter turn raise one arm, with the second turn raise the other arm, with the third turn lower one arm, with the fourth lower the other arm.
6. Repeat #1, #2, and #4 raising arms above the head, in front of the body or out to the sides. Use various combinations with each hop.
7. Repeat #6 hopping backward.

Drill Two:
1. Leap down the length of the mat.
2. Repeat #1 except hold for 2 seconds on the supporting foot after each leap.
3. Repeat #2 with the hands held behind the head with the elbows out.
4. Jump down the length of the mat leave the ground on one foot, land on two.
5. Repeat #4 doing a half twist in the air on each jump, after landing turn around and continue.

Drill Three:
1. Hop the length of the mat on one foot.
2. Repeat #1 on the other foot.
3. Repeat #1 with the arms and the opposite leg outstretched.
4. Repeat #3 on the other foot.
5. Repeat #3 hopping sideways down the mat.
6. Repeat #4 hopping sideways down the mat.
7. Repeat #1 alternately bending and straightening the other leg with each hop.
8. Repeat #1 on the other foot.

Drill Four:
1. Bend left knee so you can grasp left toe with both hands up in front of you, then hop length of mat. (Sore toe position, use for relay racing).
2. Same as #1 but grasp right toe and hop length of mat.
3. Assume one-legged man position by bending left leg backward at knee, grasp foot with left hand, hold leg against back of thigh, then hop length of mats.
4. Same as #3, but grasp right leg instead of left and hop to end of mats.
5. Bend forward with knees slightly bent, grasp toes with both hands, walk length of mats, without letting go of toes, mostly on heels.

6. Series of broad jumps length of mats, keeping legs in stride-stand position all the time.

Drill Five:
1. Gallop the length of the mat.
2. Repeat #1 galloping on the other foot.
3. Repeat #1 doing a forward roll at the end of the mat.
4. Repeat #3 on other foot.
5. Gallop swinging arms alternately above the head then to the sides.
6. Gallop swinging arms alternately in front of the body and to the sides.

15 SECOND SKILL DRILLS

Equipment: Whatever is necessary for the skill used.

Instructional Procedure:
1. Select the skill to be developed (ex. bouncing a ball)
2. Give every class member the necessary equipment (one ball for each child)
3. After instruction in the proper skill technique, have the child practice the skill as many times as possible in a 15-second period.
4. Have them keep their own scores.
5. Repeat 15 second drill many times to allow students to compare early performance with later performance.

Suggestions:
1. Emphasize proper technique.
2. Make it clear to children that they are not being evaluated.
3. Discourage comparison with others, compare your own performances.
4. Other time intervals can be used (30, 45, 60 seconds).

POSSIBLE SKILLS FOR 15 SECOND DRILLS

1. Hopping back and forth over a line.
2. Run back and forth between lines.
3. Same as #1 on one foot.
4. Throwing a ball in the air (self catch).
5. Throwing a ball against a wall.
6. Striking a ball in the air (self).
7. Striking a ball against the wall.
8. Two hand bouncing.
9. One hand bouncing.
10. Kicking a ball against the wall.
11. Jump rope (all variations).

SMALL GROUP DRILLS

Equipment: Whatever is necessary for the skill used.

Instructional Procedures:
1. Divide the children into small homogenous groups.
2. Using the circle, semi-circle, or facing straight line formations, have the students practice the skill with in the group.
   a. around the circle (ex. kicking).
   b. leader to semi-circle (ex. striking).
   c. partner to partner (ex. throwing).
3. Practice any of the skills listed under the 15-second drills.

References

1. Wells, Katharine F.: *Posture Exercise Handbook.* New York, The Ronald Press, 1963, p. 4.
2. Morehouse, L. E. and Cooper, J. M.: *Kinesiology.* St Louis, C. V. Mosby Co., 1950, p. 270.

Bibliography

PERIODICALS

Boyd, Barbara, Cox, Gloria, Ghens, Carol and Williams, Sandra: What Ever Happened To Basic Movement Skills?, *JOHPER,* May 1966. p. 21.

BOOKS

Dauer, Victor: *Fitness For Elementary School Children.* Minneapolis, Burgess Publishing Co., 1965, Chapter 9, p. 63–71.

Boyer, Madeline H.: *The Teaching Of Elementary School Physical Education.* New York, J. Lowell Pratt & Co., 1965, p. 10–174.

12

Movement Exploration Activities

The reader is referred to Chapter 7 for a more comprehensive coverage of movement exploration. In using movement exploration the following procedure may be used:

1. *Pose the Movement Problem.* In each activity listed in this chapter, a series of problems are posed. A period of movement by the children follows the statement of the movement problem. *Do not try to use all of the movement questions in one lesson.* Those are suggestions. Be careful not to restrict movement with too many questions. Create questions of your own concerning the type of movement being studied.
2. *Time for Exploration.* Each child works independently to solve the problem. Plenty of time should be available for the creation of movements as well as practice of movements. It is *not* enough just to create if proficiency is not gained. *Allow practice.*
3. *Use Demonstrations.* Children may demonstrate different movements. Pick students who demonstrate proper techniques *but* try to have all students demonstrate at some time.
4. *Give Instruction.* After a series of movement problems, suggest the best way to do certain movements. *Do not* give instructions too early or you will restrict responses.
5. *Find a Solution.* If one skill is correct or the "right way", have students learn the skill the proper way and practice it.

Moving Body Parts—Exploring Space

Objectives.
1. Learning what space is.
2. Learning the value of utilizing space in movement performance.
3. Development of "space" as an active word in the vocabulary.

Equipment. Large play area.

Basic Movement Problems. Without moving the feet, how far can you reach? Use your whole body as you reach with the arms. Can you reach further when you use the whole body? Can you reach outer space? In what different directions can you reach into space. Reach with one arm. Reach with both arms. Which way can you reach the furthest. How many body parts can you use to reach into space. Use different body parts. How much outer space can you take up? See how little "space" you can take up. Cover a large space on the floor. Cover a very small space on the floor. Move one small body part in a small space. Move the same part in a large space. Move a large body part in a small space. Move the same part in a large space. Shake the body parts in a small space. Make yourself stretch into space like a rubber band. Let the rubber band snap back into a small space.

Some Possible Responses. Reaching, swinging arms, swinging legs, circling with the head, circling with the trunk, curling up on the floor, spreading out on the floor, stretching all body parts.

Specific Instructions.
1. Do not move from your spot on the floor. Explore the space around you without leaving your own space.

Teaching Suggestions.
1. Do not ask all of the above questions during one lesson. Select specific questions for your own situations.
2. Have "good" performers or "creative" performers demonstrate periodically.
3. Be consistent in using the word, space.

Locomotor Movements—Exploring Space

Objectives.
1. Learning to use space efficiently.
2. Learning how to keep space between performer and others in games.
3. Learning the use of the word space.

Equipment. Large play area.

Basic Movement Problems. Every one in the class move together into the smallest space possible. Now spread out and use up all of the space in the gymnasium. Can you find a space which is not close to anyone elses space? This is your "Play Space." Now everyone move to one small space. Now move to your own play space. Are you sharing a play space with anyone? Now, everyone move to find a new and different play space. Why is it good to find your "own" play space? How much space can you cover before I count to 10? This time cover as much space as you can and get back to your original play space before I count to 10. Are you in a good "play space."

Some Possible Responses. All children gather in a small area. All children spread out in the gym. Movement in all areas of the gym.

Specific Instructions.
1. The "Play Space" should be one where each child is as large a distance as possible from the other children *so* he can later perform other stunts without running into the other children.

Teaching Suggestions.
1. Instead of having children line up for exercises or skill drills, merely have them find a "play space."

Moving Body Parts—Exploring Force

Objective.
1. Learning what force is.
2. Learning how we move—a result of force.
3. Learning specific movement skills.
4. Development of "force" as an active word in the vocabulary.

Equipment. Play area.

Basic Movement Problems. Can you move the arms softly? Can you imagine pushing a very light box? Now push a very heavy box. Can you bend and straighten the legs very softly? Imagine kicking a very light box. Does it take much force to kick a light box? Now kick a heavy one! Does it take more force? What is force? Can you move the arms very hard (with great force) without moving them very fast? (isometric contraction). Can you move the arms softly (with little force) but move them faster? Pretend you are a pendulum on a clock. Do not move your feet and swing the pendulum with a lot of force. Now swing the pendulum with very little force. Do you know what a jack hammer is? What is it? Can you move like a jack hammer? Make it work hard! Make it work softly.

Specific Instructions.
1. Use the body parts but do not move from your play space.

Locomotor Movements—Exploring Force

Objectives.
1. Learning the value of force in moving.
2. Learning specific skills.

Equipment. Play area.

Basic Movement Problems. What makes you move forward when you walk? What parts of the body provide the force? Can you move with great force in the legs? Now with a little bit of force? What ways can you move using force of body parts other than the legs? Can you move forward without using the force of the body parts? What ways, other than walking and running, can you use to move forward? Now find another way! Now another! Can you apply force only with your toes to make you move? Can you use the force of your legs to move in different directions? How can you use force to move the body without leaving your play space? (jumping).

Some Possible Responses. Walking, running, crawling, rolling, squirming, skipping, hopping, leaping, jumping, galloping and modifications or combinations of these.

Teaching Suggestions.
1. When pointing out good performance or when making suggestions refer to the proper ways of performing the fundamental skills as outlined in Chapter 11.

Moving Body Parts—Exploring Time

Objectives.
1. Learning the importance of time to movement.
2. Development of "Time" as an active word in the movement vocabulary.

Equipment. Play area.

Basic Movement Problems. Can you make a small body part move slowly? Can you make a large body part move slowly? Can you make a small body part move quickly? Can you make a large body part move quickly? How much time does it take you to bend over and touch your toes? Can you take more time to do it? Can you tell me the difference between time and force? Can you move your arm softly but quickly? What body parts can you move slowly? Which ones can you move quickly? Pretend you are a helicopter. Can you make your propeller move slowly. Now quickly?

Specific Instructions.
1. Make sure the children learn the difference between "force" and "time" before proceeding.
2. Use the body parts but do not move from your play space.

Locomotor Movements—Exploring Time

Objectives.
1. Learning the value of time in moving.
2. Learning specific movement skills.

Equipment. Play area.

Basic Movement Problems. Can you walk in slow motion? Can you run in slow motion? Now walk normally, walk faster, even faster. In what ways can you move slowly across the play area? Try another way! Can you move in slow motion in these types of movement? How fast can you move in a way other than running? What is the fastest way to cross the play area? What is the next fastest way? Can you move like a turtle? Can you move like a rabbit? Which of the two would win a race?

Moving Body Parts—Exploring Levels

Objectives.
1. Learning what "level" means.
2. Learning the usefulness of level in movement performance.
3. Development of "level" as an active word in the movement vocabulary.

Basic Movement Problems. Without moving from your play space. Can you put the body on a very low level? Now put the body at a medium level. How can you put the body in higher level than normal standing? Can you move the body parts at different levels without changing the body level? Can you move the body without changing the level of some of the body parts? Which ones? How high can you jump? Can you jump to a higher level from one or two feet?

Some Possible Responses. Lying on the floor, on hands and knees, standing on the toes, standing on an object, jumping, etc.

Locomotor Movements—Exploring Levels

Objectives.
1. Learning the value of level in moving.

Equipment. Play area.

Basic Movement Problems. Can you walk very low? Can you walk very high? How can you move forward to reach a very high level? Be a snake— how does a snake move? On what level? What animals move on a high level? Demonstrate how one of these animals moves. Now another. On what level does a bird move. Can you reach the level a bird moves in? What level does a giraffe move in? Move like a giraffe. Can you change level as you walk?

Can you walk low—now high? Can you change level slowly? Now quickly? At what level are you when you crawl? When you are an ape? When you are an elephant?

Moving Body Parts and Locomotor Movements—Exploring Posture and Direction

Objectives.
1. Learning the meaning of posture and direction.
2. Learning the value of 'good' posture.
3. Development of "posture" and "direction" as active words in the movement vocabulary.

Equipment. Play area.

Basic Movement Problems. Can you stand with "good" posture? (see pages 123–124.) Does your leg have posture? Make your legs have straight posture. Now crooked. Find different postures for different body parts. Can you walk with the legs in a straight posture? Can you move using both the arms and legs in a straight posture? Move around with different body postures! Can you lean forward? What other directions can you lean? Can you walk with the body leaning in different directions? Draw the body parts in. Now how can you move? Extend the body parts away from the body in all directions. Now how can you move? When you run does the body lean? How about when you walk? Can you walk in directions other than forward? Is "up" a direction? Can you move in that direction? Move in different ways in different directions. What different ways can we move in a sideways direction? Can you move to the left? What other sideways directions are there?

Locomotor Movements—Exploring Path

Objectives.
1. Learning what "path" is.
2. Learning the value of utilizing "path" in movement performance.
3. Development of "Path" as an active word in movement vocabulary.

Equipment. Play area.

Basic Movement Problems. What is the quickest way to get from one end of the play area to the other? Why is a straight line the quickest path? Investigate other paths you can follow in getting across the play area. Follow a curved path. Can you make your path even more curved? What happens if you keep walking in a very curved path? Can you get to the other end of the play area by walking in a circle? What is the best path to use to cross the play area without being tagged? Can you develop a game that involves using different paths? If some one is chasing you, is the best path a straight one?

Specific Instructions.
1. Make sure the children learn to distinguish the difference between Direction and Path. Direction refers to forward, backward, sideways, up, etc., while path refers to the course of movement (*i.e.,* straight, curved, crooked, etc.).

Teaching Suggestions.
1. Have students divide into small groups. Have a leader plan a path and the others follow. Periodically change leaders.
2. Use a simple tag game to help illustrate an evasive path.

Moving Body Parts—Body Support

Objectives.
1. Learning what "body support" means.
2. Learning how body support is important to movement.
3. Development of "body support" as an active term in the movement vocabulary.

Equipment. Play area.

Basic Movement Problems. On what body parts do we normally support the body? Can you support the body on one body part? Do it! Can you support the body with two parts, other than both feet? Try some other ways. Now try supporting the body on 3 parts. How many ways can you discover to support the body on three parts? Can you use four body parts for support? Try several other ways. Now try 5 body parts. How? Demonstrate!

Try to answer the following movement questions by working with a partner. How can you make the body most sturdy? Try to move your partner from his spot. Are you more sturdy on 2, 3, or 4 parts? How far apart should we put the body parts in standing? How should we support the body to get ready to run? How stable are you when you have one support? When you trip someone, what happens to his body support?

Possible responses. All kinds of support positions including, one leg stand, all four stand, head stand, etc.

Teaching Suggestions.
1. Have students demonstrate their discoveries frequently.

Locomotor Movements—Body Support

Objectives.
1. Learning about the role of body support in various movement activities.

Equipment. Play area.

Basic Movement Problems. Can you move on one body part? On two? On three? On four? On five? How many ways of movement can you discover for each number of body parts? Which number of body supports is best for fast movement? Which number of body supports is best for stable movement? Why do football players start from 3 or 4 parts? Can you move, changing frequently, the number of parts supporting the body? How can you stop most effectively? Where do you place the body supports when stopping? What if you put them too close together?

Teaching Suggestions.
1. Have students move around the play area using different numbers of body supports. When you say "freeze", they stop where they are, keeping the same number of supports. Ask questions: Which number of supports is best? How can we stop best to have good balance?

Moving Implements and Objects—Basic Skills

Objectives.
1. Learning basic skills.
2. Learning to use all elements of movement or patterns.

Equipment. Balls, ropes, hoops.

Basic Movement Problems. Balls. Can you impart force to the ball? In what different directions can you make the ball move? What different body parts can you use to make the ball move? Move it with one hand! Now two! Move it with one foot! Now two! What different ways can you use to impart force to the ball? What does spin do to the ball? Can you make it spin? Is it easier to throw a large or small ball?

Teaching Suggestions.
1. At first have children work with their own ball (one to a child). Later divide these into two groups. Have one group stand in one half of the play space and the second group stand in the other half of the play space. Using all size balls, have them throw, kick, etc. any and all balls into the other half of the gym. Use many balls.
2. Emphasize proper techniques for throwing, kicking, etc. (See Chapter 11)

Ropes. Lay the rope on the ground. Can you jump it? Jump over the rope slowly. Now jump more quickly! Lay the rope in a different way so it is harder to jump and so you can jump different ways. Now pick up the rope. Hold it at both ends. Can you jump over it without swinging it. How can you hold it differently to make it more difficult to jump? . . . . . Can you swing the rope and jump it? How many different ways can you swing it?

How many different ways can you jump it? Can you move around the room while jumping? What different ways can you move and jump over the rope?

Teaching Suggestions.
1. Emphasize the proper techniques for jumping rope as outlined in Chapter 11.

Hoops. Lay the hoop on the floor. Can you get in the hoop? Can you get out of the hoop? What different ways can you move in and out of the hoop? What is the fastest way to get in and out of the hoop? Pick up the hoop. Now how can you move in and out of the hoop? Find several ways. What other things can you do with the hoop?

Possible Solutions. Hula hoop, roll the hoop, jump the hoop (like a jump rope).

Teaching Suggestions.
1. Have small groups develop simple games using several hoops.

Moving with Others

Objective.
1. Learning to control all elements of movement for the benefit of total group performance.
2. Learning to move with others.
3. Learning patterns of movement.

Equipment. Play area.

Basic Movement Problems. Partners. Grasp hands with a partner, only one hand. How can you move around the gym with your partner? Can you move as fast with a partner? How can you move the fastest? Can you skip together? What paths can you follow? How must you work together to know what path to follow? Join hands with both hands. Now how can you move together? Is it easier or harder than with one hand joined? Why? What is the fastest way to move together? Can you find ways to move while joined together other than with hands joined?

Circles of Three. Work in a circle of threes. Can you move in a circle without changing your groups play space? How? Other than walking around a circle how can you move? Can you tie your circle in a knot? Can you move around the play area in groups of 3? Is it easier then groups of two? Why? Can you discover other ways of moving? What is the fastest way? Can you find different paths? Can you move with only 2 people working? How? Is it easier?

Patterns of Movement

Objectives.
1. Learning to use many movement elements together.
2. Learning basic skills.
3. Learning to use the movement terms effectively.

Equipment. Play area.

Basic Movement Problems. How many elements of movement can you use at once? Can you combine the use of space, time and force? Can you add level, posture and direction? Can you do any movements without body supports? What elements are involved in walking? Running? Skipping? Hopping? Can you combine some of these movements? Skipping is a combination of walking and hopping. What other combinations can you find? Can you hop, then step, then jump? Galloping is a combination of running and leaping. Can you gallop? Can you add another movement to galloping? Can you hop on one foot, then the other and then both feet? Develop other patterns like this. . . .

Teaching Suggestions.
1. Add any of the fundamental skills to these patterns by asking questions about their use. (See Chapter 11.)

Patterns of Movement—Rhythmic

Objectives.
1. Learning to synchronize basic movement to rhythm.
2. Learning basic skill.
3. Further developing an understanding of movement terms.

Equipment. Tom-Tom, Hoops.

Basic Movement Problems. Can you move to the tom-tom beat? What does the tom-tom tell you to do? (slow beat) Now what does it tell you to do? (fast beat). What elements of movement are important in moving to the drum beat? What movements can you do to this? (irregular beat) Can you take more than one step for each beat? How did the indians move to the tom-tom? Can one of you find a new drum beat? (have a child beat the drum) Is it easy to move with that drum beat? Why? Do we have rhythm when we do normal every day movements? Practice some every day movements to the beat of the drum. Can you move with a hoop to rhythms? Can you develop an indian hoop dance of your own?

Teaching Suggestions.
1. Children may provide the drum beat when practical.

Patterns of Movement—to Music

Objectives.
1. Learning to synchronize basic movement to music.
2. Learning to interpret music in movement.
3. Learning basic rhythmic skills.

Equipment. RCA Rhythms Vol. I (E-71), Record Player.

Basic Movement Problems. What the music tells you to do. This one is entitled "Galloping Horses", can you hear the horses? Can you be one of the horses? Repeat with other segments of the record volume (ex. birds, tip-toe, etc.).

Teaching Suggestions.
1. At first children move as they desire to the music.
2. Next suggest the title of the music to further structure this movement.
3. Ask them questions related to the music.
4. Finally ask them to develop movement patterns to the music.

Records Available From
RCA Victor Educational Sales
155 E. 24th St.
New York, N.Y. 10010

Moving Implements and Objects—Retrieve the Ball

Objective.
1. Development of specific ball skills.
2. Learning use of movement element in controlling a ball.

Equipment. A ball for every child.

Basic Movement Problems. From your own play space throw a ball far away from you. Can you retrieve the ball with your feet without letting the ball touch anyone? Can you control the path of the ball? What happens if you use too much force in kicking the ball? Return to your play space with your ball. Can you stop the ball in your own play space? This time kick your ball far away from your own space. Can you tell where the ball will go? What level should you kick the ball to make sure it doesn't touch anyone? Can you retrieve it again without touching anyone with the ball?

Teaching Suggestions.
1. Refer to Chapter 11 for proper technique for controlling a ball. Point out good performance to the children.

Patterns of Movement—Slow Motion

Objective.
1. Learning to combine elements of movement.
2. Learning to control specific movement elements.
3. Understand social behavior through movement.

Equipment. Play area.

Basic Movement Problems. Find a play space. Can you demonstrate how a pitcher, pitches the ball, in slow motion? After you pitch the ball, become the batter, again in slow motion. What movement element must you control to perform in slow motion? After you hit the imaginary ball, run the bases in slow motion! Do not leave your own play space. Is it hard to run in slow motion without moving from your play space? Can you play the part of the fielder? Now the catcher at home plate? Can you play the part of the umpire calling the play at home plate? Can you play the part of the coach? Be the coach when the umpire calls the runner out! Be the coach when he calls him safe. In slow motion can you demonstrate how the losing players walk off the field. Now the winners? Why do they walk like they do? Can you play the part of a person in the crowd in slow motion, after a home run? After a strike out?

Teaching Suggestions.
1. After each child has played each role, the teacher may want to select certain students to enact a full scale slow motion game with, umpire, crowd, etc. One student can act as narrator indicating whether the batter hits a single, a double, etc.
2. Discuss the reasons why losers and winners walk differently.

Patterns of Movement—Dodging

Objectives.
1. Learn to combine elements of movement.
2. Learn the skill of dodging.

Equipment. Balls.

Basic Movement Patterns. Divide the class into groups of three. Have one child stand between two others spaced 15 to 20 feet apart.

Can you keep the ball from hitting your feet as the members of your group roll the ball between themselves? How close can you allow the ball to come to you without being hit? When you "dodge" the ball, what movement elements do you use? Can you dodge the ball when the members of your group throw the ball in the air between each other? Can you dodge the ball on a low level? Can you dodge a rolling ball on a low level? Now can you dodge the ball if your group members try to hit you with it? What elements of movement will the throwers use to make it easier to hit you? What elements must you use to dodge? Can you invent a dodging game?

Teaching Suggestions.
1. Play circle or team dodge ball after going through this with them.
2. Change dodgers frequently.

Shadows

Objectives.
1. Learn to control body movements.
2. Learn some basic movement patterns.

Equipment. Unshaded lamp with a large bulb.

Basic Movement Problems. The children stand between the lamp and a large wall so that their shadows are projected on the wall.

Can you make your shadow move? Can you make your shadow small? Can you make it large? Is your shadow bigger or smaller than you really are? How could we change the light to make your shadow bigger? Smaller? Can you make your shadow taller by moving? Shorter? Make your shadow into different shapes. Make an L. Make a Z with your shadow. Can you make your shadow look like an animal? Try several. Can you make your shadow leave the ground? How? Can you touch someone elses shadow with yours? Can you keep your shadow from being touched? How? Can you develop a game using shadows?

Poems

Objectives.
1. Learning to interpret poems in movement.
2. Learning to understand the basic movement elements.

Equipment. Play area.

The Bear Hunt[1]
by
Margaret Widdemer

I played I was two polar bears
Who lived inside a cave of chairs,

And Brother was the hunter-man
Who tried to shoot us when we ran.

The tenpins made good bones to gnaw,
I held them down beneath my paw.

Of course, I had to kill him quick
Before He shot me with his stick.

So all the cave fell down, you see,
On Brother and the bones and me—

So then he said he wouldn't play—
But it was teatime, anyway!

Can you become one the polar bears? Can you walk like a bear? Can you do what the bear did in the poem? Can you play the part of the hunted? Now can you play both parts?

Teaching Suggestions.
1. Select several children to act out the total story above.
2. Ask questions and have the children act out the following poems in the same manner as above.

The Squirrel

Whisky Frisky,
Hippity hop,
Up he goes
To the tree top!

Whirly, twirly,
Round and round
Down he scampers
To the ground.

Furly, Curly,
What a tail!
Tall as a feather,
Broad as a sail!

Where's his supper?
In the shell,
Snap, cracky,
Out it fell.

Holding Hands
by
Lenore M. Link

Elephants walking
Along the trails

Are holding hands
By holding tails.

Trunks and tails
Are handy things

When elephants walk
In Circus rings.

Elephants work
And elephants play

And elephants walk
And feel so gay.

And when they walk—
It never fails

They're holding hands
By holding tails

The Monkeys And The Crocodile
by
Laura E. Richards

Five little monkeys
Swinging from a tree;
Teasing Uncle Crocodile,
Merry as can be.
Swinging high, swinging low,
Swinging left and right:
"Dear Uncle Crocodile,
Come and take a bite!"

Five little monkeys
Swinging in the air;
Heads up, tails up,
Little do they care.
Swinging up, swinging down,
Swinging far and near:
"Poor Uncle Crocodile,
Aren't you hungry, dear?"

Four little monkeys
Sitting in a tree;
Heads down, tails down,
Dreary as can be.
Weeping loud, weeping low,
Crying to each other:
"Wicked Uncle Crocodile
To gobble up our brother!"

3. Find other poems or stories to help children develop movement skills.

Pictures

Objectives.
1. Learning to interpret pictures through movement.
2. Learning to understand basic movement elements.

Equipment. Pictures and a play area.

Basic Movement Problems. (Provide the children with a picture of a clown and/or a puppet, etc.) Can you play the part of the clown shown in the picture? What stunts and tricks can a clown do? Can you perform some? Can you make people laugh with your movements? How? Walk like a clown? Can you be a marrionette? What is so unusual about how the puppets walk? Can you walk that way? Can you do other movements the same way? What else can you do like the puppet in the picture?

Teaching Suggestions.
1. Select other pictures such as cartoon characters in action and have children act out the parts.
2. Emphasize proper movement when skills are performed in acting out pictures.

Develop a Game

Objectives.
1. Development of usable movement patterns.
2. Development of specific skills.
3. Development of creativity through movement expression.

Equipment. Whatever is desired by the children creating the game, most likely balls, bean bags, duck pins, etc.

Basic Movement Problems. Can you develop a game using _____? (Insert the name of any piece of equipment in the blank.)
Can you develop a game using _____ element of movement? (Insert the name of one movement element in the blank.)
Divide the class into groups of 2, 3, 4, 5, or 6. Ask them the same questions as above.

Teaching Suggestions.
1. As children develop specific games which use movement elements effectively, allow the total class to play the game.

Develop a Relay

Same as above except the children try to develop movement relays instead of games!

Reference

1. Ferris, Helen (Ed.): *Favorite Poems Old and New.* New York, Doubleday and Co., Inc., 1957.

Bibliography

Anderson, M., Elliot, M., and LaBerge, J.: *Play With a Purpose.* New York, Harper & Row, 1966, Chapter 1 (p. 5–36), Chapter 10 (p. 371–409).

Andrews, G.: *Creative Rhythmics Movement for Children.* Englewood Cliffs, N.J., Prentice-Hall Inc., 1954, Chapter 5 (p. 45–56).

Andrews, G., Saurborn, J. and Schneider, E.: *Physical Education for Today's Boys and Girls.* Boston, Allyn and Bacon, 1960, Chapter 4 (p. 47–72).

Brown, C., and Cassidy, R.: *Theory in Physical Education.* Philadelphia, Lea & Febiger, 1963, Chapter 7 (p. 124–178).

Halsey, E., and Porter, L.: *Physical Education for Children.* New York, Holt, Rinehart & Winston, 1963, Chapter 9 (p. 171–218).

Mosston, Muska: *Developmental Movement.* Columbus, Ohio, Charles E. Merrill Books, Inc., 1965.

13

Experiments and Discussion
Questions for Use
in the Classroom

The following chapter is divided into six groups of activities including five groups of experiments and one section which includes questions for promoting discussion of topics pertinent to physical education. Like earlier chapters, the educational experiences suggested here are not intended to be the only available activities for meeting knowledge objectives in physical education, rather these activities are suggested as representative of experiments and discussion activities which can be used to aid elementary school children in becoming physically educated.

The following experiments are intended to illustrate these concepts (See Chapter 8 for detailed discussion):

1. How to move. (Experiments 1–6)
2. Understanding personal movement capabilities. (Experiments 7–10)
3. The health benefits of exercise. (Experiments 11–13)
4. Making appropriate movement decisions. (Experiments 14–15)
5. The value of efficient movement. (Experiment 16)

Experiment #1—Posture*

Problem: What is good posture? What are the effects of poor posture on the body?

*Credit is given to Linda Hughes, a student, for developing this experiment.

Expected Results:
1. Students will be able to assess their own posture.
2. The children will discover that an "easily erect" posture is the best from all points of view. Such a posture requires less energy than a "military" posture and does not cause undue strain on the ligaments as does a slouching posture.

Equipment Necessary: 3 or 4 large wooden blocks or the same number of cardboard boxes with tops. Also, several strips of cheap elastic will be needed.

Data Collection:
1. Have the children observe the two sketches that are drawn on the black board (see below).

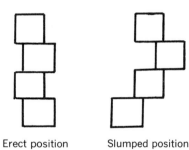

Erect position   Slumped position

A. Discuss: This is how the spine looks in two types of posture, one erect, one slumping. The spine is never completely straight but the erect posture requires a straighter spine than the slumping posture.
2. Have the children stack the blocks in a manner similar to the black board diagrams.
   A. Discuss: What is the difference between the two columns of blocks? How does this relate to good posture. (The crooked column is harder to support and causes stretch on the ligaments.)
   B. Discuss: What happens when one block is out of place? (It means that other blocks must be stacked crooked if the column is to balance. Thus one posture problem can create others.)
   C. Discuss: How does the crooked stack of blocks look? Would you like your posture to look like the crooked stack of blocks?
   D. Discuss: The muscles support posture. Which stack of blocks would be easier to support?
3. Have the children stretch the strips of cheap elastic until it becomes overstretched and loses its elasticity.
   A. Discuss: What happens to the elastic when it is continually overstretched? What happens to the body's ligaments when you have

poor posture? (The elastic is "strained" by continued overstretch just as the ligaments which support good posture are overstretched by poor posture.)
4. Have the children slump their shoulders and assume other positions of poor posture to illustrate how the ligaments are overstretched.

The Solution: Use "easy erect" posture.
1. It makes you look better.
2. It keeps you from getting tired so easily.
3. It may prevent future aches and pains.

Teaching Suggestions:
1. Keep explanations simple.
2. Let the children supply the answers whenever possible.

Experiment #2—Efficient Pushing, Pulling, and Lifting.

Problem: What is the best way to lift? What is the best way to push? What is the best way to pull?

Expected Results: The children will be able to visualize the best way to pull, push, and lift.

Equipment Necessary: Several cardboard boxes, some square and some long and narrow. Also needed are several short lengths of clothesline.

Data Collection:
1. Have the children push against several of the boxes of different shapes.
   A. Discuss: What happens when you push the top of a box, especially a tall one?
   B. Discuss: What happens when you try to push on a box at a low level without bending your legs? (It reduces your pushing force and strains the back.)
2. Have the children pull several of the boxes by attaching the ropes to the box at different levels.
   A. Discuss: Same topics as for pushing including the danger of pulling an object over on yourself.
3. Have the children lift several boxes using the following postures: legs straight, back bent forward, and legs bent, back straight.
   A. Discuss: Notice the strain on the back when lifting in the legs straight, back bent position. Have the children feel the tenseness in the bent back.
4. Have one child lift a light box with his arms extended at full length. Now have him stoop down and lift the box with the arms vertical to the ground, bending the knees so the straightening of the legs lifts the box (See Chapter 11 for illustration).

A. Discuss: Which way is easier? With the arms straight one must lift the weight of the box multiplied by the length of the lever (the arm). The longer the lever, the harder it is to lift the box. In the second lifting technique, the lever is shortened as the box is lifted near the body and the task is easier.

B. Example: A good way to illustrate the idea of the arm being a lever is to have each child hold a book on his hand with his arm close to the body (bent), then have him hold the same book with the arm extended in front. The added work caused by lengthening the lever is easily noticed.

The Solution:
1. The best way to push is with the legs bent, leaning into the object, pushing near the center of gravity.
2. The best way to pull is near the center of gravity with the legs bent and back straight.
3. The best way to lift is with the legs bent and the back straight.
4. Lifting is easiest when body levers are shortest.

Experiment #3—Stability of the Body

Problem: Should your body assume a stable position in performing physical education skills? In what position is the body most stable? Why do different sports use different body stances?

Expected Results: Some sports require stability, others do not. Some body positions are stable, others are not.

Equipment Necessary: None.

Data Collection:
1. Have the children work with a partner. Each child performs several maneuvers with his partner.
   A. Stand up straight—Have your partner push softly on your shoulders.
   B. Bend the knees and lean forward in a semi-squat position. Have your partner push softly on your shoulders.
   C. Get in an all fours position—Have your partner push softly on your shoulders.
   D. Stand with the feet spread apart—Have your partner push softly on your shoulders.
2. Which of the above positions is the most stable—Which stance was the easiest to push over? Why?
3. Get in a track runner's stance. In this stance your hips are high in the air and you lean the weight forward.

A. Is this stance stable? What would happen if you were pushed from behind? Should this stance be stable?
4. Discuss: What is the best stance for basketball? What is the best stance for a tennis player? What is the best stance for other sports?

The Solution:
1. The most stable position is one with a low center of gravity, with the weight over the center of gravity, and with a wide base of support. The all fours position is an example.
2. The least stable is just the opposite. Standing straight up on one foot is an example.
3. Some sports require stability, such as a defensive basketball player or a football lineman.
4. Some sports require instability such as a runner in track or a pitcher in baseball.

Teaching Suggestions:
1. Explain that it is important to learn stance in basketball, baseball, etc. Note the similarity between sports stances such as basketball defensive stances, baseball infielder's stance and a tennis stance.
2. Explain: Stances will be similar if stability is wanted but different if instability is wanted.

Experiment #4—Feedback, Using Your Senses to Learn Skills.

Problem: When we perform skills we use our senses, particularly sight, hearing and touch. We use these senses to "feedback" information to the brain so that we can make our next performance better. The purpose of this experiment is to explore the use of our senses in feeding back information about the performance of a simple skill. (Feedback is the use of one's senses to make adjustments in future skill performance.)

Expected Results: The children will need the use of their senses to perform simple skills.

Equipment Necessary: Paper and pencil.

Data Collection:
1. Have the children draw any of the following figures:

 or write their names.

2. Next have them draw the same figure with their eyes shut.
   A. Discuss: Why does drawing get poorer when we do not look at what is drawn? (Visual feedback is lost.)

B. If you have had experience in performing a skill, the skill becomes habit and you do not need as much feedback. (Example: It is easier to write *your* name without looking than to write a name of someone not familiar to you.)

C. The more difficult the task, the more feedback you need. (Example: The more difficult figures (above) are more distorted than the simple ones when drawn without use of the eyes.)

D. Discuss: Learning a physical education skill is very similar to what one does when drawing the figures. Our skills are better when we use our senses. (Example: If you watch the ball closely in a game of baseball, it is easier to hit than if you swing with the eyes closed.)

E. How do we use sight for feedback in sports? How do we use hearing? touch?

The Solution: All senses supply feedback for learning skills. The more we do the skill, the more it becomes habit and the less we need the feedback. Example: When we first learn to dribble a basketball, we must always watch the ball (use of sight feedback), but as the skill becomes a habit we no longer need to watch the ball.

Teaching Suggestions:

1. After the children have drawn the figures by themselves without looking, let them work with a partner. Have the partner tell the child where to make the lines. The partner's voice will substitute for their sight.

2. Have the children draw the figures one at a time first with sight then without. Proceed from the most simple figures to the more complex.

Experiment # 5—Friction and Skill Learning

Problem: What is friction? How does friction effect performance of a skill?

Expected Results: Friction will benefit the performers in some ways but in other ways friction is undesirable in learning skills.

Equipment Necessary: One smooth 6 foot board, some sawdust, one smoothly planed block (4 x 4 x 2), one rough block (4 x 4 x 2), and one block with very rough sand paper fastened on one side.

Data Collection:

1. Make a ramp with the 6 foot board by placing one end of the board on the floor and the other end on a chair.

2. Have the children slide the blocks down the board ramp.

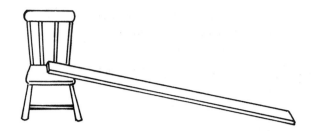

   A.   Slide the sand paper block.
   B.   Slide the rough block.
   C.   Slide the smooth block.
   D.   Sprinkle some sawdust on the ramp and slide the smooth block
        again.
3. Have the children determine which block slides the best.
   A.   Discuss: Why does one slide fastest? What is friction?
4. Have the children discuss: How friction is used in physical educa-
   tion class and in sports.
   A.   Could you ice skate if the ice was like the sand paper block?
   B.   If you have to stop quickly in a game, can you do it best in
        leather sole shoes or in tennis shoes? Why?
   C.   What would happen in shuffleboard if the puck was not smooth?

The Solution:
1. In sports like ice hockey or shuffleboard, we do not want much
   friction.
2. In sports like basketball we want friction. It allows us to stop.

Experiment #6—How does spin effect a ball?

Problem: How does spin effect a ball?

Expected Results: Different kinds of spin effect a ball in different ways.

Equipment Necessary: One ball for every child and a reasonably large
play area.

Data Collection:
1. Give each child a ball. Have the children roll their balls toward
   a wall so that it will bounce back to them. Now roll the ball, turning the hand as the ball is released so that the ball spins sideways
   as it rolls.
   A.   Discuss: What happens to the ball? What makes the ball curve?
2. Repeat the above. Spin the ball in the opposite direction.
3. Have the children work in pairs. One child passes the ball to the
   other (bounce pass), so that the ball spins to the left. Repeat with

spin to the right. Repeat with overhand spin. Repeat with back spin.
  A. Discuss: What happens when you spin the ball?
4. How can spin help you in a ball game?

The Solution: Spin aids the baseball pitcher by making the ball curve. The bowler also uses spin to make the ball curve. Games such as football, pool, billards, and others also use spin.

Teaching Suggestions:
1. Demonstrate ball spinning for the children.
2. Hula Hoops can also be used to demonstrate the effects of spin.
3. Relate friction (see experiment #5) to spinning the ball.

Experiment #7—Calories Used in Exercise and Play.*

Problem: When we eat food we consume calories (see definitions below). If a person eats too many calories, he gets fat. We know how he consumes calories (eating) but how does he use calories? Does exercise use calories?

Explanation of Terms: Calorie—A calorie is a measure of heat. However, commonly a calorie is used to describe stored energy in the human body. Fat, for example, is stored energy or stored calories. When carbohydrates or fats are used by the body in work or play, we say we use calories. When we eat food, we say we consume calories. The calories we consume may be used immediately or stored in the body as fat or fuel for later use.
  Calories and oxygen—One way to determine how many calories the body uses is to determine how much oxygen the body is using. Just as a candle cannot burn without oxygen, the body cannot use calories without oxygen. For this reason we can determine how many calories we are using by determining how much oxygen we are using.

Expected Results: The more vigorous the exercise, the more calories the body uses.

Equipment Necessary: Several large plastic bags, and a watch with a sweep second hand.

Data Collection:
1. Select one child to be the experimental subject. Have the other children observe the performance of the experimental subject.
2. Have the experimental subject sit still in a chair. Have the subject practice breathing in through his nose and out through his mouth.
3. Take one of the plastic bags and bunch it at the top as if you were going to blow it up and pop it. Force all of the air out of the bag.

*Credit is given to Paul Kimmelman, a student, for helping in the development of this experiment.

4. Put the bag up to the mouth of the subject. Have him breath in through his nose and out through his mouth into the bag for 15 seconds. Quickly close the bag at the top and put a rubber band around the top of the bag so the air stays in the bag. Save the full bag.
5. Now have the subject do the pogo hop for 30 seconds. (See Experiment 8 for pogo hop details.) At the end of the hopping period, put a bag to the subjects mouth and have him breath in through the nose and out through the mouth into the bag as above. After he has breathed into the bag for 15 seconds, close the bag and seal it with a rubber band. Save the full bag.
6. Repeat the same procedure using several exercises of different intensity. Exercise for 30 seconds and collect air for 15 seconds.
7. Have the students compare the size of the bags. The more vigorous the exercise, the more the air in the bag and therefore, the larger the bag.
8. Explain: The body needs oxygen to burn calories. The more oxygen used, the more calories are used. The more oxygen used, the more air in the bag. Thus the exercises which cause the bag to fill require the body to use up calories. These vigorous exercises which cause you to use calories are the ones which help you use the calories you take in when you eat.

The Solution: Vigorous exercises require a big expenditure of calories as measured by the amount of air used in the exercise.

Teaching Suggestions: As another measure of calories expended count the numbers of breaths taken in each 15-second period.

Experiment #8—Evaluating Endurance Performance*

Problem: How much endurance do you possess?

Expected Results: The children will vary in the endurance performance.

Equipment Necessary: A stop watch or watch with a sweep second hand.

Data Collection:
1. Have the children put their hands behind their head standing with one foot in front of the other. The children Pogo Hop (see diagram), stepping forward with the opposite foot each time they jump into the air. Each child counts the number of Pogo Hops he can do in $1\frac{1}{2}$ minutes. (One hop is counted each time the right foot is forward.)
2. Score the children on the following scale.

*Credit is given to Martha Nan Dowell, a graduate student, for helping in the development of this experiment.

Excellent—215 or more hops
Very Good—190–214 hops
Good—150–189 hops
Poor—149 or below

3. Discuss what the score means.
   A. High scores give an estimate of endurance capacity.
   B. A strong healthy heart is necessary for endurance performance.
   C. You can improve endurance by exercising.
   D. Different people have different endurance levels but everyone can improve his endurance.

The Solution: Each child should know his endurance level, should know what endurance means, and should know how to improve his endurance.

Teaching Suggestions:
1. Emphasize that you are not grading the children on the test. Let them know the test is for their own information.
2. Explain that the best and most efficient pace in taking the endurance test is a steady pace.

Experiment #9—Evaluating Balance Performance

Problem: How good is your balance? Can all people perform equally well on balance tasks?

Expected Results: The children will vary in their balance performance. Some should pass all tests, while some may fail them all. (Explain: practice in some physical education activities improves balance.)

Equipment Necessary: None.

Data Collection:
1. Have the children perform the following balance tests:

Test	Description
Diver's Stance	Stand on the toes with the feet together. Hold the arms straight out in front of the body. Hold for 10 seconds.
One Foot Stand	Perform the same as the diver's stance except that one foot must be held 10 inches off the floor and the leg must be straight.

Test	Description
Swan Stand	Bend forward at the waist. Lower the head to waist height. Lift the left leg to waist height behind you. Hold 10 seconds without shifting the foot.
Jumping Half Turn	Jump into the air. Turn a half turn in the air and land on one foot. Hold for 10 seconds without moving the foot.
Tip Up	Do a hand stand placing the knees on your elbows. Hold for 10 seconds (see page 209).

2. Discuss: How many tests did you pass? Could you get better with practice? Do some people naturally have the ability to perform balance tasks? Do people with good endurance have (necessarily) good balance?

3. Explain and discuss: People are not the same in their abilities. Some people are good in reading, others are good in spelling, some are good in baseball, and some are good in other sports. Each person has a different ability to perform in balance. The more balance tasks you can perform, the better your balance. The more you practice, the more tasks you can perform. It is possible that you may be good in balance but poor in other aspects of physical fitness or visa versa. Like other aspects of fitness, practice will improve performance. Each person should practice especially hard in the area of his weakness.

Excellent—Pass all five
Very Good—Pass Four
Good—Pass three
Poor—Pass two or one or none

Solution: Each child should know his balance potential, know what balance means and know how he can improve his balance.

Teaching Suggestions:
1. Have the children practice the items at home as a method of improving balance.

Experiment #10—Evaluating Reaction Time*

Problem: How good is your reaction time? Do all people have the same reaction ability?

*Credit is given to Martha Nan Dowell, a graduate student, for helping in the development of this experiment.

Expected Results: The children will vary greatly in their reaction time scores.

Equipment Necessary: One stop watch and a light bulb which can be controlled with an on-off switch.

Data Collection:

1. Mark off a 5-foot area in the classroom. Draw a line at each end of the 5-foot area. Place the light bulb (red if possible) where a child standing behind one of the lines, can see it. Have the child watch the light bulb. Turn the switch on, simultaneously starting the stop watch. When the bulb goes on, the child runs to the opposite line and back. Stop the watch as he crosses the starting line. The time it takes the child to complete the task is his reaction time. Test each child's reaction time in this manner.
2. Discuss: What is your reaction time? (see below) Could you get better with practice? Do some of us naturally have better reaction time than others? Do people with good reaction time necessarily have good balance or endurance? (see preceding experiment)

The Solution: Each child should know his own reaction time, know the meaning of reaction time, and understand individual differences in reaction time. It is doubtful that reaction time will improve with practice as much as endurance or balance.

> 2.5 seconds or less—Excellent
> 2.6 seconds—Very Good
> 2.7 to 2.9 seconds—Good
> 3.0 to 3.3 seconds—Fair
> 3.4 seconds or more—Poor

Teaching Suggestions:

1. Involve the children in recording scores and marking the area.
2. If more than one watch and light are available, have the children test themselves as you test them.

Experiment #11—The Overload Principle

Problem: Overloading a muscle is the *only* way in which we can make a muscle stronger. How does overload make a muscle stronger?

Expected Results: The children will develop a better understanding of the overload principle and an understanding of the value of exercise.

Equipment Necessary: None.

Data Collection:

1. Explain the overload principle. "If you want to make a muscle stronger, you must make it work harder than it regularly works. This is why we do exercises, to make the muscle work harder than in our regular daily routine."

2. Explain the converse of the overload principle. "If a muscle is used less (underloaded) than usual, it gets weaker."

3. Explain that a muscle must be overloaded regularly and that the overload must be progressive (a little at first and more as the muscle gets used to the overload).

4. Discuss the following examples and relate it to the overload principle:

   A. What happens to your hands when you work hard with a shovel or a hoe all in one day? *YOU GET BLISTERS.*

   B. What happens to your hands when you gradually build up to a full days work with a hoe or shovel? *YOU DEVELOP A CALLOUS.*

   C. Nature has a way of overcompensating for overworked tissue. When a muscle is overworked too much, it gets sore, much as the hands get blisters when they are overworked. When the overload is gradual (a little bit at a time), the muscle gets stronger just like the hands get stronger with a callous. The progressive overload causes small amounts of break down in the muscle tissue. The body is not bothered by this small break down. The body replaces the broken down tissue with more and stronger tissue as in a callous.

5. Discuss: When you do push ups and chin ups everyday, the muscle gets bigger and stronger. Have the children measure their arms and follow a program of progressive overload to see if their arms get bigger.

The Solution: The best way to make a muscle stronger is to make it work harder than usual. This overload should be regular and progressively more difficult.

Experiment #12—Exercise and the Heart

Problem: How does exercise effect the heart rate? Does exercise make the heart stronger?

Expected Results: The heart rate is one of the best indicators of the amount of work the heart is performing. During exercise the heart rate should increase because the heart is working harder.

Equipment Necessary: A watch with a sweep second hand.

Data Collection:

1. Have the students learn to take their carotid pulse by placing their finger tips next to the Adam's apple, on either side (the radial or wrist pulse may be used also).

   A. Carotid pulse is the movement caused by the artery (carotid) of the neck. The blood being ejected by each beat of the heart causes a movement in the artery known as pulse. Thus pulse is one measure of the rate of the heart. The carotid is easy to locate (next to the Adam's apple), and is for this reason, one of the better methods to use in taking heart rate.

   B. The radial or wrist pulse is located on the inner surface of the wrist just below the heel of the hand. Like the carotid pulse, movement of the blood from the heart can be felt with the finger tips and can be interpreted as representative of the rate of the heart.

2. Discuss the pulse. Explain that each pulse represents one beat of the heart.

3. Have the children count the number of heart beats (pulse) for 30 seconds at rest.

4. Have them do 50 pogo hops (see experiment #8) and then count their heart beats again.

5. After a rest, count the heart beats again for 30 seconds.

6. Now have the children do 50 jumping jacks (side straddle hops) and then count the heart beats.

7. Discuss:

   A. What happened to the heart rate after exercise?

   B. What happens to the heart rate after a rest?

   C. What does a harder exercise do to the heart rate?

8. Explain:

   A. The heart works harder during exercise.

   B. Explain that the heart is a muscle which gets stronger when it is exercised and has to beat more during exercise. This is the same as the Overload principle for other muscles. (Experiment #11)

The Solution: Exercise overloads the heart and makes it stronger. However, like any other muscle, the heart needs to be overloaded regularly and progressively through exercises which make it work hard.

Teaching Suggestions: The teacher may want the children to work in pairs, taking each others pulse after each exercise.

Experiment #13—Weight Control and Caloric Balance

Problem: How can a person control his weight? What causes weight gain or weight loss?

Expected Results: The children should be able to visualize and understand the concept of "balancing caloric intake with caloric expenditure" for weight control.

Equipment Necessary: One fulcrum scales or an improvised fulcrum (see below).

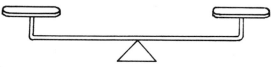

Data Collection:

1. Make several small weights. Label them as specific foods with specific calorie contents (see below). The weights should be proportional in weight to the amount of calories in the food. Also make some weights for activities, labeling them as specific activities weighting them according to the calorie expenditure of the activity. Make the following weights.

   Calorie Expenditures:

   Basal Metabolic Rate—1800 calories
   School Work and normal activity—500 calories
   One hour of basketball—500 calories
   ½ hour of bicycle riding—330 calories
   Dancing for 1 hour—330 calories

   Calorie Consumption:

   Breakfast—700 calories
   Lunch—700 calories
   Supper—900 calories
   Cola drink—170 calories
   Milk shake—342 calories
   Candy bar—55 calories
   Cake—100 calories
   10 potato chips—50 calories

2. Have the children place different combinations of weights on the scale. If the scale balances, this represents a balance between intake and expenditure. Start with the activities and foods listed below on the diagram:

   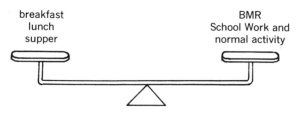

   breakfast
   lunch
   supper

   BMR
   School Work and
   normal activity

The scale should balance with the above weights. Explain that the meals you eat represent calorie intake and the play and other activities during the day equal calorie expenditure.

3. Let the children discover what would happen to the scales if several of the "goodies" were added. The scales would go out of balance indicating weight gain.
4. Let the children discover what happens when extra activity or exercise is added.
5. Explain the meaning of BMR (Basal Metabolic Rate), the amount of calories that must be expended merely to live without extra movement.

The Solution: To lose weight more calories must be expended than are taken in. To maintain weight, calorie intake and expenditure must balance.

Experiment #14—What is the Best Way to Throw for Distance?

Problem: What is the best way to throw a ball for distance? Should you throw with a little arch on the ball or high with a lot of arch?

Expected Results: The children should be able to visualize the best angle of release for throwing the ball for distance.

Equipment Necessary: A protractor and a rubber garden hose attached to a water outlet with good water pressure. (A small rubber tube attached to a water spigot inside the classroom may be used instead of the hose.)

Data Collection:
1. A rubber hose or a rubber tube is attached to a water outlet. Turn on the water and hold the hose parallel to the ground. Allow the children to gradually raise the angle of the hose. Measure the angle formed by the ground and the hose with a protractor (see diagram below):

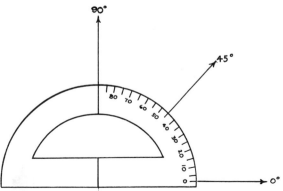

2. Have the children record the distance the water squirts in the air at each of the different angles.

3. Discuss: The water squirts farthest at a 45 degree angle. Throwing a ball works the same way. The ball will travel farthest if thrown at a 45 degree angle.
4. Discuss and Re-measure: If a ball is thrown too high, much of the force of the throw is wasted in making the ball travel upward. Re-measure the distance the water squirts at a 75 degree angle to illustrate the point. If the ball is thrown too low, gravity forces the ball to the ground before it can travel very far. Re-measure the distance the water squirts at a 25 degree angle to illustrate the point.

The Solution: A ball will travel the greatest distance if thrown at approximately a 45 degree angle.

Experiment #15—Pacing Performance

Problem: If you run a race or play a game, you may use up your energy too fast and fail to finish if you do not pace yourself. What can be done to make sure that you will not use up all of your energy too early in the game or race?

Expected Results: The children will understand the concept of *PACING* performance.

Equipment Necessary: Same as experiment #12.

Data Collection:
1. As in experiment #7, one child is selected as the experimental subject. He practices breathing in through his nose and out through his mouth.
2. Have the experimental subject do the pogo hop 50 times as fast as he can. Immediately after the exercise, have the subject breath into a plastic bag (inhaling through the nose) for 15 seconds. Seal the bag with a rubber band as in experiment #7.
3. After a period of rest, have the experimental subject perform 50 pogo hops slowly (one every second or slower). Immediately after exercise have the subject breath into a plastic bag for 15 seconds. Seal the bag with a rubber band.
4. Discuss: Why does the bag have more air (oxygen) after the fast hop than after the slow hop?
5. Explain:
   A. The more air in the bag the more energy used (see experiment 7).
   B. In some cases we want to expend calories as in controlling weight. However, in playing a game or running a race we want to use the calories efficiently so we can finish the race. This is pacing.
   C. Pace means spreading the vigorousness of the exercise over the

entire race. In a long race or a long game you should exercise at a steady pace for the whole race or the entire game.

D. The best way to exercise is much like the best way to drive a car. If you drive too fast, you get poor mileage and you may run out of gas before you reach your destination.

The Solution: The best pace is a steady pace.

Experiment #16—Picking the Best Exercise

Purpose: Whenever you do an exercise, it should be done for a purpose. For example, we may want to make our arms or legs strong. The purpose of this experiment is to help children understand how to select an exercise to accomplish a specific objective.

Expected Results: The children should learn how to determine which muscles are used in a specific exercise done in the physical education class.

Equipment Necessary: None.

Data Collection:
1. Select several (2 or 3) exercises that are normally done during the physical education period. Ask the children why they do these exercises. Discuss this topic.
2. Have the children work with a partner. One partner begins by performing one of the exercises. The second partner tries to identify which muscles are working during the exercise. For example, in doing a push up he will observe and feel the muscles of the arms.
3. Explain:
   A. The hard muscles are the working muscles.
   B. The working muscles are the ones that get stronger.
   C. If you cheat on an exercise or do it improperly, it probably will not do you any good.
4. Continue having partners work together. Have them try to determine which muscles are working in each exercise by observing and feeling the muscles.

The Solution: Exercises do not build all muscles. Certain exercises make specific muscles work and these working muscles are the ones that get strong. To be a fit person, one should select different exercises so that all of the different muscles are developed.

Teaching Suggestions:
1. Carry this over to the class when exercises are given. Have the children attempt to discover the value of the exercise by the method described above.

DISCUSSION QUESTIONS

Topic	Specific Questions	Activity
First Aid	What can be done for a person who has stopped breathing? What can you do if you find someone who has been injured and has no heart beat?	Teach the children how to perform mouth to mouth artificial respiration.
Rules of Games	How do you score the game of _____? How many people play on each team in _____? What are the positions of the players in the game of _____? Are there any illegal procedures in the game of _____? What special rules are involved in the game of _____? What is the penalty for violation of the rules in the game of _____? What equipment do you need for the game of _____?	Fill in the name of the specific activity. Discuss.
Strategy	What different tasks do the different players have in the game _____? What special manuevers can you make to help a team mate in the game of _____? Are there any predetermined strategies that are normally used in the game of _____? What does team balance mean?	Fill in the name of the specific activity. Discuss.
Safety	What special rules do we have in our games that make them safe? What equipment should you have specifically for safety in various games? What are some of the most common reasons for accidents on the playground and in games? List the DO's and DO NOT's for safety in games.	Select specific activities needing special equipment and discuss its safe use. Discuss the questions in column 2.

Topic	Specific Questions	Activity
How to watch a sport.	What is the object of the game of _____? What are the basic rules of the game of _____? What signals do referees use in the game of _____? What do the referee's signals mean? How is play started in the game of _____? Who starts the ball in play? How do you score the game of _____? What are some of the special techniques that players use in the game of _____? What special words have been coined which apply only to this game? What do they mean?	Have the children go to a game or watch a game on television and report the results.

14

Low Organization Games

Games are tools which the teacher can use to help children progress toward accomplishing physical education objectives. The games included in this chapter are of simple nature involving little organization and few rules.

Included with the description of each of the games is a list of behavioral objectives which might be fulfilled through the use of each particular activity. It is, however, important to emphasize the following points when selecting a game for use in the physical education program:

1. The games may and probably will help children meet other objectives than those listed in this chapter.
2. The games should be selected *after* the objectives have been determined rather than before objectives are determined.
3. The method of teaching the game is as important as the nature of the game in helping children meet physical education objectives. Keep objectives in mind as you teach!

The games in the following section are organized into four groups: basic skill games, ball games, circle games, and running games, in that order. Within each of the four game catagories the games are arranged with those for primary children preceding those most applicable for the intermediate grade children.

Basic Skill Games

NORTH POLE

Grade Level: 1–2

Objective: To run. To stop and maintain balance. To follow rules of a simple game.

Equipment Needed: None.

Procedures: All children line up behind one boundary line. On "go" they advance to the opposite boundary. At the command "Freeze" the children must stop where they are and maintain the position prior to stopping. Continue alternately suggesting "GO" and "FREEZE". The first child to the opposite boundary is the winner.

Teaching Suggestions:
1. Allow the winner to give the commands.
2. Pick the most unusual position on each "FREEZE".
3. Pick the best stopper on each "FREEZE".

FOLLOW THE LEADER

Grade Level: 1–2

Objectives: To learn specific motor skills (specifically the skills used by the leader). To imitate performances of animals, indians, airplanes, etc. To move creatively.

Equipment Necessary: None.

Procedures: The children follow a leader in single file. Whatever the leader does the children do. Begin with walking, stretching, toe touching. Continue with walking faster, then jogging, hopping, leaping, galloping, etc. Use different types of arm motions while moving forward. Use different trunk movements as well. Youngsters may also do animal and other types of imitations such as indians, airplanes, etc. As students become more proficient allow them to perform as leaders.

PULL THE TAIL

Grade Level: 3–6 ✔

Objective: To develop agility and skill in running. To develop skill in hand-eye movements. To develop skill in offensive and defensive tatics used in sports.

Equipment Necessary: Ropes or flags similar to those used in flag football. Flags should be 18 to 24 inches in length. Two per student.

Procedures: The class is divided into three teams. One team becomes the group of runners. The two remaining teams line up facing each other 4 yards apart. Runners run between the lines twisting and spinning while attempting to keep line players from pulling their "tail". Each tail that remains unpulled counts one point for the runners. Change line players with runners until all teams have run. The team with the most points is the winner.

Variations: Allow each team to run several times before scoring.

Teaching Suggestions:
1. Tie a knot in the "tail" so that all tails are tucked in to the knot and thus are tucked in a uniform distance.
2. Draw lines on the ground over which tail pullers may not cross.

CHINESE WALL ✔

Grade Level: 2–4

Objective: To run. To dodge and tag.

Equipment Necessary: Properly marked playing area.

Procedures: The children line up on one boundary line facing the other line. Between the boundary lines two lines are drawn parallel to the boundaries. These lines represent the chinese wall. One player, called the "coolie", stands in the wall area. The "coolie" calls, "scale the wall" and all players run from their boundary to the opposite boundary. As they cross the middle or "wall" they may be tagged by the "coolie". All tagged players become "coolies". Continue until only one player remains. This player starts the next game as the "coolie" and is the caller for the entire game. Players may delay after the call before crossing the wall.

Teaching Suggestions:
1. If players delay before crossing the wall, allow the coolies to count 10 after which the player must cross the wall. Only one coolie may count on one runner at a time.

JUMP THE DITCH ✔

Grade Level: 2–4

Objectives: To jump and run. To dodge. To use personal abilities to best advantage in a game.

Equipment Necessary: Properly marked play area.

Procedures: Children line up on one boundary line facing the opposite boundary line. Between the boundary lines two lines, narrow at one end and wide at the other, are drawn. These lines represent "the ditch". One player is the "ditch digger". He gives the command go. All players try to run to the opposite boundary line. The ditch digger may roam anywhere between the boundaries but the other players must jump the ditch. Players tagged by the ditch digger or landing in the ditch become ditch diggers. The last person to become a ditch digger is the ditch digger and caller for the next game.

ON ALL FOURS

Grade Level: 4–5

Objective: To use and refine fundamental skills. To follow the rules of the game.

Equipment Necessary: Properly marked play area.

Procedures: Players are grouped as hoppers or skippers. The play area is divided into four areas: two Hoptowns and two Skipsvilles. On "go" all players move forward toward the opposite end of the play area. Hoppers tag skippers in Hoptown and Skippers tag hoppers in Skipsville. Any player tagged in the opponents territory must get down on ALL FOURS. Players must remain on ALL FOURS until they tag a member of the other team (any where in the playing area). Both teams are free from being tagged when they are over the end line. The team to get all opponents on all fours is the winner.

Hoptown
Skipsville
Hoptown
Skipsville

Teaching Suggestions:
1. Periodically change the names of the teams and of the areas by changing the task to be performed, *i.e.,* Leaping, galloping, etc.
2. Have each team wear a separate color arm band.

GUARD THE PIN

Grade Level: 4–5

Objectives: To develop defensive skills and body stability. To use skill in accurate throwing.

Equipment Necessary: Two or three balls for every eight children. Two or three bowling pins for every eight children.

Procedures: Children form several circles of eight children each. A bowling pin is placed in the middle of the circle. One child stands in the middle of the circle to keep the pin from being hit and knocked over. The other children attempt to bowl the pin over. Add more balls and more pins as proficiency is developed.

STEAL THE BACON

Grade Level: 4–5

Objectives: To use game strategy within one's ability. To play as a team member. To tolerate different performance levels among peers. To develop agility.

Equipment Necessary: Four or five large bean bags.

Procedures: Divide the class into two teams. Number the members of each team consecutively from 1 to 15 or as high as necessary. One team lines up behind a line 50 feet from another line behind which the other team stands. Between the two lines a small circle is drawn. The bacon (bean bag) is placed in this circle. The teacher then calls one number. The team members from each team having that number advance toward the bacon. The object of the game is to carry the bacon over one's own boundary or to tag a player in possession of the bacon before he crosses his own boundary. The player on the team who accomplishes the objective scores one point for his team. Continue to call numbers until a predetermined score is reached.

Teaching Suggestions:
1. As the children gain proficiency in the game call several numbers at the same time.
2. Make sure you call all numbers an equal number of times.
3. As children become proficient, have several games going at the same time with 8 to 12 people in each game. Allow a student to call the numbers. This allows more children to be active.

Ball Games

BALL BASE

Grade Level: 2–3

Objective: To dodge a ball. To throw at a moving target. To respond to a signal.

Equipment Necessary: One base for each student and one ball for each 10 students.

Procedures: Bases are distributed at equal distances throughout the play area. Each student finds a base. Three or four students are left without a base. These students become the throwers. Each thrower has a ball. On the whistle each player must run to a different base. Any player may be hit while off base. When a runner is hit, he becomes a thrower. The thrower then becomes a runner.

Variations:
1. Have runners who have been hit become throwers adding more balls to the game. The last one hit is the winner.

Teaching Suggestion:
1. Have bases closer together at first. Lengthen them as students gain proficiency.

2. Add more throwers as the game progresses.

TUNNEL BALL

Grade Level: 2–4

Objective: To give practice in ball rolling. To develop flexibility of the hamstring muscles. To develop team work in moving toward the game objective. To develop skills in using the hands defensively.

Equipment Needed: One ball for every two players.

Procedures: Children are divided into two teams. One team forms a circle with each child spreading his legs and standing foot to foot with the child next to him. Keeping his legs straight he bends forward at the waist allowing his hands to hang in front of his legs. The other team stands in the center of the circle. On the whistle the team in the middle tries to roll one of several balls through the legs of the circle players. One point is scored each time the ball goes through the legs of a player. After a designated time the teams change positions with the circle players becoming the ball rollers.

Variations:
1. Same game except players are not divided into teams. When the ball is rolled through the legs of a circle player, he must go into the middle.

Teaching Suggestions:
1. Enforce the legs straight rule.
2. Start with few balls and increase later.
3. Decrease circle size as children become more proficient.

GUARD THE BASKET

Grade Level: 2–4

Objectives: To develop accuracy. To defend a simple goal. To learn the proper time to throw in scoring on a guarded target.

13

Equipment Necessary: One waste basket or small box for each 6 or 7 players. One bean bag for every player.

Procedures: Children form in circles of 6 or 7 players each. A waste can or box is placed in the center of the circle. One child stands in the center of the circle to defend the basket, while the circle players each try to toss a bean bag in the basket. Center players get one point for each bag which drops to the floor outside the basket. The center player changes with a circle player until each player has been center player.

Teaching Suggestions:
1. When proficiency is gained, add a tossing time limit.

BOUNDARY BALL

Grade Level: 2–4

Objective: To throw and kick. To work together in large teams.

Equipment Necessary: One ball for every two players, various sizes.

Procedures: Group the children in two teams. Each team stands on its own side of a middle line. Each team has a boundary line to protect. On command, children pick up balls from the center line and attempt to throw the balls over the end or boundary line of the other team. The ball may not cross the boundary line on the fly. One point is scored for each ball which crosses the opponents boundary line.

Variations: Children kick or serve (as in volleyball) the ball rather than throw it.

Teaching Suggestions:
1. Add more balls as play progresses.
2. Alternate players between throwing and defending.

BALL THROW

Grade Level: 2–6

Objectives: To throw. To catch. To cooperate in small group play.

Equipment Necessary: One ball for every two players.

Procedures: The two teams line up facing each other. The distance between lines should be determined according to the grade level of the children. Each student on Team A stands directly opposite a player on Team B. Team A throws the balls, one for each player, to players on Team B. Team A scores on ball dropped by Team B and Team B scores on bad throw from Team B. Continue with Teams A and B throwing alternately. Vary the ball size according to age.

Procedures: Several small circles are marked in different locations on the play area. These are "home" for the sheep. One half of the class comprises the "sheep" and the other half the foxes. As play begins the sheep spread out on the play area as do the foxes. When the leader fox feels that the sheep are lured far enough from home, he yells "RUN, SHEEP, RUN" at which time the foxes try to tag sheep before they reach home. Tagged players become foxes.

Teaching Suggestions: If trees or other hiding places are available on the playground, allow the sheep to hide from the foxes.

STAND IN PAIRS

Grade Level: 2–3

Objectives: To react to the situation. To develop skill in running and tagging.

Equipment Necessary: None.

Procedures: The children group in twos and distribute themselves over the play area. The children stand one in front of the other. One child is "IT" and the other is the "RUNNER". The "IT" player chases the "RUNNER" trying to tag him. The runner may stop at the back of any line for safety. When he stops, the front person in that line becomes the runner and is eligible to be tagged.

Teaching Suggestions: Set up several games of approximately 10 players each. Have children play the same game in different areas of the playground. This allows more children to be active.

TRAIN TAG

Grade Level: 2–4

Objective: Learn to work as part of the group. Endurance through vigorous running. Agility and balance while running.

Equipment Necessary: None.

Procedures: Draw a large circle on the ground or on the gym floor. Divide the children into two teams. Each team joins with one leader and the remainder of the team members grasp the waist of the other members in line behind the leader. Each "train" moves clockwise around the circle with the leader of each team trying to tag the last player of the other train. Each tag is worth one point.

Variations: Have "trains" stand without grasping and call either "clockwise" or "counterclockwise". The students react to the command by running as a train in the proper direction. The above rules hold true.

GET MOVIN'

Grade Level: 2–4

Objectives: Develop skill and fitness depending on the type activities required of students in this game. To give and take directions. To work with a partner.

Procedures: Children grouped by two. Working with a partner, they follow the commands of one leader. "Stoop Down", "Face Together", "Join Hands and Turn Under", etc. When the signal "GET MOVIN'" is given all children find a new partner and the remaining ones gives the commands.

Teaching Suggestions:
1. Give the commands yourself the first few times to give the children some ideas of what to do.
2. Select activities which are vigorous and which develop types of skill or fitness.

CROWS AND CRANES

Grade Level: 2 to 4

Objectives: To improve reaction and movement time. To follow directions. To learn the difference between safe and unsafe tagging.

Equipment Necessary: Properly marked play area.

Procedures: The children are assigned to one of two groups, the crows and the cranes. The crows line up on one side of a middle line which is drawn between two boundary lines. The cranes line up on the other side of the middle line. The teacher then calls either crows or cranes. If the call is crows, the crows run for the boundary behind them. The cranes attempt to tag them. Those players that are tagged become cranes. The same procedure is repeated. If "cranes" is the call, the crows are the taggers and the cranes are the runners. Continue calling until all players become members of one team.

Teaching Suggestions:
1. Periodically call "crackers", "crawdads", or some other similar word to keep teams from anticipating the call.
2. Encourage all players to play hard no matter which team they are on.

PRISONER BASE

Grade Level: 3 to 4

Objective: To develop agility and general body coordination. To develop team strategy. To work in small groups. To follow basic rules and report personal violations. To run.

Equipment Necessary: Properly marked play area.

Procedures: Children are divided into two teams. The play area is marked so that there are two end lines, a middle line and two jail areas. Five players from each team are placed in the jail of the other team. All other players line up on their own half of the playing area. Play begins at the command of the instructor. Students attempt to free those players that are in jail by tagging them on the hand. Only one prisoner can be freed at a time. The prisoner and the team mate attempting to free the prisoner then try to

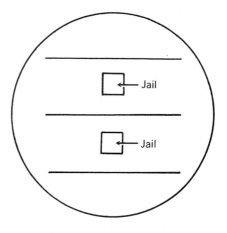

escape to their own territory at their own risk. Any player tagged while trying to free a prisoner must go to jail (may be caught only when in opponents territory). The first team to free all prisoners or to capture the entire opposing team is the winner. Players may cross the end line of the opponent to rest without risk of being tagged.

Teaching Suggestions:
1. Have students wear colored shirts or arm bands so that team members can recognize their own team mates.
2. After students become proficient set a time limit and score one point for each prisoner held at the time limit. This keeps more children active.

FLIP THE LID

Grade Level: 3 to 4

Objective: To react. To follow directions. To learn the difference between safe and unsafe tagging.

Equipment Necessary: Cardboard circle colored red on one side and blue on the other side.

Procedures: The play area is marked with three lines, a middle line, and two end lines. The children are divided into two teams, the reds and the blues. The reds line up on one side of the middle line and the blues on the other. The cardboard circle is thrown into the air. If it lands blue, the blues chase the reds. If it lands red, the reds chase the blues. Tagged players become members of the other team. Continue until all players are on one team.

14

HOOK ON

Grade Level: 3 to 4

Objectives: To play together in small groups. To help children understand personal limitations as well as those of other children. To develop strength and agility.

Equipment Necessary: None.

Procedures: Several groups of 3 to 5 members are formed. Each group forms a single file line with each child grasping the waist of the child in front of him. One player is the HOOKER and tries to hook on to the end of one of the lines. Line players may run around the play area trying to keep the HOOKER from joining their line. However, they may not break hands. The front player in the line becomes the new HOOKER if the end of his line is hooked by an "IT" player.

Teaching Suggestions:
1. As the game progresses add several hookers.

SAFETY LINE TAG

Grade Level: 3 to 4

Objectives: To learn to control movement behavior. To run, dodge, and tag. To follow simple game rules.

Equipment Necessary: Properly marked play area.

Procedures: Two boundary lines are drawn on the play area. A middle or "safety" line is drawn between the two boundary lines. The children line up behind one boundary. One child is "IT". At any time the non "IT" players may run from one boundary to the other. They may stop on the safety line if they desire. When on the safety line or behind an end boundary, the players are safe. Players tagged between lines become "IT" and help tag the non "IT" players. The last child caught is the "IT" player for the next game.

Teaching Suggestions:
1. Children should be encouraged to run from boundary to boundary as many times as possible. The teacher may award 1 point each time a child runs from boundary to boundary. Any child running 5 times without being caught can be awarded one "free". In other words, a child with a "free" saved up must be tagged twice before he becomes "IT".

✗ BUGS

Grade Level: 3 to 4

Objectives: To follow more difficult game rules. To react to appropriate signal. To run, dodge and tag.

Equipment Necessary: Properly marked play area.

Procedures: Mark four circles on four corners of the play area. Divide the class into four groups. Each group moves to one corner of the play area and stands in one of the circles. Each group then decides on a team name (some type of bug, *i.e.;* spiders, ants, stink bugs, etc.). The teacher then calls two team names. These players must switch circles without being tagged by the Bug Bomb (the IT player). Any player tagged by the Bug Bomb becomes a Bug Bomb and a tagger. Continue to call team names until only one person remains. The team of which he is a member is declared the winner.

Teaching Suggestions:
1. Call several team names at once after players become proficient.
2. Let players call team names. Help the caller remember to call all team names.

✗ BASE TAG

Grade Level: 3 to 6

Objectives: To take a reasonable chance in a simple game. To use simple game strategy. To cooperate in competitive situations. To develop balance and agility.

Equipment Necessary: One base for every child.

Procedures: One base is needed for every player. The bases are distributed throughout the play area. One is picked up so that one person will be without a base. On the call "change", all children run to a different base. The one person left without a base is in the "mush pot". Continue each time removing one base to leave more children in the "mush pot".

Variations:
1. Allow two players to be in the middle without a base. Have one player chase the other attempting to tag him. The runner may at any time stop on any base to keep from being tagged by the tagger. The person on that base then becomes the runner and must vacate the base. If the tagger tags the runner, the runner becomes the tagger and must try to tag the new runner. Gradually increase the number of taggers and runners.

2. Allow several players to be in the middle without bases. Some will be throwers and the others will be runners. The game is played like Variation 1 except runners must be hit with the ball rather than being tagged. Throwers carry a ball attempting to hit runners between bases.

CAPTURE THE GOLD

Grade Level: 5 to 6

Objectives: To follow rules and strategy of a somewhat complex game. To learn to self enforce rules. To provide experience in running, dodging and tagging.

Equipment Necessary: Properly marked play area.

Procedures: Play area is divided in half. Each half has a prison and a gold storage area. Players are divided into two teams, one on each half of the play area. When play starts, each team directs its efforts to capturing the other team's gold. Players may cross into the opponents territory at their own risk. They may be captured if tagged in opponents territory with two hands. Captured players must go to prison. The gold is captured when one player lifts the gold from the "bank" and returns it over the middle line to his own territory. Prisoners may be freed by being tagged by a free team mate or by having the gold thrown to them by a free team mate. A prisoner with the gold gets free passage to his own territory in exchange for the gold. The team carrying the gold to their own territory is the winner.

Teaching Suggestions: Have opposing teams wear different shirt colors.

BARLEY BREAK

Grade Level: 6

Objectives: To work with a partner in a game situation. To learn the limitations of self and of others. To change direction effectively. To provide an opportunity for running.

Equipment Necessary: Properly marked play area.

Procedures: The children find a partner. One pair lines up in the middle of the playing area (see below). The remainder of the players stand with their partners in either of

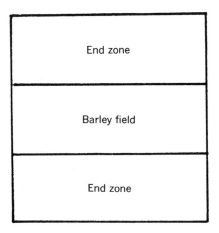

End zone

Barley field

End zone

the two end zones. The pair in the middle are the wardens. They attempt to protect the barley fields (middle area). The other players try to trample the barley. These players run through the middle of the play area with their partner. The wardens try to tag them. Players tagged by the warden become barley and must stand as obstacles in the barley field until all runners are caught. The last pair caught becomes the new warden pair.

References

AAHPER: *How We Do It Game Book.* Washington, National Education Association, 1964.

Bancroft, J. H.: *Games.* New York, The Macmillan Co., 1937.

Eisenberg, H. and Eisenberg, L.: *The Omnibus of Fun.* New York, Association Press, 1956.

Geri, F. H.: *Illustrated Games and Rhythms for Children.* Englewood Cliffs, N.J., Prentice-Hall Inc., 1955, pp. 71–102, pp. 147–196.

Hindman, D. A.: *Complete Book of Games and Stunts.* Englewood Cliffs, N.J., Prentice-Hall Inc., 1956.

Hunt, S. E.: *Games Around the World.* New York, Ronald Press, 1964.

Kraus, R. G.: *Play Activities for Boys and Girls—THROUGH 12.* New York, McGraw-Hill Book Co., 1957, Chapter 5.

Mulac, M. E.: *Games and Stunts for Schools, Camps, and Playgrounds.* New York, Harper & Row, 1964.

Van Hagen, W., Dexter, G., and Williams, J. F.: *Physical Education in the Elementary Schools.* Sacramento, California State Department of Education, 1958, Chapters 13 through 21.

15

Gymnastics and Tumbling

Gymnastics and tumbling can serve as excellent activities for meeting the objectives of elementary school physical education. This chapter includes a presentation of the following gymnastics and tumbling activities: tumbling on the mats, stunts, ladder balancing, tumbling table, tube tumbling, horizontal bar stunts, and balance beam.

Tumbling On The Mats (Individual)

Objectives: Strength, agility, flexibility, balance, sense of body relocation, provides physical challenge, and experience in evaluating self limitations.

Equipment: One mat for every 3 to 6 children.

Grade: 1 to 6, the first stunts for the lower grades and the latter for the higher elementary grade levels.

Procedures:
1. *Log Roll:* Lying face down on the mat with the hands out-stretched above the head the student rolls laterally along the mat, keeping the feet together and the hands straight above the head. Emphasis is placed on rolling straight along the mat without the head or feet moving faster than each other.

measo

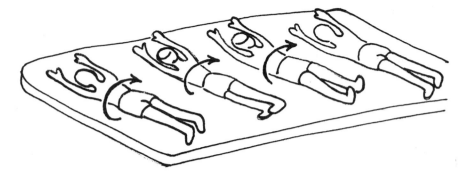

2. *Forward Roll (Tuck Position):* From a squat position the student places his hands in front of him a shoulder's width apart. Pushing forward with the feet and taking the body weight on the hands the student ducks the head placing the chin near the chest and allowing the weight to be taken on the shoulders and the rounded back. The forward movement provides the impetus for rolling up to the feet. Emphasize keeping the head off the mat, the knees against the chest and continuing forward until the student reaches his feet.

3. *Dive Roll:* Same as the forward roll except the stunt is executed from a standing position. After a forward lunge, the body weight is taken on the hands and the forward roll is executed. As the stunt is perfected the lunge can be done from a higher position and over a greater distance. This stunt can be performed after taking a running start.

4. *Forward Roll (Pike Position):* Done the same as the forward roll (tuck) except the stunt is executed from a standing position bending for-

ward at the waist at a 90° angle (pike position). As the lunge is made forward the 90° angle or pike position is maintained until the roll is completed and the student returns to his feet. A simple modification can be made by straddling the legs in the pike position and maintaining this position throughout the forward roll.

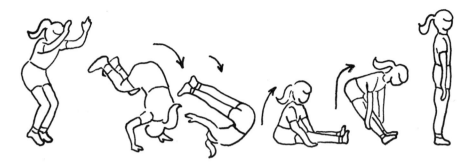

5. *Backward Roll (Tuck):* From the squat position the student rolls back onto the shoulders. Reaching over the shoulders and placing the hands on the mat above the shoulders. While maintaining the tucked position the student rolls on over to his feet. The student pushes with the hands to aid him in continuing up to his feet. Emphasize the push with the hands and the maintenance of the tight tuck position.

6. *Backward Roll (Pike):* Same as the backward roll in the tuck position except that a pike position is maintained throughout. See forward roll, pike position.
7. *Back Roll With Extension:* Done as a regular backward roll except that an additional push is applied with the hands and the feet are pushed into the air so that the student lands on his feet in the standing position.

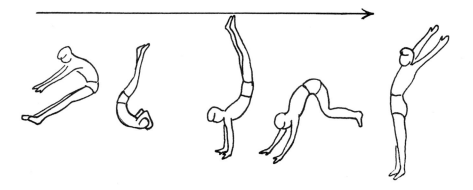

8. *Fish Flop:* Done from the back roll with an extension. Instead of landing on the feet the legs are kept straight and the student drops his whole body on his stomach with a flat flop against the mat.

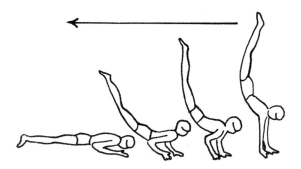

9. *Forward to Backward Roll:* On coming up from the forward roll the legs are crossed. Stand up with the legs crossed, make a half turn by uncrossing the legs and continue on with the backward roll.

10. *Tip Up:* From a squat position place the hands at shoulder width on the mat. Spread the knees placing the elbows against the knees. Push forward with the feet placing the forehead against the mat forming the third part of a triangle on the mat. Keep the knees on the elbows and maintain a head stand in this position.

11. *Frog Stand:* From the tip up position push forward pressing the knees against the elbows keeping the head off the mat while balancing on the two hands. Keep the knees on the elbows and maintain the hand stand in this position.

12. *Cartwheel (To The Right):* Start with the right side facing down the mat with the arms and legs spread apart like the spokes of a wheel. Rock onto the right foot, bend at the right side placing the right hand on the mat two feet from the right foot. Throw the left leg in the air straight over the head while pushing off with the right hand. Place the left hand on the mat while swinging the right leg over head. The momentum pushes the body into a handstand position. Keeping the legs and arms spread, the head is kept up so that the eyes can focus on a spot between the hands. The momentum carries the student through the hand stand. As the left foot lowers to the mat, bend at the waist lifting the right hand off the mat as the left foot makes contact. The right foot sways over to return to the standing position facing the same direction as at the start of the cartwheel. Emphasize keeping the arms and legs straight and spread. Also emphasize a vigorous thrust at the beginning to provide the momentum to complete the maneuver. The stunt can be performed in either direction.

13. *Headstand:* Performed much the same as the tip up. Form a triangle with the hands and the head. Place the hands at shoulder width with the head (at the hairline) forming the peak of the triangle. Lift the legs overhead until they are extended directly above the head. Arch the back slightly and hold. The beginners may kick the legs up into the headstand if there is a spotter. If the performer begins to fall forward, he should duck the head and perform the forward roll.

14. *Handstand:* Place the hands on the mat at shoulder width. Keep the head up. Throw the legs into the air so that they are held directly over the hands. The weight is borne on the hands. The back should arch slightly. Balance control is maintained with the pressure applied by the fingers. Students may spot each other while learning the stunt or use the wall as a spotter (kick up allowing feet to touch the wall).

15. *Headspring (On Rolled Mat):* Place a rolled mat across the length of mats on which the stunt is performed. From the standing position

in front of the rolled mat place the hands on the near side (top) of the rolled mat. Lower the head to the far side (top) of the rolled mat while allowing the feet to lift off the floor in the pike position. Moving through the headstand throw the feet overhead (thrusting from the waist). As the feet move over, arch the back and push with the hands. Land on the feet. A spotter should be present for beginners. Poorly skilled performers may place the hands and head in front of the rolled mat. Then the performer moves through the headspring maneuver. The rolled mat catches the middle of the back helping the performer over.

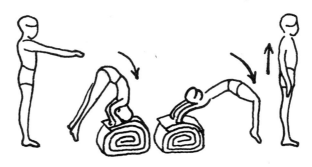

16. *Headspring:* The same as the above described maneuver except the performer may begin with a run and the rolled mat is removed.
17. *Handspring (Over Rolled Mat):* After a run, skip with one foot then stepping forward with the other. Bend forward at the waist placing the hands on the floor in front of rolled mat. Kick the lead foot down and back. Kick the back foot overhead following it with the front foot as the body moves through the handstand position, push with the shoulders and hands. Arch the back slightly and continue to the feet. A spotter should be present at this stunt.

18. *Handspring:* Same as the above stunt without the rolled mat.
19. *Roundoff:* This stunt is much the same as the cartwheel except the body makes a one-fourth turn before landing so that the performer

is facing the opposite of the starting direction instead of sideways. The roundoff is a method of changing direction in performing a series of stunts. It is a lead in to back maneuver.

20. *Suggestions for teaching*
    A. Provide a "spotter" for students who have difficulty.
    B. Practice simple stunts across the width of the mat rather than along the length to allow more students to be active.
    C. Encourage proper technique to every detail because the advanced stunts are based on proper execution of the more simple maneuvers.
    D. Allow students to spot each other on simple stunts.

Tumbling and Stunts (Dual or Group)

Objectives: Same as for individual tumbling.

Equipment: One mat for every 3 to 6 children.

Grade: 3 to 6, the easier stunts are listed first and the more difficult last.

Procedures:

1. *Double Forward Roll:* One performer lies on his back with his feet in the air. The second performer straddles the head of the first performer facing his feet. The partners grasp each others ankles. From this position, the standing performer dives to a forward roll bringing the bottom performer to his feet. The maneuver is repeated several times.

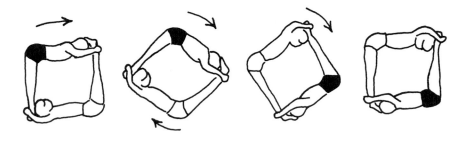

2. *Three Man Log Roll:* Three performers lie face down across the width of the mat. The center person log rolls toward either of the outside performers. As he nears the outside performer, that performer jumps over the middle man and log rolls toward the other outside man. The middle man stops now becoming the new outside man. As the rolling man reaches the otherside, the 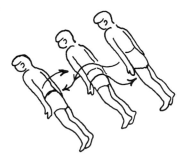 outside man jumps and log rolls to the outside. Continue to jump and roll.

3. *Chest Balance:* One performer stands on the mat in the all fours position. The second performer grasps under the chest of the first performer allowing his head to extend over his back. From this position the second performer kicks his feet above his head in a similar way to performing the hand stand. With the feet overhead and the back slightly arched the top performer maintains a balanced position.

4. *Thigh Stand:* Two performers face in the same direction. One performer places his head between the legs of a second performer standing directly in front of him. The front man places his

feet in the back mans thighs. The top man then stands up while the bottom man holds the top man slightly above the knees. The bottom man keeps his knees bent to aid the top man in maintaining the standing position. The top performer then arches the back, spreading the arms and holding this swan position.

5. *Knee-Shoulder Balance:* One performer lies on his back on the mat with his knees and the arms raised. The second performer places his hands on the knees of the bottom performer. He leans forward placing his shoulders in the hands of the bottom performer. The top performer leans forward until the arms are fully extended. Keeping the head up he kicks into a position similar to the hand stand with the feet balanced above his head. The bottom performer supports the top man. The balance position is maintained.

6. *Pyramids:* Three performers get on the mat in all-four position. About 4 inches apart. Two smaller performers get on all-fours position on the backs of the three bottom performers. These performers place their knees and hands on the backs of the bottom performers. A smaller performer gets to a similar position on the two middle performers.

Two performers get in a hands and knees position next to each other. A third performer stands with one foot on the back of the two bottom men. The other two performers perform headstands on either side of the bottom performer so that the standing performers can hold their feet.

Two performers do a thigh stand. One on each side two performers demonstrate the knee shoulder balance. The top performer on the thigh stand holds the feet of the top performer in the knee shoulder balance.

Ladder Balancing

Objectives: Same as for tumbling.

Equipment: One 12 foot ladder for each 7 students.

Grade: Grades 5 and 6.

Procedures:

1. *The Back Arch:* In this stunt the children grasp the vertical piece of the ladder directly opposite their hips, and then with their hips against the ladder and their arms held straight they arch backward as far as possible.

2. *The Leg Hang:* To put themselves into position for the leg hang, the children, in unison, first place one leg over the rung above the one they are standing on. Then they hook the foot of this leg over the outside of the lower rung and move the other foot down one rung. Finally, they arch backward slowly, and release their handgrip and place their arms into the position illustrated. Their heads should be pulled back.

3. *The Half Eagle:* To accomplish the half eagle the children stand with their sides toward the ladders and then slowly extend arms and legs to complete the stunt.

4. *The Full Eagle:* This stunt is a continuation of the half eagle, with the children slowly extending their arms to achieve the effect illustrated.

5. *The "L":* The children should first turn around on the ladders, placing their backs toward the ladder. Next they should reach up, one hand at a time, to grasp the rung and lift their legs to the horizontal position to complete the stunt.

6. *The "O":* The hand grip on the rung is with palms up. While holding onto one rung and standing on another the children simply arch.

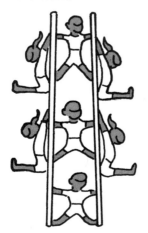

Tumbling Table

Objective: Same as basic tumbling with emphasis on body relocation balancing, coordination and agility.

Equipment: One mini-tramp (trampolette) and a tumbling table (sturdy mat covered table).

Grade: Grades 3 to 6.

Procedures:

1. *Spring On The Mini-Tramp:* After a run, the performer leaps from one foot to the center of the mini-tramp. He then bounces using a two foot take off from the mini-tramp. He jumps into the air landing with both feet on the mat. If the balance is not maintained after the landing, a forward roll is performed as a safety measure.

2. *Jack Spring From The Mini-Tramp:* Performed in the same way as the regular spring except that the performer straddles the legs in the air after the jump lifting the leg as high as possible. He touches his feet with his hands before returning to the mat.

3. *Jump To Table:* Performed the same as the regular spring except that the tumbling table is placed behind the mini-tramp. The performer lands on top of the table on two feet. He then jumps off the table to the mat.

4. *Vault From the Table:* Once on the table the performer can get off using this maneuver. He leans forward placing his hands on the table at the back end. Swinging the legs to one side the weight is taken on the hands and the performer drops off the table to his feet.

5. *Jump to hands and Knees Position:* After jumping from the mini-tramp the performer reaches over the table catching his hands on the back side of the table. The arms bend, acting as shock absorbers, lowering the knees to the table. Once in this position, the performer vaults off.

6. *Forward roll on Table:* After jumping from the mini-tramp the performer places the hands on the near side of the table. He ducks his head performing the forward roll over the table, dropping off the back side to his feet after performing the roll.

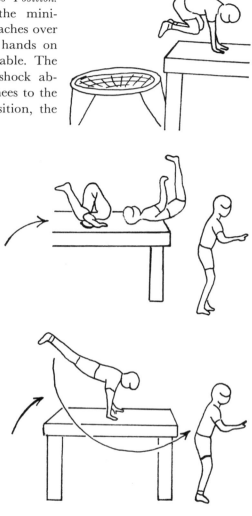

7. *Wolfe Vault:* After jumping (vigorously) from the mini-tramp the performer reaches over the table placing the hands on the back side of the table. Keeping the head up, he swings both legs to one side over and to the side of his hands, dropping his feet on the floor on the far side of the table.

8. *Straddle Vault:* Performed with the same way as the Wolfe Vault except that one leg is spread on each side of the hands as the performer passes over the table.

9. *Squat Vault:* Performed in the same way as the Wolfe Vault except that both feet swing between the hands as the performer passes over the table.

10. *Cartwheel Vault:* Performed in exactly the same way as the cartwheel on the floor except that is done over the table after a spring on the mini-tramp.

11. *Roundoff Vault:* A regular roundoff performed over the tumbling table after a jump on the mini-tramp.

12. *Handspring Vault:* A regular handspring performed over the tumbling table after a jump on the mini-tramp.

Tube Tumbling

Objectives: Same as basic tumbling with the emphasis on body relocation, balancing, coordination and agility.

Equipment: Mats and large tractor inner tube.

Grades: 1 to 6.

Procedures:

1. *Bounce Over the Hole:* The performer runs up to the tube and bounces on the front side (land on two feet). Bounce again landing on two feet on the back side of the tube. Finally bounce off the back of the tube to the mat.

2. *All The Way Over:* Bounce on the near side of the tube, springing all of the way over the tube landing on the mat.

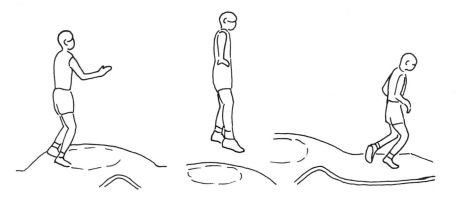

3. *Jack Spring:* Bounce on the near side of the tube, springing into the air. While in the air lift and spread the legs touching the toes with the hands.

4. *Swan Spring:* Bounce on the near side of the tube, springing into the air. While in the air hold both arms at full length back and to the sides. Arch slightly backward. Land on the far side of the tube.

5. *Straddle Around:* Stand on the tube straddling the hole. Bounce into the air. Give a half body twist in the air, land on the tube straddling the hole facing the other direction.

6. *Half Twist Spring:* Bounce on the near side of the tube, springing into the air. Half turn in the air, landing facing the tube.
7. *Full Twist Spring:* Same as above with a full twist in the air.
8. *Jump To Seat:* Bounce on the near side of the tube, springing into the air. Lift the legs into the air in a "seat" position. Drop on top of the tube hole in a "seat" position.

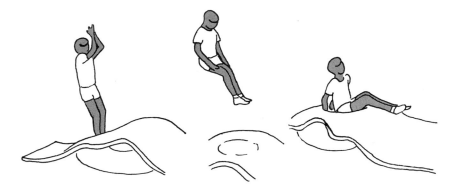

9. *Forward Roll Over The Hole:* Run toward the tube, place the hands on the near side of the tube. Do a forward roll over the tube, land on the feet.

10. *Knee To Roll:* Same as roll over the hole except that the performer does a knee drop on the near side of the tube before rolling over it.

11. *Head Spring Over The Tube:* Place the head and hands on the near side of the tube. Swing the legs over the head, push with the hands, land over the tube on the feet.

12. *Knee To Seat:* Bounce on the knees on the near side of the tube. Duck the head after springing in the air. Flip in the air, dropping in the "seat" position on the hole.

13. *Headover:* Done in the same way as the head spring except the hands are not used.

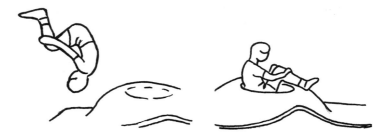

Horizontal Bar Stunts

Objectives: To develop upper arm strength, to develop self confidence, to develop agility.

Equipment: Horizontal bar.

Grades: 3 to 6.

Procedures:
1. *Swing:* Hang by the hands lift the legs forward, kick them out and up, then arch the back prior to swinging backward. Swing back then forward. Swing back then forward, repeating the kick and back arch.

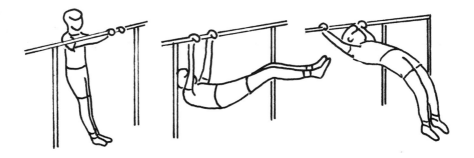

2. *Skin The Cat:* Hang from the bar with both hands. Lift the legs through the hole formed by the legs and the arms. Lower the legs as close to the ground as possible. Lift the legs back through the hole to the starting position.

3. *Monkey Hang:* Skin the cat but *do not* return. When legs have been lowered through the hole as far as possible, let go with one hand. Allow the body to turn until the starting position is reached. Regrasp the bar with the free hand.

4. *Knee Hang:* Lift the legs up to the bar. Lift the feet over the bar until the back of the knee is draped over the bar. Let go with the hands. Hold! To dismount regrasp the bar and lower the legs.

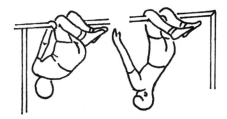

Dismount

5. *Front Support:* Face the bar supporting the body weight above the bar on both arms (held straight). The body should lean slightly against the bar at the stomach. *Lower the body to pull up position and land with slightly flexed knees to prevent jarring the body.*

6. *Forward Circle:* From the front support, lean forward over the bar. Bend the knees drawing the legs in close to the body. Allow the body to continue to fall over the bar. Hang on with the hands. The body will drop to the two hand hang position. *Dismount*

SAme AS ChiNNiNg the Bar

7. *Backward Circle:* From the hanging position, kick the legs up in front and over the bar. The bar should hit at the waist. Bend at the hips holding the body on the bar at a 90° angle. Lift the head until the body is in the front support position. Suggestion: Help the children kick up to the bar during early learning stages. *Dismount*

same as front support

8. *One Leg Kick Up:* From the hanging position, lift one foot through the hold formed by the hands and the bar. Lock the knee around the bar. Keeping the free leg straight, kick it down vigorously. At the same time pull with the arms until the body moves into a front support position. *Dismount same as chin the*

Cat

9. *One Leg Forward Circle:* From the front support position, place one leg over the bar inside the arms and hands. The performer falls forward from the position. As the body drops below the bar, kick the leg and pull with the arms as in the one leg kick up. Finish in the starting position. *Dismount same as skin the cat*

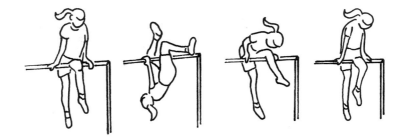

10. *One Leg Back Circle:* Begin from the same position as the one leg front circle. The performer falls backward from this position holding on with the hands. As the body falls directly under the bar, grab the bar with the knee and kick the other foot forward over the bar. Pull the chest over the bar to the starting position. *Dismount same as skin the cat*

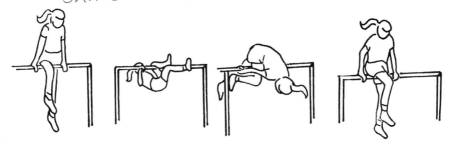

Balance Beam *yes*

Objectives: To develop balance and agility, to develop foot eye coordination to develop understanding of self limitation, to develop self confidence.

Equipment: Balance beam of 2 x 4 feet securely suspended.

Grades: 1 to 6.

Procedures:
1. *Walk:* Stand on the beam walk across get off the other end.

2. *Two Foot Turn:* Stand on toes (on the beam). Twist both feet at the same time until facing the opposite direction. Lower back to total foot support.

3. *One Foot Turn:* Lift one foot off the beam. Stand on the toe of the other foot. Twist turning on the foot. When 180° is complete lower both feet to the beam.

4. *Backward Walk:* Walk backward across the beam.

5. *Side Shuffle:* Stand sideways on the beam. Slide the right foot sideways then the left foot sideways down the beam. Take steps of approximately 18 inches. Move faster as skill develops.

6. *Crawl The Beam:* Crawl the length of the beam on the hands and knees.

7. *Skip The Beam:* Skip the length of the beam.

8. *Alternate Knee Touch:* Face the length of the beam. Take a long step forward with one foot. Stoop until the other knee touches the beam. Stride forward with the other foot placing it well ahead of the front foot. Again stoop until the knee touches. Continue stepping and kneeling on alternate knees.

9. *Dip Walk:* On an elevated beam lift one foot supporting the body weight on the other. Stoop, lowering the lifted leg as close to the floor as possible. Return to stand, step forward on the other foot as repeated.

10. *Stork Stand:* Stand on the beam. Lift one foot up and backward. Bend forward at the waist while standing on one foot. Hold for several seconds.

11. *Seal Walk:* Suspend the body on the beam on the hands and feet with the body bent at about 120°. slide the feet forward, then alternately walk the hands forward. Continue across the beam.

12. *Leap To Leap:* Leap in the air landing on one foot. Repeat landing on the other foot. Continue across the beam.

13. *Bounce Ball Across The Beam:*
14. *Teaching Suggestions:*
    A. After children have learned the above skills have them combine several skills.
    B. Have students improve stunts on the beam.
    C. If no balance beam is available, have the children perform the stunts on a line on the floor.

Bibliography

Anderson, M., Elliot M., and LaBerge, J.: *Play With a Purpose.* New York, Harper & Row, 1966, Chapter 3, p. 79–121.

O'Quinn, Garland: *Gymnastics for Elementary School Children.* Dubuque, Iowa, Wm. C. Brown & Co., 1967.

Lohen, N. and Willoughby, R. J.: *Complete Book of Gymnastics.* Englewood Cliffs, N.J., Prentice-Hall, Inc. 1959.

Dauer, V.: *Fitness for Elementary School Children.* Minneapolis, Burgess Publishers, 1965, Chapter 12, p. 118–135, Chapter 20, p. 224–247.

16

Relays

This chapter includes a discussion of various relays and relay formations which can be used in meeting elementary school physical education objectives.

Relay Formations

STRAIGHT LINE RELAY FORMATION

Students stand in single file lines. One person participates at a time—after finishing, each person goes to the end of the line and the person in the front of the line performs the same maneuver—continue until each person has participated once and the line is back to the original position.

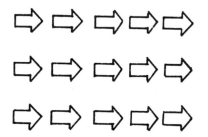

CIRCLE RELAY FORMATION

Students divide into small squads and form squads in circles. One person performs at a time—when he returns to his original position, the next person begins—continue until each person has participated.

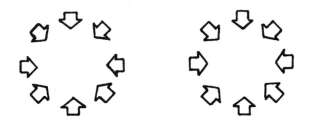

SHUTTLE RELAY FORMATION

Each team forms two single file lines facing each other. #1 performs finishing near person #2—#2 then performs finishing near person #3, etc. When finished, the performer goes to the end of the opposite line. Continue until each person has performed once.

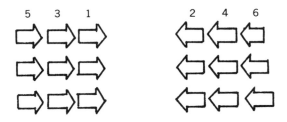

SEMI-CIRCLE RELAY FORMATION

Teams form in semi-circle with one person standing opposite the semi-circle facing in (leader)—each person in semi-circle performs then the leader performs, the next then the leader, etc. Until all have performed once.

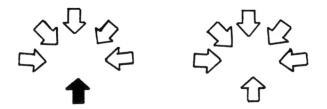

Relays

DOWN AND BACK RELAYS

Objective: Learn to follow directions and to cooperate as a team. Learn specific skill involved in relay variation. Develop agility and balance.

Grade Level: Any grade from 1 to 6 depending on performance level of children. Variation progress from simple to difficult. Relays are probably most effective as a tool beginning in Grade 3.

Equipment: Jump ropes, balls, bean bags, baseball bats or wands.

Formation: Straight line relay formation.

Procedures: Beginning in the straight line relay the first performer in each line runs to a line 30 to 50 feet away. The runner returns to the beginning position, tagging the next person in line. Continue until each team member has performed once and the line is back to the original position. When all performers are finished, they all sit down. In skill learning situations no winner should be declared. If the situation is competitive, the first team to complete is the winner.

Variations:
1. *Two Leg Hop:* The same as above except performers hop down to the line and back on two feet.
2. *One Leg Hop:* As above hopping on one foot.
3. *Skip:* As above skipping.
4. *Jump Rope:* As above except each performer jumps a rope while running to and from the line. The same rope is handed to the next team member.
5. *Ball Carry:* As above except performer carries a ball as he runs to and from the line.
6. *Bean Bag Carry:* As above except as he walks or runs to and from the line, the performer carries a bean bag on his head.
7. *Hold the Toe:* As variation #2 except the performer holds the big toe of one foot as he hops to and from the line on the other.
8. *Between the Knees:* As variation #1 except the performer holds a ball between his knees as he hops to and from the line.
9. *Balance the Bat:* As above except the performer balances a bat on a finger as he walks to and from the line.

Teaching Suggestions:
1. Place a bowling pin or marker at the line—require performers to run around the marker so that there is no doubt about each person traveling the proper distance.
2. In variations, the performer must stop forward progress if he drops

the ball, the bat or fails to perform proper maneuver. Forward progress resumes only when performer again begins the proper maneuver.
3. Distance can be varied in accordance with abilities of the students.

ANIMAL WALK RELAYS

Objective: To develop skills in stunts. To develop team cooperation. To develop flexibility, agility and balance.

Grade Level: Grades 3 to 6 depending on previous skill learning of students.

Equipment: None.

Formation: Straight line relay formation.

Procedures: Beginning in the straightline relay formation, the first performer in each line walks on all fours (using both hands and feet) to a line 15 to 25 feet away. The participant touches the second person in line who then dog walks (same maneuver) to and from the line. Continue until each team member has performed once and line is back to the original position.

Variations:
1. *Crab Walk:* Same as above except participants crab walk to and from line.
2. *Wheelbarrow:* Same as above except participants wheelbarrow to and from the line. Performers work in pairs.
3. *Camel Walk:* Same as above except participants camel walk to and from the line. Reach between the legs and grab the outside of each ankle—walk in this position.
4. *Seal Walk:* Same as above except each participant seal walks to and from the line.

Teaching Suggestions:
1. Keep teams small so that more children are participating at one time.
2. Do not use relays as a method of teaching skill.

BALL PASS RELAYS

Objectives: To develop skilled play in a competitive situation. To give drill in specified ball skills. To develop team cooperation.

Grade Level: Grades 4 to 6.

Equipment: One ball for each relay squad.

Formation: Straight line relay formation except for variations #5 and #6.

Procedures: Each team stands in the straight line relay formation with an arms distance between team members. The first performer passes (hands) the ball to the second performer, etc. Pass the ball on down the line until the ball reaches the last player. The last player runs to the front of the line and the same procedure is repeated—continue until the line is back to the original position. Team members all sit down when the team is finished.

Variations:
1. *Overhead:* Same as above except the ball is passed backward over the head instead of from the waist height.
2. *Roll It Through:* Same as above except all team members stand with the legs straddled and the ball is rolled through the legs rather than being passed.
3. *Underleg Pass:* Same as variation #2 except the ball is passed backward through the legs rather than being rolled on the ground.
4. *Over and Under:* Same as above except it is a combination of variation #1 and #3. The first team member passes the ball backward overhead. The second under and through the legs. The third back and over, etc. Alternate over and under until the ball reaches the end of the line. Continue as above.
5. *Foot Pass:* Done from the semi-circle formation. The leader kicks the ball alternately to each circle member. When the ball reaches the end of the circle. The first circle member becomes the leader. Repeat until each team member has been the leader.
6. *Circle Ball Pass:* Same as above except the teams form in the circle relay formation—the ball is passed around the circle. The ball must travel around the circle once for each team member.

Teaching Suggestions:
1. If the competitive relay situation is to be used, allow teams to practice several times—this will aid their skill performance and aid in developing team cooperation.
2. Do not use relay situations unless skills have been previously learned.
3. As referee, do not allow illegal play—emphasize fair play.

OBSTACLE RELAYS

Objectives: To develop balance, power and agility. To develop skill in total body control. To develop team cooperation.

Grade Level: Grades 4 to 6.

Equipment: Markers (Bowling pins or chairs), tires, balance beam.

Formation: Straight line relay formation.

Procedures: Same as down and back relays described earlier except each performer must zig-zag around staggered markers while running to and from a line.

Variations:
1. *Through the Tires:* As above except each participant must step in the hole of each of several tires on the way to and from a line.
2. *Walk the Beam:* As above except each participant must walk down and back a balance beam.
3. *Jump the Line:* As above except each participant jumps over several lines while running down and back.

Teaching Suggestions:
1. Add several obstacles as children become accomplished at single obstacles.

GO FETCH IT RELAY

Objectives: To develop agility. To learn the basic skill involved. To learn to follow directions.

Grade Level: 1 to 6.

Equipment: One bean bag or one ball for each team.

Formation: Straight line relay formation.

Procedures: The first performer runs to a line 30 to 50 feet away picking up a bean bag then running back to his line passing the bag to the next team member—the second team member runs to the line and places the bag on the line—he then runs back to his line tagging the next team member who runs to the line and picks up the bag—repeat until each team member has participated.

Variation:
1. *Roll It Back:* Each performer carries a ball to the line he then rolls the ball back to the next team member—repeat until each has participated.

Teaching Suggestions:
1. For low grades do not make it competitive—allow each person to participate several times.

RESCUE RELAY

Objectives: To develop team cooperation. To develop ability to follow directions.

Grade Level: 3 to 6.

Equipment: None.

Formation: Straight line relay formation.

Procedures: The first two persons on each team or squad run, holding hands, to a line 30 to 50 feet away, then they return—the second person in the line joins hands with the third person and these two run to and from the line—the third team member then joins hands with the fourth person in line—these two run to and from the line—this is continued until the first and last team members complete their run together.

Variation:
1. *Carry Them All:* Same as the above except that team members one and two run down and back, then team members #3 joins on. All three run to and from the line. Continue until all team members run together to and from the line.

RAILROAD RELAY

Objectives: To develop agility and balance. To develop alertness to commands.

Grade Level: 2 to 6.

Equipment: None.

Formation: Straight line relay formation or circle relay formation.

Procedures: Each team member sits down in the straight line relay formation with his legs straddled. Each team member is given a number. The teacher then calls a number—the members of each team with that number stands up, then runs down the line alternately stepping over the "Railroad" ties formed by the legs of his team members. Continue until returning to the starting position where he sits down—the first runner seated earns one point for his team.

Variations:
1. *Down and Around:* Similar to the above except the team members lie face down on the floor in a circle. As above players respond to the call of their number and run around the circle stepping over the legs of team members. The first person finished earns one point for his team.

NUMBER CALL RELAY

Objectives: To develop alertness to commands. To develop agility.

Grade Level: 2 to 6.

Equipment: None.

Formation: Straight line relay formation or circle relay formation.

Procedures: This relay is performed similar to the railroad relay. Each team member is given a number. As the instructor calls one number, the performer in each line with that number runs completely around his line and back to his original position. The first one back scores one point for his team.

Teaching Suggestions:
1. Keep track of numbers called so that every child gets equal opportunity to participate.

Stop

CHARIOT RELAY

Objectives: To develop group cooperation. To develop ability to work in small groups. To develop balance and agility.

Grade Level: 5 to 6.

Equipment: None.

Formation: Modified straight line relay formation.

Procedures: Students form in teams of multiples of three. Each team has several chariots formed by three performers, two horses and one driver. One chariot runs for each team at a time. Running with all three performers joined by the hands. The chariot must run to and from a marker. After completing their run, the next chariot begins. Continue until each chariot (group of three) has run.

Teaching Suggestions:
1. Have children run this race several times. Each time allowing a different student to "drive" the "chariot".

AROUND THE BASES RELAY

Objectives: To develop agility. To develop ability to follow directions. To develop lead up skills to softball (base running).

Grade Level: 5 to 6.

Equipment: 4 bases.

Formation: Modified straight line relay formation.

Procedures: Participants form in lines behind four bases—each team member begins running at the word "go". The performer runs around the bases, touching each one, until he returns to his starting position where he tags the next performer who runs the bases. Continue until each team member has run.

Teaching Suggestions:
1. Have a line behind each base so that there are fewer in each line, thus each performer gets more running opportunities.
2. Add bases as needed to cut the number of performers on each team.

SHUTTLE RELAYS

Objectives: To develop specific track skills. To develop team cooperation. To develop agility.

Grade Level: 4 to 6.

Equipment: Batons and jump ropes.

Formation: Shuttle run relay formation (see page 232).

Procedures: Performers #1 runs and tags performer #2 etc. Until each performer has run at least once. The first team to have all performers finish running is the winner.

Variations:
1. *Baton Pass:* Same as above except the performers pass a baton to the next performer instead of tagging him. He must have the baton before he can begin running.
2. *Jump Rope:* Same as above except performers jump rope instead of running.
3. *Any of the Down and Back can be used:* Perform the same as any of the down and back relay but use the shuttle run relay formation. (See page 233.)

Teaching Suggestions:
1. Have each team run through each activity several times for each race.

LEADER-SQUAD RELAYS

Objectives: To teach specific sports skills.

Grade Level: 4 to 6.

Equipment: Nets, volleyballs, soccerballs, basketball, other type balls.

Formation: Semi-circle relay formation (see page 232).

Procedures: The leader begins for each team by passing a ball (one hand, two hand, or bounce pass) to the first circle member. The ball is then passed back to the leader, then to the next circle member, back to the leader, etc. Continue until all circle members have caught the ball. The first circle player then becomes the leader and the old leader moves to the end of the circle. Continue until all players have been leader. The first team finished is the winner.

Variations:
1. *Over the Net:* Same as above except a net is placed between the leader and the circle.
2. *Ball Kick:* Same as above except the ball (a soccer ball) is kicked back and forth between the leader and the circle.
3. *Volley Back:* Same as variation #1 except the ball is volleyed rather than thrown.

Teaching Suggestions:
1. This same basic relay can be used for most ball skills.
2. For developing skills do not use this relay as a competitive race.

DRIBBLE RELAYS

Objectives: To develop dribbling skill. To develop ball control skills.

Grade Level: 5 to 6.

Equipment: Basketballs and soccer balls.

Formation: Straight line relay formation.

Procedures: The relay is performed as any other down and back relay except the ball must be dribbled to and from the line. Continue until each performer has dribbled. In this variation the performer may use both hands at the same time.

Variations:
1. *One Hand Dribble:* Same as above except only one hand may be used at a time.
2. *Soccer Dribble:* Same as above except the ball must be dribbled with the feet—(right, left or both).

Bibliography

State of New Mexico, Division of Health Physical Education and Recreation. *Aids in Physical Education for Teachers.* Santa Fe State Department of Education: 1961. Bulletin 9, p. 44–50, Bulletin 10, p. 59–64.

Van Hagen, W., Dexter, G., and Williams, J. F.: *Physical Education in the Elementary School.* Sacramento, California State Department of Education, 1951.

Dauer, V.: *Fitness for Elementary School Children.* Minneapolis, Burgess Publishing Co., 1965, Chapter 13, p. 136–138, Chapter 21, p. 248–256.

17

Sports and Lead Up Games

Before the children begin playing the sports and lead up games as presented in this chapter, they should have had instruction in the basic or fundamental skills involved in these activities. Suggestions as to how these skills should be taught are given in the chapters on Fundamental Skills (Chapter 11) and Suggestions for Teachers (Chapter 10).

Skill instruction may take place as part of a unit in fundamental skills, a unit in movement exploration, or in other units such as relays or games. However, many fundamental skills could be taught in association with and/or immediately prior to the participation in a sports type activity. Instruction in a skill includes: teaching or describing the skill, demonstrating, practicing, and reinforcing the skill. The children should have sufficient practice so that they are able to *perform* basic skills *before* they are placed in game situations.

A list of the basic skills required for participation in each activity is presented with the discussion of that activity.

SET BACK ✓

Grade Level: 4 to 6.

Sport Type: Football.

Equipment Necessary: One football and a play area for every 10 players.

Objectives: To practice the skills of throwing, and kicking a football. To understand simple game strategy. To play with teammates.

Procedures: Two boundary lines are drawn on the playground 30 to 50 yards apart. The children are divided into teams of five. One team kicks off to the other from its own goal line. Members of the other team attempt to catch or touch the ball as near the opponents boundary line as possible. The ball is then kicked or passed alternately toward the opposing teams boundary line. Each team tries to touch the ball or catch it as soon as possible. Continue alternately throwing or kicking until one team is successful in throwing or kicking the ball over the opponents boundary line (in the air without being touched or caught). Basic rules are as follows:

1. A ball thrown over the end line without being touched or caught counts 2 points. A punt counts 1 point and a place kick 3 points.
2. If a ball is caught, in the air, 5 steps can be taken toward the other team's goal. Up to 15 steps can be saved and taken all at one time.
3. Players on each team are numbered 1 to 5. Players take turns kicking or throwing with 1 going first, 2 next, etc.
4. The ball is kicked or thrown from the place where it was touched or caught unless the ball was caught or touched behind the boundary line in which case the ball is brought up to the boundary line.
5. Several games can be conducted between the same boundaries.

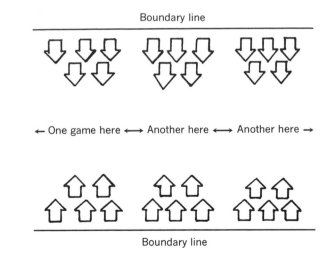

Boundary line

← One game here ⟷ Another here ⟷ Another here →

Boundary line

Basic Skill Prerequisites:
1. Throw or pass a football.
2. Punt a football.
3. Place kick a football.
4. Catch a football.
5. Hold ball for a place kick.

TIRE END BALL

Grade Level: 5 to 6.

Sport Type: Football.

Equipment Necessary: One football for each game, one properly marked play area for each game, one or two suspended rubber tires at each end of each play area.

Objectives: Participation in basic skills of football in a game situation. To learn basic position play and strategy of a sport type game. To learn defense techniques and strategy. To provide an opportunity for all children to be active.

Procedures: A large play area is marked so that the area is divided into five sections. Two end zones and three play areas. On each end of the field, one or two rubber tires are suspended as goals. (The tire may be supported on an archery target holder or hung below a basketball backboard.) The children are divided into teams of 8 to 12 players. One to 3 players are designated as ends. The ends play in there own end zone and attempt to defend the suspended tire. In the quarterback zone the players (2–4) play both offensively and defensively. In the halfback zone the players (5) are primarily offensive.

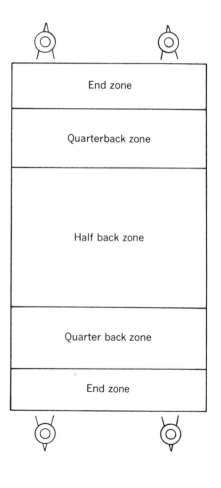

Play is started with a jump ball at mid-field between two half backs. The object of the game is to hit the tire with the football. Any ball hitting the tire scores a point. When thrown by a quarterback and two points when thrown by a halfback. A ball thrown through the hole in the tire counts 3 if thrown by the quarterback and 5 if thrown by a halfback. Ends may not score. The basic rules are as follows:

1. Players can run backwards or laterally but not forward.
2. A loose ball is in play as long as it is in bounds. If two players from opposite teams are both in possession of the ball, a jump is called.
3. Fouls for tackling, rough guarding, offsides are penalized with a free throw.
4. Balls thrown out of bounds are played in by the opposing team with a throw in.
5. Goals must be several feet beyond the end zone to keep the ends from standing directly in front of the tire.

Basic Skill Prerequisites:
1. Throw football.
2. Catch football.
3. Defensive Stance.
4. Defensive Guarding.
5. Throw while running.

FLAG FORWARD PASS

Grade Level: 5 to 6.

Sport Type: Football.

Equipment Necessary: One football and one play area for each 12 to 14 children.

Objectives: To play a simple football type game. To use simple game strategies. To practice catching, throwing, centering and lateraling a football. To practice dodging and running. To use defensive techniques including pulling flags.

Procedures: A 40 yard playing field is marked off into five sections 5, 5, 10, 10, and 20 yards in width. (See diagram.) The children are divided into two teams of 6 or 7 players. Players are designated as end(2), center(1), quarterback(1), halfback(2) and fullback(1). The game is played much like regular football except that running with the ball is illegal. A player may run with the ball after a completed pass. Every

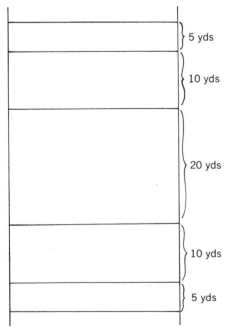

5 yds

10 yds

20 yds

10 yds

5 yds

player is eligible to receive a pass. Only ends and the center may rush the passer and these players must audibly count one thousand one, . . . , through one thousand five before they may rush. Basic rules are as follows:

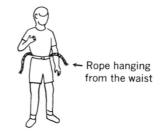

← Rope hanging from the waist

1. Each score counts 1 point with no extra point attempts.
2. Each player has a 12 inch length of rope inserted in his or her pants on each side (left and right). Eight inches of the rope must be exposed. A player is stopped when the rope (either one) has been pulled free.
3. Each time a team crosses a line on the playing field they are awarded a first down. Three downs may be attempted before turning the ball over on downs.
4. One game consists of 30 total plays by both teams.
5. Teams may not punt on third down or any down but may give up their third down and the ball and place the ball on the 15 yard line of the opposing team.

Basic Skill Prerequisites:
1. Pass a football.
2. Catch a football.
3. Center a football.
4. Flag pulling.
5. Defensive maneuvering.

ROTATION FORWARD PASS

This activity is the same as *Flag Forward Pass* with one major modification. The players on each team are numbered from one through 6 or 7 depending on the number on each team. On the first series of downs number 1 plays end, number 2 plays center, number 3 plays end, number 4 plays quarterback, number 5 plays halfback, number 6 plays halfback, and number 7 plays fullback. On the next series of downs the players move one position (end to center, center to end, end to quarterback, etc.) This is done both on offense and defense to give every child a chance to play every position.

CENTERING A BALL

Centering a football is performed in much the same manner as throwing a ball except that the performer throws the ball between his legs from an all fours position.

1. The throwing hand (dominant hand) should be placed near the middle of the ball toward the top end. The other hand is mainly used to guide the direction of the ball and is placed below the middle of the ball.

2. Some weight is placed over the ball (see illustration) but not as much as is on the feet.
3. The ball must stay in contact with the ground until it is centered.
4. The knees should be bent and the head up.
5. To center the ball thrust both arms back—use the top hand as if throwing the ball. Slightly straighten the legs as the ball is centered.

FOOTBALL POSITION PLAY (OFFENSE)

Ends—lineman, blocker, pass receiver
Center—centers the ball, blocker
Quarterback—receives ball from center, handles ball, runs ball, passer
Halfbacks—runs ball, pass receiver, blocker
Fullback—runs ball, blocker

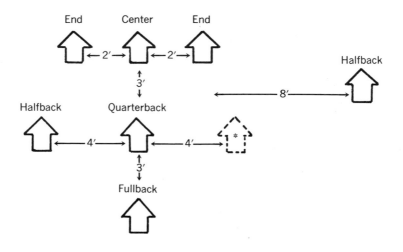

* This halfback may play either position.

FOOTBALL POSITION PLAY (DEFENSE)

Ends—rusher
Center—rusher
Linebacker—rusher, pass defender
Halfback—pass defender

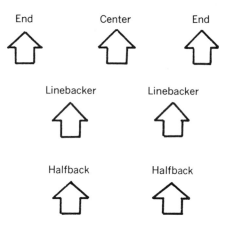

ZONE SOCCER √

Grade Level: 4 to 6

Sport Type: Soccer

Equipment Necessary: Properly marked play area and one ball for every four players.

Objectives: To dribble with the feet, kick a ball, and trap a ball. To overload for leg strength and endurance. To practice defensive position and stance. To play positions in a soccer type game. To use strategy of a soccer type game in a game situation.

Procedures: A 40-yard square playing area is marked off with 8 five yard (width) zones (see diagram). The children are divided into two teams. One half of each team become kickers and the other half goal keepers. The goal keepers for each team line up along the end line of one of the zones marked on the field. Each zone will then have a goal keeper at each end. The kickers line up so that one kicker from each team lines up in a zone. A ball is started in play by the instructor or referee who throws the ball into the middle of the play area. The kickers attempt to kick the ball over the opponents boundary line past their goalie. Kickers may kick the ball only when it is in their zone. Goalies may catch the ball and throw it to a member of their own team but may not throw the ball over the opponents end line. If the ball goes over either of the two side lines, it is thrown in by the players of the end zone. A point is scored if the team kicks the ball over their opponents end or boundary line.

A penalty kick is taken from mid field if a player touches the ball with his hands (except goalies) or if any other penalty is called.

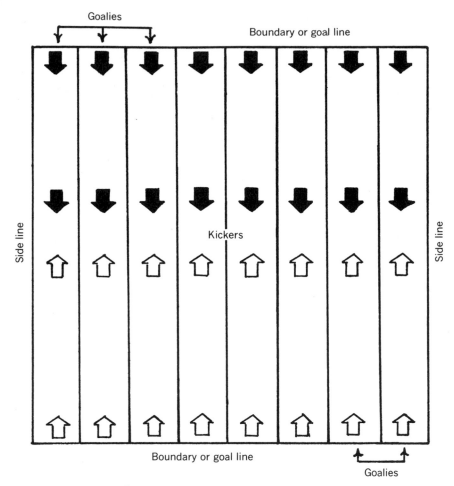

Teaching suggestions:

1. Add one or more balls when the children become more proficient.

Basic Skill Prerequisites:

1. Soccer Dribble
2. Soccer Kick
3. Soccer defensive tackle
4. Goalie play

CRAB SOCCER √

Grade Level: 4 to 6

Sport Type: Soccer

Equipment Necessary: Properly marked play area and a ball.

Objectives: To overload for arm and leg strength. To practice agility and total body coordination. To practice in kicking a ball.

Procedures: A crab soccer field 40 to 50 feet long is marked off either indoors or outdoors. The entire end line or boundary line on either end of the area represents the goal. Players are divided into two teams. Each team lines up at their own goal line in the crab position. A ball is placed in the middle of the playing area. On the whistle, players crab walk (see diagram) toward the ball and attempt to kick the ball over the opponents goal line. A point is scored if the ball is kicked over the opponents goal line. When a goal is scored the children *crab walk back* to their boundary and the procedure is repeated.

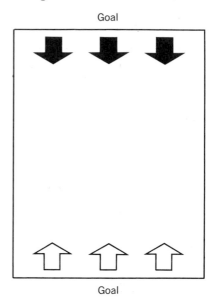

Goal

Goal

Teaching Suggestions:
1. Award a free kick for a hand ball or unnecessary roughness.
2. If the same players continually linger near the goal line so they will not have far to crab walk, number the players so that low numbers are kickers and high numbers defenders one time and positions change later in the game.
3. Make sure children have soft soled shoes.
4. Penalize dangerously high kicks.

Prerequisite Skills:
1. Crab walk
2. Kicking

Crab walk

SOCCER THROW IN

The legal throw in is performed as follows:

1. Both feet *must* be in contact with the ground when the ball is thrown. In teaching beginners, the feet should be spaced at about shoulder width.
2. The ball must be thrown with *both* hands from *behind* the head.
3. The upper body and arms should be snapped forward prior to releasing the ball to get maximal distance.

LINE SOCCER

Grade Level: 4 to 6

Sport Type: Soccer

Equipment Necessary: Properly marked play area and soccer balls.

Objectives: To practice dribbling, passing, kicking, and trapping a soccer ball. To practice defensive goalie play. To practice throwing a soccer ball in play legally. To work together with a team mate offensively. To use strategy of a soccer type game.

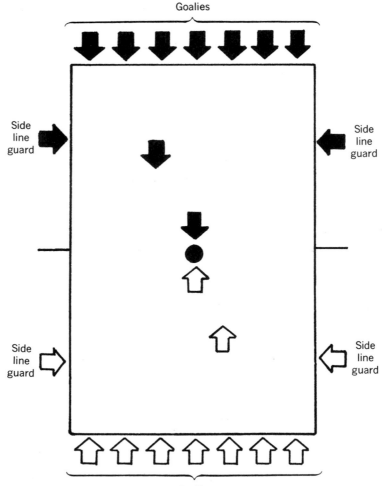

Procedures: A 40 x 60 foot field is marked off as illustrated in the diagram. The children are divided into two teams. Each team lines up across its own end boundary or goal line so that there is an equal distance between all players. Four players from each team do not line up on the end line but line up at different locations on the field. Two of these players are side line goalies. They guard the two side lines nearest their own goal line. The other two players are kickers and may run anywhere inside the play area.

The object of the game is to have one of the kickers kick the ball over the goal line between any of the players defending that line. One point is scored each time the ball crosses the line below shoulder level. The side line guards attempt to keep the ball in play. If the ball goes out of bounds in their half of the field (see diagram), these players may either throw or kick the ball into play. The remainder of the players are lined up across their own goal line and are assigned the task of defending this line. They may use their hands or their feet to keep the ball from crossing their own goal line. The ball is started in play when the referee drops the ball between two kickers at mid-field. Other rules and procedures follow:

1. Every 2 minutes the players on each team rotate so that different players are playing side guards, kickers and goalies. Thus every one gets a chance to play every position.
2. A penalty kick from mid-field is awarded for the following offenses: hand ball, unnecessary roughness and a ball kicked over the end line above the goalies' head.

Basic Skill Prerequisites:
1. dribbling
2. kicking
3. trapping
4. goalie play
5. legal throw in
6. kick from drop ball by referee

SOCCER KICK BALL

Grade Level: 4 to 6

Sport Type: Soccer

Equipment Necessary: One soccer goal or simulated goal and a ball. A properly marked play area and a set of bases.

Objectives: To practice the skills of heading, trapping, kicking, and passing a soccer ball. To learn the value of the short accurate soccer pass. To play as a team defensively.

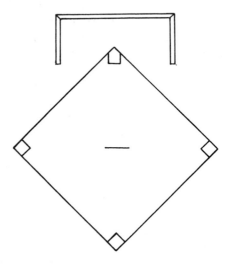

Procedures: A play area is marked as shown in the diagram. A soccer goal is located behind home plate. The children are divided into two teams. One team starts as fielders and the other team as kickers. The fielders distribute themselves much as they would in a game of softball. The batters stand behind home base. One member of the fielding team, the pitcher, rolls the ball toward the first kicker in line. The kicker kicks the ball onto the play area. He then runs around the bases. If he rounds the bases without being put out, he scores one point. Fielders attempt to keep the kicker from scoring a point by making him out. A kicker is out when:

1. Any fielding player heads (hits the ball with his head) a fly ball.
2. The ball is played by the fielders through the goal behind home base before the runner reaches home base.

Each team is allowed three outs per inning. Five innings constitutes a game. If a fielder touches the ball with his hand, it is an automatic point.

Teaching Suggestions:
1. Number the kickers so they are sure of their turn at bat.
2. Encourage children to play different fielding positions each inning.

Basic Skill Prerequisites:
1. Heading the ball
2. Passing the ball
3. Kicking
4. Dribbling

FOUR SQUARES

Grade Level: 4 to 6

Sport Type: Volleyball

Equipment Necessary: Properly marked play area and a rubber ball.

Objectives: To practice the skills of underhand volleying, underhand serving and the skills of defensive volleying. To practice strategy of a volleyball type game. To use proper position play. To play a game which can be used during free play time. To arbitrate rules in a group situation.

Procedures: A square of 15 feet is drawn on the play area. The square is divided into four equal sections and the sections are numbered from 1 to 4 (see diagram). One player stands in each of the four squares with the remainder of the players waiting in line behind square number 4. The player in square number 1 is the King and is the only person who can score points. The King begins play by dropping the ball to the ground and volleying it on the first bounce to any of the other three squares. Each player plays the ball when it lands in his square by volleying the ball to any of the other squares. The volley continues until one player misses the ball in his square, hits the ball out of bounds, or hits a line with a volleyed ball. That player leaves his square and goes to the end of the line outside square 4. If the King is eliminated, the person in square 2 becomes King, the person in square 3 moves to square 2,

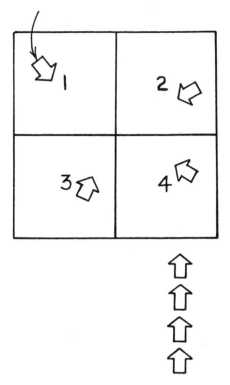

the person in square 4 moves to square 3, and the first person outside square 4 moves in to square 4. If the person in square 2, 3, or 4 misses a similar procedure for "moving up" is followed. If any player other than the King is eliminated, the King scores 1 point, even if the King did not cause that person to be eliminated. Thus the purpose of the game is to be King and score points while the other players attempt to advance toward the King spot. The following rules should be enforced:

1. The ball must be volleyed underhanded.
2. The ball must follow an upward arch before it falls in the square of an opponent.
3. Line balls are *not* good.
4. A player may stand outside his square if he desires.
5. The ball must bounce before it is played.

Teaching Suggestions:
1. Once instruction has been given allow the children to start several games so that more children are active.

2. Enforce the rules. If they are not enforced early, the game can deteriorate.
3. Alter the size of the ball and the size of the square in accordance with the abilities of the children.

Basic Skill Prerequisites:
1. The underhand volley
2. The underhand bounce and serve
3. Practice in moving to play the ball before the ball hits the ground

⭐TETHER BALL √

Grade Level: 4 to 6

Sport Type: Volleyball

Equipment Necessary: One tether ball pole and ball for each 5 children.

Objectives: To practice the basic skills of volleying and serving a ball. To use positioning in a volleyball type game. To use strategy in a one on one game situation. To play a vigorous jumping activity. To play a game which can be used during free play time.

Procedures: A large circle is drawn on the play area around the tether ball pole. This circle is divided in half by a line drawn through the center of the circle (see diagram). Each of the two players must stand in his own half of the play area. Other players stand outside the circle waiting to play the next game. A coin is tossed to determine who serves the first game. The winner of the coin toss serves by holding the ball in one hand and striking it so that the ball and rope begin to wrap around the pole. The server attempts to wrap the ball and rope completely around the pole in the direction of the serve. His opponent attempts to wrap the ball and rope around the pole in the opposite direction. The first of the two players to wrap up the rope completely is the winner. The players may strike the ball once on their side of the pole in attempt to wind the rope. Either a fist or an open hand may be used as long as the ball is not carried or thrown. The following rules must be followed:

1. Each player must stay in his half of the circle. Violation results in a free serve by the opponent.
2. Players may not strike the rope. Violation results is a free serve by the opponent.
3. An intentional striking of the rope results in loss of the game.
4. The ball may be struck with two hands.
5. The loser of a game goes to the end of the line. The next person in line, the "challenger" takes on the champ. The challenger gets the serve and choice of side. Each time the champ wins a game he gets one point.
6. Carrying or throwing the ball results in a free serve by the opponent. Two violations in the same game results in loss of game.

Teaching Suggestions:
1. Divide children into homogeneous groups so that the children at each pole are of about the same ability.
2. Have as many poles as possible to get more children active.
3. Label the poles AAAA, AAA, AA, A, etc. When a child wins 20 games on one pole in the same period, he may advance to the next pole. A child may move to a lower level pole at any time.

Basic Skill Prerequisites:
1. One and two hand volleying skills
2. Serving and striking skill
3. Blocking skills

BALLOON VOLLEYBALL✓✓

Grade Level: 4 to 6

Sport Type: Volleyball

Equipment Necessary: Several large thick rubber balloons and nets.

Objectives: To practice the basic skills of volleying, setting, digging, spiking, and serving a volleyball type object. To play a lead up to regular volleyball type skills. To use a system of volleyball position rotation. To use volleyball position play. To work with other players.

Procedures: Children are divided into several teams of 4 players each. The game is played on a 10 by 20 foot rectangle with a net or rope suspended over the middle of the play area (see diagram). One team stands on either side of the net. The game is played in the same way as volleyball except a large balloon is used instead of a ball. The ball is served from behind the rear boundary of one team. The serve may be played again by the members of the server's team. The balloon must cross the net in five hits. If the balloon touches the floor, is hit out of bounds, or is struck more than five times, the other team gets the serve. If the ball hits the floor, is hit out of bounds, or is struck more than five times by the nonserving team, the serving team scores a point. A game consists of 10 points scored by the same team.

Players rotate or change position each time they regain the serve from the other team. The rotation sequence is illustrated to the right.

Teaching Suggestions:
1. Add a penny or some other nonsharp object inside the balloon as the children gain proficiency at the game.

Basic Skill Prerequisites:
1. Volleying an object
2. Striking an object
3. Serving an object

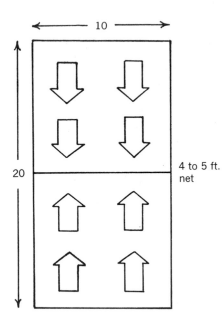

4 to 5 ft. net

Rotation

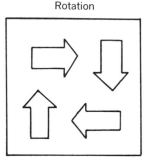

NEWCOMB √

Grade Level: 4 to 6

Sport Type: Volleyball

Equipment Necessary: Volleyball courts, volleyballs and nets.

Objectives: To practice the skills of throwing a ball accurately, catching a ball and serving a ball. To play modified volleyball. To learn to pass the ball to team mates in a more advantageous position for scoring. To practice rotation of volleyball positions. To use volleyball position play.

Procedures: Children are divided into teams of six players each (if too few courts are available up to 9 may be placed on a team). A standard volleyball court or a smaller court may be used. A net or rope should be suspended across the play area at a height of 5 to 7 feet depending on the ability of the players. One team of 6 players stands on either side of the net. The play proceeds as in volleyball with one team serving (or throwing) the ball over the net. Players may catch the ball and throw it over the net or to a player on their own team. A player *may not hold the ball for more than 3 seconds.* The ball may be handled four times on each side of the net. Only the serving team may score. If the ball touches the ground, hits out of bounds or is caught more than four times, the opposing team gains the serve. If the opposing (nonserving) team allows the ball to hit the ground, hits it out of bounds or catches the ball more than four times in a row, the serving team scores a point. Continue until one team scores 15 points. Each time a team regains the serve they rotate or change positions according to the diagram at the right.

The ball may not touch the net when thrown.

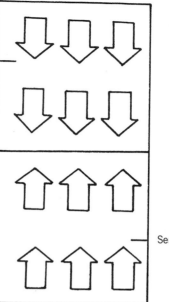

Serve line

Basic Skill Prerequisites:
1. Ball throw for accuracy
2. Catch a ball
3. Serve a ball
4. Rotating positions

Rotation

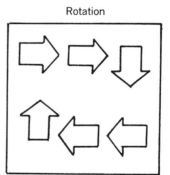

MEDICINE BALL VOLLEY

This activity is very similar to Newcomb except that a medicine ball is used. The ball is started in play by throwing the ball. Players on the serving team may touch the initial throw. A lower net may be used.

IN THE AIR FOUR SQUARE

Grade Level: 5 to 6

Sport Type: Volleyball

Equipment Necessary: Volleyball court and two nets or ropes.

Objectives: To practice the skills of underhand volleying, and underhand serving. To use strategy of a volleyball type game. To use position play.

Procedures: The volleyball court is divided with a net placed at 4 to 5 feet. Another net is draped over the first net so that the volleyball court is divided into four sections (see diagram). The second net may be cut in the middle (up to the top rope) so that it may be draped over the first net (see diagram). Three players stand in each of the four sections of the court. The four sections are numbered from one to four. Play is started when one member of the team in square one bounces the ball and volleys it underhanded over the net into any of the other three squares. Players in each square keep the ball in play by volleying the ball underhanded to any of the other three squares. The ball may strike the floor before it is volleyed but it may also be volleyed in the air. The ball may be played twice in each square and may touch the ground between each touch by a player. Any ball which hits the net, hits a line, goes out of bounds or hits the floor two times in succession in the same square results in a point gained for the serving team. If the serving team causes the infraction, they lose the serve and team two serves. Only the serving team may score. Any of the nonserving teams may cause the error or loss of point but the serving team still receives the point. The serve goes from team 1 to 2 to 3 to 4 to 1 etc.

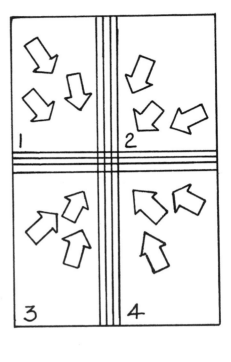

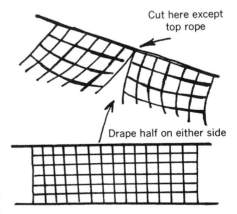

Cut here except top rope

Drape half on either side

The first team to 15 points is the winner.

Basic Skill Prerequisites:
1. Underhand volley
2. Underhand volley serve

AROUND THE BASES VOLLEYBALL

Grade Level: 5 to 6

Sport Type: Volleyball

Equipment Necessary: One volleyball and a properly marked play area.

Objectives: To practice serving a volleyball. To practice catching and throwing. To perceive distances of a ball's flight. To place a struck ball to best advantage.

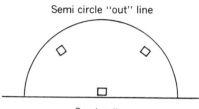

Semi circle "out" line

Serving line

Procedures: The children are divided into two teams. The play area is marked with a large half circle and three bases (see diagram). One team begins in the field as in baseball. The other team is the serving team. The fielders distribute themselves behind the semicircle marked on the play area. The first server serves the ball as he would in a game of volleyball. The ball must travel in the air beyond the semicircle. If it does not, the server is out. If the ball travels beyond the semicircle, the fielders must play the ball as if they were playing a volleyball game. The first player to the ball volleys it to another player on his team but does not catch it. If two players (defensive) volley the ball in succession without catching it or without allowing the ball to drop to the ground, the server is out. If the ball hits the ground before two players have volleyed it, the server may be made out by throwing the ball around all three bases before the server can run around them. Each time a server circles the bases without being put out he scores a point for his team. An inning includes one serve for each player. The team with the most runs or points is the winner.

Teaching Suggestions:
1. Encourage the servers to serve the ball where the fielders are not located.
2. Make the bases located so that it is difficult to get a server out if two volleys are not made.

Basic Skill Prerequisites:
1. Serve a volleyball
2. Volley a volleyball
3. Catch a volleyball
4. Throw a volleyball

BIG MAN VOLLEYBALL

Grade Level: 4 to 6

Sport Type: Volleyball

Equipment Necessary: Volleyball Court, net and ball

Objectives: To provide practice in the skills of catching a ball, throwing a ball, and serving a ball. To vary the way in which you attack the opponent offensively. (Throw the ball to different places each time.) To work together as a team.

Procedures: The game is played in the same manner as Newcomb with a different scoring system. Before the start of the game each of the two teams gets together and gives a special name to several of their players. One player is the Big Man, one is the Small Man, and One is the Little Dog. The teams spread out one on either side of the net as in Newcomb and begin to throw the ball back and forth across the net. No points are lost if the ball touches the ground, but an attempt is made to keep the ball in play. Each time one of the three specially named players catches the ball the team scores points. The Big Man scores 15 per catch, the Small Man 10 per catch and the Little Dog 5 per catch. If any other member of the team catches the ball, *no* points are scored. A special scorer counts the points for each side. When a team accumulates 100 points, they are declared the winner. Opposing teams *do not* know which of the opposing players are the scorers.

Teaching Suggestions:
1. Keep the net low so throws across the net are easy.
2. Balls thrown over out of bounds should be rethrown by the same team to give a point scorer a chance to catch the ball.
3. Encourage the teams to throw the ball to many different places on the other side of the net so that points do not mount up rapidly by repeated throwing to a scorer.

Basic Skill Prerequisites:
1. Serve a ball
2. Catch a ball
3. Throw a ball

PIN BOMBARDMENT ✓

Grade Level: 4 to 6

Sports Type: Basketball

Equipment Necessary: 5 to 15 balls and 10 to 20 bowling pins.

Objectives: To practice throws for accuracy, and ball catching. To practice defensive stance and technique. To use game strategy. To cooperate with team members by passing to them.

Procedures: The game may be played inside or outside. A large play area is divided in half. At one end of the play area 5 to 10 bowling pins are lined up on the boundary line. The same number of pins are lined up at the other end of the play area. The children are divided into two teams. The teams line up in front of their own bowling pins in their own half of the play area. The balls are placed on the middle line. On the whistle players may run forward and pick up the balls. Players throw the balls attempting to knock down the bowling pins of the opposing teams. Any pin that is knocked down scores one point. The following are the basic rules of the game:

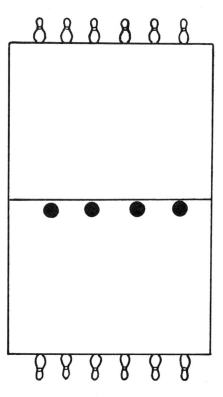

1. Players may not cross the center line.
2. If a player knocks down his own pin, it still scores one point for the opponent.
3. A team may not score when one of their own pins is on the floor. (Pins must be re-set immediately so that the team may score.)
4. A 5-yard restraining line should be marked in front of the pins on each end. A defender may not touch a thrown ball behind this line.

Basic Skill Prerequisites:
1. Throw for accuracy
2. Defending
3. Catching

BOMBARDMENT √√

    Grade Level: 4 to 6

    Sports Type: Basketball

    Equipment Necessary: Five to 15 rubber balls.

Objectives: To practice the skills of throwing, dodging, catching and leaping. To throw the ball most effectively in a specific game situation. To develop agility and general body coordination.

Procedures: The play area is divided into two halves. The children are divided into two teams with each team lining up in their own half of the play area. Five to 15 balls are placed on the middle line of the play area. On the whistle players from either team may advance to the middle line to retrieve a ball. Members of each team throw the balls at members of the other team, attempting to hit them with the thrown ball. If a player is hit with a thrown ball, he is eliminated from the game and must sit down on the side line. The ball must hit the player in the air (it may not bounce first) and must hit him below the shoulders. If a player catches a thrown ball in the air before it hits the floor, the thrower is eliminated. Play continues until all players on one team have been eliminated. The team with players remaining is the winner.

Teaching Suggestions: The teacher may wish to award points to teams hitting other players with the ball rather than having these players eliminated. Points would also be awarded for catching a thrown ball in the air.

Basic Skill Prerequisites:
1. Catch
2. Throw
3. Dodge

HULA HOOP BALL

Grade Level: 5 to 6

Sports Type: Basketball

Equipment Necessary: Four hula hoops and a rubber ball.

Objectives: To practice the skills of throwing at a target, dribbling a ball with the hands, catching a ball, and defending against a thrown ball. To experience playing a basketball type game. To pass the ball to team mates who are in a more advantageous position. To use strategy of a basketball type game.

Procedures: The playing area is divided into four zones. Two guard zones and two forward zones (see diagram). Goal lines are the end lines of the play area. The children are divided into two teams. Each team consists of 5 guards, 5 forwards and 2 hoopers. Guards stand in the guard zones and are defensive players. Guards may not score. Forwards stand in the forward zones and are offensive players. Forwards are the only players who may score points.

The hoopers stand beyond the end lines of the play area holding hula hoops. Players may not run with the ball in their possession. They may take three dribbles. Play begins with a jump ball between two forwards at mid-court. Forwards attempt to throw the ball toward a hooper in attempt to have the ball pass through a hoop. Hoopers may stand anywhere behind the end line and may move the hoop as they desire in attempt to have the ball pass through the hoop. A ball which passes through the hoop scores a point. Guards attempt to deflect the ball so that forwards will not score. If they intercept the ball, they try to pass it to their own forwards. Passes may not be thrown above the level of the head. After a score the ball is given to the guard of the team which did not score.

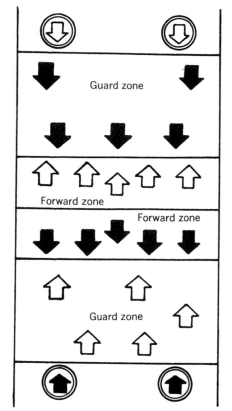

Prerequisite Basic Skills:
1. Dribble
2. Throw
3. Catch
4. Defend
5. Jump at center court

DRIBBLE TAG

Grade Level: 4 to 6

Sports Type: Basketball

Equipment Necessary: At least 2 balls for every 3 children.

Objectives: To practice the skill of dribbling a ball with the hands. To react to a change in direction while dribbling. To develop agility and hand eye coordination.

Procedures: Children are divided into three groups. One group of children become standers. The standers stand in different spots around the play area. The second group are the dribblers. The players dribble basketballs or rubber balls around the play area between standers. The third group (2 or 3 children) are IT. IT players dribble a basketball around the play area attempting to touch a dribbler with their free hand. If they are successful in touching a dribbler, the dribbler becomes IT. A dribbler may become a stander by handing the ball to a stander. A stander becomes a dribbler when the ball is handed to him. When a stander becomes a dribbler, he must dribble the ball at least three times before he can hand off to another stander. Beginners may use two hands to dribble the ball.

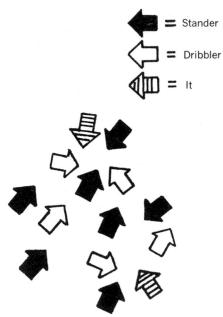

= Stander

= Dribbler

= It

Basic Prerequisite Skills:
1. Dribble with the hands

4 FLY AWAY BALL

Grade Level: 4 to 6

Sports Type: Basketball

Equipment Necessary: One ball for 12 children.

Objectives: To pass a ball with deception. To play a basketball type defense. To work with team mates toward a common goal.

Procedures: The play area is marked with a 25-foot circle. The children are divided into three teams of 4 players each. Two teams join together to make a circle around the line drawn on the play area. The other team stands inside the circle. Circle players pass the ball around to other circle players attempting to keep the 4 players in the center of the circle from intercepting the ball. If the circle players pass the ball successfully for 8 consecutive times without having the ball intercepted, both circle teams score 1 point. If the

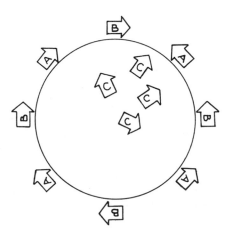

players in the center of the circle intercept the ball 5 times, they change places with one of the circle teams and the game continues. When all teams have been in the center once, the teams count their points. The team with the most points is the winner. The following basic rules apply:

1. The ball may not be thrown to the circle player standing immediately on either side.
2. The ball may not be passed above shoulder level by circle players.
3. If the ball is dropped by a circle player, it is dead and cannot be intercepted by a center player until it is thrown again.

Basic Prerequisite Skills:
1. Pass a basketball
2. Defensive stance
3. Defensive shuffle
4. Catch

HIT THE POLE

Grade Level: 4 to 6

Sports Type: Basketball

Equipment Necessary: A tether ball or volleyball pole with two concentric circles drawn around it, and one ball.

Objectives: To practice the skills of accurate throwing, faking and defending. To pass the ball to team mates with a better chance to score than yourself. To practice many different types of passes. To use team strategy in a basketball type game.

Procedures: Two concentric circles are drawn on the play area around a pole (see diagram). The circles are divided in half with a line. The children are divided into two teams of 5 players each. There are 3 forwards and 2 guards on each team. The guards stand in the guard zones (see diagram) and defend against a score. Guards may not score points. Forwards stand in the forward zones and attempt to score by hitting the center pole. Guards try to block shots by the forwards. If a guard intercepts the ball, he attempts to throw it to one of the forwards on his own

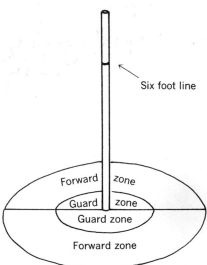

Six foot line

Forward zone

Guard zone

Guard zone

Forward zone

team. A ball must hit the pole below a line drawn on the pole at 6 feet.

The ball is started in play with a jump ball between 2 guards. If the ball goes out of bounds, it is played in from the guard zone by a guard of the opposite team. After a score the opposite team plays the ball in just as if the ball had gone out of bounds.

Since only 10 players can play in one game, several games must be started.

Basic Skill Prerequisites:
1. Jump at center
2. Throw
3. Pass chest and bounce
4. Catch
5. Defensive stance and footwork

STEAL THE BACON BASKETBALL

Grade Level: 4 to 6

Sports Type: Basketball

Equipment Necessary: Two basketballs and two 7 foot baskets.

Objectives: To practice the skills of dribbling, shooting at a basket, and passing a ball. To develop reaction time to a specific stimulus.

Procedures: A regular basketball area can be used. The baskets should be lowered to 7 feet. The children are divided into two teams. The members of each team are numbered from one through the number necessary to assign one number to each player. The teams line up on opposite sides of the basketball court. The teacher calls two or three numbers. Those three players step one step forward. The player with the lowest number runs forward and picks up the ball placed in the middle of the court. He dribbles the ball to his team's basket and shoots at the basket. He shoots until he puts the ball through the hoop. He then dribbles back to the middle of the court, puts it down and goes back to

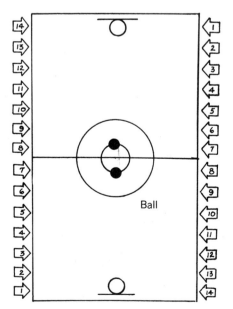
Ball

his place in line. The next lowest number which was called does the same task. Continue until all numbers called have completed the dribble and shot. The first team to have all players back in line is awarded one point. The same procedure is repeated until one team scores 15 points. Different combinations of numbers are called each time.

Basic Skill Prerequisites:
1. Dribble a basketball
2. Shoot a basketball at a basket (lay up)
3. Stop during a dribble.

WHIFFLE END BALL

Grade Level: 4 to 6

Sport Type: Basketball

Equipment Necessary: One plastic half gallon bottle without a bottom (see diagram) for each child. One 3-inch whiffle ball.

Objectives: To practice the skills of throwing a whiffleball with an implement (bottle without a bottom), to catching a ball with the implement, and defending against the thrown ball. To use the strategy of a basketball type game. To play in an activity which allows participation by all children. To work with other members of the same team.

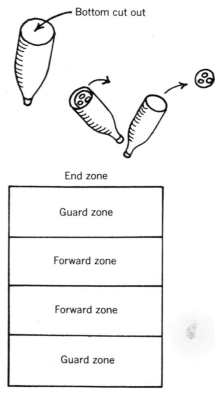

Bottom cut out

End zone

Guard zone
Forward zone
Forward zone
Guard zone

End zone

Procedures: The play area is marked off into four zones. Two forward zones and two guard zones. The area beyond each end line is the end zone. The children are divided into two teams. Each member of each team has a bottle (see diagram). Three players are assigned to each of the four zones on the floor. Two players from each team play in the end zone or beyond their own end line. Thus each team has 14 players. Play begins when the referee throws the whiffle ball high into the air between the two forward zones. Players attempt to catch the ball in the scoop made with an empty bottle. The object of the game is to throw the ball to the players in your own end zone. A ball caught in the bottle scoop by an end-zone player counts as one point for the team catching the ball. A player may throw the ball toward his end zone from anywhere on the floor but he may not leave his own zone, touch the ball with his hand or run with the ball in his possession. If a ball is dropped to the floor, it is a free ball and may be scooped up by any player. A ball that goes out of bounds is played in as in basketball, but the player must use the bottle scoop to throw the ball in. Players should alternate positions periodically.

Prerequisite Basic Skills:
1. Throw with a bottle scoop
2. Catch with a bottle scoop

THREE MAN BASKETBALL

Grade Level: 5 to 6

Sport Type: Basketball

Equipment Necessary: One 7-foot basket for every 6 children and 1 basketball for every 6 children.

Objectives: To practice the skills of dribbling, shooting, passing and catching a basketball. To experience a basketball type game. To develop agility, hand eye coordination and movement time. To work together in small teams. To use strategy and position play of a basketball type game.

Procedures: The game is played on one half of a basketball court. The basket should be 7 feet high. The rules are the same as regular basketball with the following exceptions:

1. Each player is limited to 5 dribbles in a row. (A player may be allowed to double dribble or to use two hands to dribble depending on skill level.)
2. The ball must be taken back behind the free circle when the ball changes hands from one team to the other.
3. Players must play a zone defense. Two players defend under the basket, one on each side and the other player covers the area in front of the basket.
4. At least two players must touch the ball before a shot can be taken. This makes sure the players pass the ball at least once after bringing the ball in or after a rebound.
5. Fouls count one point automatically for the team being fouled.

Basic Skill Prerequisites:
1. Dribble a basketball
2. Pass a basketball

3. Shoot a basketball
4. Rebound a basketball
5. Defensive shuffle
6. Defensive footwork and stance

BOUNCE AND BAT ✓

Grade Level: 4 to 6

Sport Type: Softball or baseball

Equipment Necessary: One tennis ball and 4 cardboard boxes of equal size.

Objectives: To practice the skills of hitting a moving ball, catching, throwing accurately, running the bases, and pitching a ball. To use basic strategy of a softball type sport. To work with members of the team to put opposing players out. To use the rules and position play of a softball type game.

Procedures: The children are divided up into two teams. One team is the batting team and the other is the fielding team. The rules of softball are followed with some basic differences. The following are the basic rule differences:

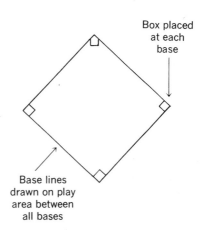

Box placed at each base

Base lines drawn on play area between all bases

1. The batter uses his hand and not a bat.
2. A tennis ball is used instead of a softball.
3. The pitcher must pitch the ball to the batter on one bounce.
4. The batter must hit the ball so that it bounces inside the baselines or he is out. (Baselines must be clearly marked—see diagram.)
5. Each batter gets only one strike.
6. Two foul balls is an out.
7. A batter may stay on any base as in softball but he is forced when the tennis ball is placed in the box in front of him in a force out situation. The ball may be thrown into the box directly or caught and dropped in the box.
8. Each player bats every inning. Outs score zero points. Men left on base score 1 point. Players making it to home base score two points.

Basic Skill Prerequisites:
1. Position skill and understanding
2. Defensive and fielding skill

3. Batting skill
4. Catching skill
5. Running skill (bases)

KICKBALL ✓

Grade Level: 4 to 6

Sport Type: Softball or baseball

Equipment Necessary: An area marked off for softball and a rubber ball.

Objectives: To practice the skills of kicking, catching, throwing and running. To use the position and strategy play in a softball type game. To use defensive team play. To play *only* your own position. To work with *all* children on your team.

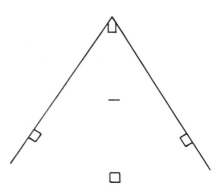

Procedures: The game is played in much the same way as softball. The basic rules are the same except a rubber ball is kicked rather than batting a softball. Also a runner may be made out by hitting him with the ball between bases. The pitcher must roll the ball to the batter so that it may be kicked. If two "balls" or bad pitches are made by the pitcher, the batter gets a free kick with the ball stationary on home plate.

Teaching Suggestions:
1. Number the players on each team and have them bat by numbers to make sure each player gets his turn to bat in the proper order.
2. Players may play a defensive position by number and alternate positions each inning.
3. If batters are too successful, lengthen the bases, if they are unsuccessful, shorten the bases.

Basic Skill Prerequisites:
1. Kicking a rolling ball
2. Catch a ball
3. Running the bases
4. Throw a ball
5. Defensive stance and fielding skills ·

ALL THE WAY KICKBALL ✔

Grade Level: 4 to 6

Sport Type: Softball and baseball

Equipment Necessary: Same as kickball

Objectives: Same as kickball.

Procedures: The rules are the same as kickball except that only one base is marked on the play area (foul lines are drawn). The kicker must make it all the way home on each turn at bat. He may be put out by having the ball reach home before he does. If he makes it all the way home, he scores a run. He may not stop on the base.

Basic Skill Prerequisites: Same as kickball

HIT PIN KICKBALL

Grade Level: 5 to 6

Sport Type: Softball and baseball

Equipment Necessary: One rubber ball and 4 bowling pins.

Objectives: To practice the skills of kicking, catching, throwing, running, and rolling a ball. To experience a game which can be played during free time. To use the position play of a softball type game. To work with other children toward a common objective.

Procedures: The game is played in much the same way as kickball. The basic difference is that one bowling pin is placed at each point where a base would normally be located. The kicker must run around the pins and back to the spot (home) where the ball was kicked. The fielders attempt to knock down a bowling pin at a base before the runner gets to that base. The fielders must throw the ball to a baseman at each base before they may knock down the pin at the next base. The kicker must make it all the way home on his turn and may not stop on the bases. The kicker may be made out by hitting him with the ball. Example: If the runner has safely made first base, the fielders must touch first base with the ball before they can knock the pin down at second base. Before they may hit the runner with the ball, they must touch each base that the runner has already touched.

Basic Skill Prerequisites: Same as kickball.

SPRINTING ✓

Grade Level: 1 to 6

Sports Type: Track and Field

Equipment: None

Objectives: To practice the skills of moving a distance in the shortest possible time. To practice the skills of starting, running, and finishing. To react quickly.

Procedures:
1. Divide children into groups of similar ability.
2. On commands "take your mark", "get set", and "go", the children go through proper starting procedure.
3. After start children run 25 yards (may extend to 50 yards) and stop. Continue until all groups have run.
4. Repeat in the opposite direction.

Teaching Suggestions:
1. Do not run competitively until the skills of starting are learned (see below).
2. Emphasize the need to run past the finish line.
3. Review proper running technique before sprinting.

Basic Skill Prerequisites:
1. Starting (standing and sprint)
2. Finishing skill
3. Running

Standing Start
1. The feet should be pointed in the direction of the run.
2. The feet should be spread from 18 to 24 inches apart, one foot ahead of the other.
3. The body should lean forward.
4. On "go", the body should fall forward and the legs should drive forward.
5. The arms should begin to swing soon after the start to stabilize the body.

Sprint Start
1. Both hands are placed even with the starting line.
2. The foot farthest forward is placed a comfortable distance (less than a foot) behind the starting line.
3. The knee of the second leg is placed beside the front foot.
   STEPS 1-3 are done on "take your mark".
   STEPS 4-6 are done on "get set".
4. The back knee lifts off the ground high enough to make the leg level with the ground (the hips may be higher than the shoulders).
5. The head should be down with the eyes looking at the ground a few inches from the start.
6. Distribute weight on hands and feet.

7. On "go" dive with legs and feet.
8. Step forward with the back leg after front leg straightens.
9. Straighten body posture slowly.

HURDLING

Grade Level: 4 to 6

Sports Type: Track and Field

Equipment: Three to 6- 18-inch hurdles or suspended bamboo poles on standards.

Objectives: To practice the skills of starting, running, hurdling, and finishing. To run an obstacle type race in the shortest possible time. To perform a combined speed-agility activity.

Procedures: This activity is done in the same way as sprinting (see above) except that the runners must clear 3 to 6 hurdles during the activity. The hurdles should be 5 to 15 yards apart depending on the capabilities of the children.

Teaching Suggestions: The children may be allowed to learn to jump the hurdles before they actually learn to hurdle (see below for hurdling technique).

Basic Skill Prerequisites:
1. Starting
2. Running
3. Hurdling

Technique of Hurdling: The children should be instructed in the following techniques:
1. Take steps of even length between hurdles.
2. Do not JUMP over hurdles but stride (modified step) over them.
3. The front leg is kicked up and stepped over the hurdle. Continue the forward movement, lifting the front leg only as high as necessary to clear the obstacle.
4. Drive forward with the back foot as the front foot reaches over the hurdle. Lift the back foot up with the knee and leg to the side of the body and parallel to the ground.
5. Regain contact with the ground as soon as possible to continue forward drive.
6. The right arm should be forward as the left foot steps over the hurdle and visa versa.

SHUTTLE RELAY

Grade Level: 3 to 6

Sports Type: Track and Field

Equipment: Batons or 8-inch pieces of broom stick

Objectives: To practice starting, running and baton passing. To handle an object while running. To react quickly. To work as part of a team to move a distance in the shortest possible time.

Procedures:
1. Divide the children into teams of 4.
2. Two children from each team stand opposite each other at opposite ends of a 35-yard track.
3. On "go", the first runner carries the baton to the opposite end of the track. He passes the baton to the next runner (see facing line formation, Chapter 10).
4. Runners may not begin running until they have received the baton.
5. Continue until all 4 runners have run the 35-yard distance.

Teaching Suggestions:
1. The children should *not* compete until they are proficient in the prerequisite basic skills.

Prerequisite Basic Skills:
1. Running
2. Baton Passing

Shuttle Baton Pass:
1. When receiving the baton, the runner should be in the standing start position with the arm on the side of the front foot reaching forward to receive the baton.
2. The hand receiving the baton should be palm up forming a V with the fingers and the thumb.
3. The passer of the baton should place the baton in the V of the receiver's hand. The baton should be placed firmly into the hand of the receiver.
4. The passer should pass on the near side of the receiver's outstretched hand.

CIRCLE RELAY

Grade Level: 4 to 6

Sports Type: Track and Field

Equipment: Batons or 8-inch pieces of broomstick.

Objectives:
1. To practice the running baton pass.
2. The others are the same as the shuttle relay.

Procedures:
1. The circle relay is performed in the same way as the shuttle relay except that the four team mates are spaced 35 yards apart around a 140-yard circular track.
2. In the circle relay the receiver of the baton may begin running before he receives the baton as long as he has not run more than 5 yards before the baton is passed.
3. Each runner runs 35 yards passing the baton to the next runner until the 140-yard track has been completely circled. (A similar relay could be run on a 140-yard straight away.)

Prerequisite Basic Skills:
1. Starting
2. Running
3. Running baton pass

Running Baton Pass:
1. When receiving the baton the runner should be in the standing start position with the arm reaching backward on the side of the rear foot.
2. When the runner gets within 3 yards of the next runner (the receiver), the receiver begins to run away from the runner. The runner passes the baton just after the receiver begins to run.
3. The remainder of the running baton pass skill is performed in the same way as the shuttle baton pass except the receiver extends his arm backward to receive the baton rather than forward.

STANDING BROAD JUMP

Grade Level: 1 to 6

Sports Type: Track and Field

Equipment: Jumping line drawn on the floor or ground

Objectives:
1. To practice the skills of jumping from 2 feet.
2. To use total body in a skill performance requiring leg strength.

Procedures: See description in Appendix F, the AAHPER Test.

RUNNING BROAD JUMP

Grade Level: 1 to 6

Sports Type: Track and Field

Equipment: Broad Jump Pit

Objectives:
1. To practice the skill of jumping after a run.
2. To use the total body in a complex skill requiring speed, leg strength and agility.

Procedures:
1. The children run to a jumping board or mark (run should be less than full speed, especially at first).
2. The take off for the jump should be on one foot, that is with one foot driving off the jumping board.
3. The jumper should push off with one foot attempting to jump in the air at an angle slightly less than 45 degrees.
4. The jumper should land on both feet so that the body swings forward over the feet and so that the jumper does *not* fall backward after the jump.
5. The jump is measured from the front edge of the jumping board to the nearest point where the jumper touched the ground, usually the heel of the proficient jumper.

Teaching Suggestions:
1. Have beginning jumpers jump without a jumping board or mark. If a measurement is necessary, measure from toe to heel.

HOP-STEP-JUMP

Grade Level: 3 to 6

Sports Type: Track and Field

Equipment: Jumping Pit

Objectives:
1. To practice a series of skills in succession while trying to attain the greatest jumping distance.
2. To test one's self in a complex skill.
3. To use total body agility and coordination in performing a skill.

Procedures:
1. Basically the hop-step-jump is performed in the same manner as the running broad jump except that a one foot hop and one step precede the jump.
2. The jumper lands on two feet after the hop-step-jump.
3. Either foot may take off first. However, the example below describes a right foot start.

Prequisite Skills:
1. Hop

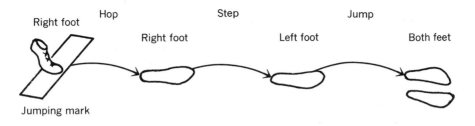

2. Step
3. Jump
4. Run

HIGH JUMP

Grade Level: 4 to 6

Sports Type: Track and Field

Equipment: Jumping Pit, standards and cross bar

Objectives:
1. To practice the skill of jumping for height after a run.
2. To use the total body in a complex skill requiring speed, leg strength and agility.

Procedures:
1. Approach the jump running at approximately 45 degree to the bar.
2. Kick up with the outside leg as if kicking a football.
3. Lean back, pushing off the ground with the inside foot.
4. As the outside foot swings over the bar, lay the body over the bar parallel to the ground.
5. As the upper body and head clear the bar, lower the head and swing the back leg high over the bar.
6. The landing in the pit is on the hands and outside foot.

HOP-KICK GOLF

Grade Level: 3 to 6

Sports Type: Golf

Equipment: Eighteen bowling pins, floor marking tape, and one $1\frac{1}{2}$ x $1\frac{1}{2}$ inch square block for each child in the class.

Objectives:
1. To play a game that can be played during leisure time.
2. To score a game of modified golf.
3. To use agility, balance and foot-eye coordination in a game situation.

Procedures:

1. Mark off an 18-hole course as indicated below. Boxes (holes) should be 1 foot square and the arrow extending from each box should point in the direction of the next hole. A bowling pin should be placed in each 1 foot box.

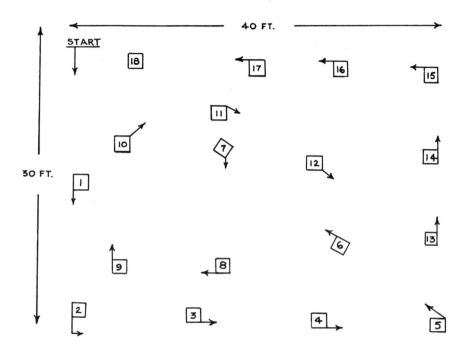

2. Divide the children so that two or three are starting at each hole at the same time.
3. When the game begins, each child stands on one foot with the other foot held in the air. With his free foot, he kicks his block as many times as is necessary to get it in the next hole (follow the arrow). The block is in the hole when it is in the square.
4. The children count the number of kicks required to get their block in each hole. A 2-strike penalty is assessed for touching the ground with the non-kicking foot.
5. Continue playing until each child has played each hole.

Teaching Suggestions:

1. Have the children make their own score cards for use in scoring.
2. For the less skilled children require the block only to enter the square

to be in the hole. For the more skilled, make the block hit the bowling pin inside each square.

3. As children become more skilled, make them kick and hop on the same foot.

References

Armbruster, D. A., Irwin, L. W. and Musker, F. F.: *Basic Skills in Sports.* St. Louis, C. V. Mosby Co, 1963.

AAHPER: *How We Do It Handbook.* Washington. National Education Association, 1964.

Hindman, D. A.: *Complete Book of Games and Stunts.* Englewood Cliffs, N.J., Prentice-Hall Inc., 1956.

Means, L. E. and Jack, H. K.: *Physical Education Activities. Sports and Games.* Dubuque, W. C. Brown & Co., 1965.

Seaton, D. C., Clayton, Leibee, and Messersmith: *Physical Education Handbook.* Englewood Cliffs, N.J., Prentice-Hall Inc., 1965.

18

Physical Fitness Activities*

There are many effective methods of helping children in developing physical fitness. Physical fitness games, physical fitness stunts, interval training, circuit training, the obstacle course, exercises and calisthenics, and isometric exercises are discussed in this chapter as effective techniques for helping children develop physical fitness.

Physical Fitness Games

FOLLOW THE LEADER

Objective: All aspects of physical fitness.

Equipment Necessary: None.

Grade Level: Any grade 1 to 6.

Procedures:
1. Line members of the class in single file.
2. Have students follow the person in front of them trying to mimic their behavior.

---

*Although activities included in other sections of this book contribute to the physical fitness objective, those activities are not designed only to develop physical fitness. The primary objective of activities listed in this chapter is the development of physical fitness.

3. Introduce hopping, skipping, running, stretching, twisting or what ever desired—emphasize movement of all body parts.

Suggestions for Teaching:
1. Precede the game with instruction in how to line up including establishment of distances between persons in line.
2. The teacher may lead the first few times the game is played to establish desirable movements and ideas.
3. Allow the students to lead but suggest certain stunts to the leader to insure total body activity.
4. Introduce stunts similar to exercises which produce specific physical fitness benefits.
5. Introduce imitations of animals, indians, etc. Use those involving especially vigorous movement.
6. Use several lines with several leaders if classes are large.

✳ HIT THE DECK

Objective: Physical Fitness development; specifically strength and endurance.

Equipment Needed: None.

Grade Level: Grades 3 to 6.

Procedures:
1. Line the students in squads or single file lines of 5 or 6.
2. Have the students spread out to allow two body lengths between each other.
3. On command of teacher the students act as follows:
   a. "Run in Slow Motion"—in place
   b. "Double Time"—run in place
   c. "Hit the Deck"—get to the ground stomach down as soon as possible.
   d. "On Your Back"—same as c, but on the back.
   e. "On Your Feet"—get back to your feet.
   f. "Slap Your Knees"—run in place slapping the knees as they come up.
4. Give different commands at different intervals with specific attention given to vigorous continuous movement.

Suggestions for Teaching:
1. Allow the students to lead.
2. Emphasize the speed of execution.
3. Stop periodically to see if all of the students are with leader.
4. Start slowly at first speeding up as you go.

STOP AND START

Objective: Endurance and agility development.

Equipment Needed: Whistle, if desired.

Grade Level: Any grade 1 to 6.

Procedures:
1. Students form one line facing the teacher with one arm's distance between each other.
2. On command "Start" or on the whistle, all students run.
3. On "stop" or the second whistle, the students stop immediately trying not to move.
4. Students moving after the "stop" command return to starting place.
5. Students move in the direction of a goal trying to be the first to reach that goal.

Suggestions for Teaching:
1. Designate first student to finish as winner and new leader.
2. Add "to right" and "to left" as desired.

JUMP THE LINE

Objective: Leg power, strength, endurance.

Equipment Needed: Lined play surface.

Grade Level: Any grade level 1 to 6.

Procedures:
1. Have the students form one line facing the teacher.
2. Play the same as "Stop and Start" except the students must jump the distances from one line to the other.

Start	Jump	Jump	Jump	Finish

Suggestions for Teaching:
1. Vary the distances between lines to the needs and abilities of the students.
2. Use long white ropes as lines if a liner is not available.
3. Introduce this game after the rules of "Stop and Start" are established.

POISON PIN

Objective: Strength and agility.

Equipment Needed: Indian Clubs or Bowling Pins.

Grade Level: Grades 4 to 6.

Procedures:
1. Form in circles of 8 to 10.
2. Place a bowling pin in the middle of a circle.
3. Students join together making a circle grabbing wrists with a double wrist grip.
4. On the command "Begin" the students pull on the arms of other students in the circle attempting to make someone else knock down the pin.
5. Any student hitting the pin or breaking hands is out.
6. The last student remaining is the winner.

Suggestions for Teaching:
1. Start a new circle for the eliminated players.
2. Make it clear that breaking hands eliminates both players involved regardless of whose fault it was.

PUSH BALL

Objective: Strength development.

Equipment Needed: Large canvas or plastic ball—3 to 6 feet in diameter.

Grade Level: 3 to 6.

Procedures:
1. Divide the students into two teams.
2. Have all students place their hands on the ball with each team facing a different direction beginning at the center of the playing area.
3. On "Go" the students attempt to push the ball over the opponents goal line.

Goal

Goal

TUG-O-WAR

Objective: Strength development.

Equipment Necessary: Ropes.

Grade Level: 5 to 6.

Procedures:
1. Divide students into two teams.
2. Have one team of students grab one end of the rope and the other team of students grab the opposite end of the rope.
3. Place a flag in the center of the rope—put the flag in the center of the game area.
4. On "Go" the students attempt to pull their opponent over a goal line.

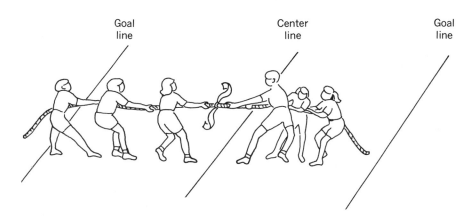

Goal line	Center line	Goal line

Suggestions for Teaching:
1. If a rope is not available, divide the group into small groups or teams (3 to 4). Have them grab the waist of the team member in front of them with the lead member of each team grabbing the wrist of the other teams leader. Follow the same procedures as above.

OVER THE ROPE

Objective: Leg Power.

Equipment Needed: Ropes.

Grade Level: Grades 2 to 4.

Procedures:
1. One player swings a weighted rope in a circle low to the ground.
2. Students jump the rope as it comes around.

Suggestions for Teaching:
1. Keep the groups small (3 to 4). Too many players in one group allows many misses and much inactivity.
2. Change twirler frequently.
3. Vary the speed of the rope as students become more proficient.

✗ Physical Fitness Stunts

The following stunts can be performed as part of the Follow the Leader Game, during pre-class exercises or in a special stunts unit. Stunts must be continued or performed for a relatively long period of time if they are to produce any overload or physical fitness benefits.

Mule Kick—Student assumes modified push up position, kicking the feet in the air then returning to starting position.

Coffee Grinder—Tip from push up position until weight is on one hand, lift the other hand off the ground, turn body sideways and walk feet in a circle around the hand touching the ground.

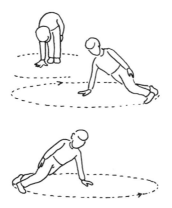

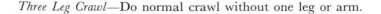

Three Leg Crawl—Do normal crawl without one leg or arm.

Seal Walk—Starting in push up position, draw legs toward the hands keeping the arms and legs straight. When feet are as close to hands as possible, walk the hands forward until normal push up position is attained. Keep feet together.

Crab Walk—From sitting position, extend the legs slightly—lean trunk slightly backward supporting upper body with the arms. Alternately step with one arm, one foot.

Camel Walk—Stand with legs spread—reach through the legs and around the ankles—grasp the ankles—walk.

Frog Jump—Begin in all fours position—lift hands slightly, reach hands forward, drive with the legs—catch body weight with the arms allowing feet to return to the ground—repeat.

Bear Walk—Same as seal walk except legs are kept apart (straight) and walked forward alternately.

Walrus Walk—Assume the push up position—walk arms alternately forward dragging the legs behind.

Inch Worm—Assume the push up position—keeping the legs straight alternately walk them forward—when the feet are close to the hands, walk hands alternately forward—repeat.

Gorilla Walk—Assume standing position with feet spread shoulder width—bend forward at the waist allowing the arms to hang free—gallop slowly swinging the arms.

Elephant Walk—Same as gorilla walk except the walk is slower and arms are held together to form a trunk—swing the arms together from side to side.

Human Ball—Sit on the floor tucking the body as close as possible keeping the knees close to the chest. Reach behind the knees and grasp the hands in front of the ankles. From this position fall to one side and allow the body to roll across the back and return to the starting position—repeat.

Rocking Horse—Lie down on the stomach—Bend legs up behind grasping the ankles with the hands. Arch the back. Rock onto chest and back to starting position—repeat.

Spider Walk—Sit on the floor—raise the hips off the floor reaching the hands through the legs placing the palms of the hands on the floor slightly behind the feet. Bend the arms allowing the back of the upper leg to rest on the back of the upper arm. Walk the feet and hands forward.

Dual Stunts

Push And Pull—Two students sit down facing each other with legs straight (slight bend may be necessary) and feet together—students grab hands and pull like rowing a boat—some resistance is given to pulling but not enough to exclude movement—the same procedure can be used substituting pushing for pulling.

Back To Back—Two students stand back to back—interlock elbows with partner behind the back—one student leans forward slowly lifting his relaxed partner on his back—return to original position—repeat with second student doing lifting—continue alternating lifting.

Wring The Rag—Two students stand facing each other grasping hands—without dropping hands one partner turns away from the other—the student #2 turns away—when each student has made one full turn you have wrung the rag.

Special Fitness Programs

INTERVAL TRAINING

Objective: Primarily endurance development.

Equipment Necessary: Marked distance, stop watch.

Grade Level: Upper Elementary.

Facts About Interval Training:
1. Interval training can be used with many activities as the basis (running, swimming, stepping the bench, jumping rope) but is traditionally associated with running programs.
2. The four variables to consider in interval training are distance of the run, time of actual running, time of rests between running (interval), and number of repetitions of the running.

3. Interval training is of particular value because of the controlled nature of the overload which places specific demands on the individual. This controlled overload helps to encourage maximal performance when performance might normally cease or diminish.

Procedures:
1. In modified interval training for elementary school children, the first procedure is to select the distance to be run and to test the student at the distance (time).
2. Secondly—group the students in small (4 or 5) homogeneous groups (ideally programs are based on individual ability).
3. Have the students run the distance at a reduced rate ($\frac{1}{2}$ to $\frac{3}{4}$ speed) with the others in their group. Time them to help them finish in the desired time.
4. Allow a rest (interval) of two to three times the running time. This rest may involve walking from the finish line back to the starting line.
5. Repeat from 6 to 12 times as desired.
6. As the running becomes easy increase the distance, shorten the rest interval, increase the number of repetitions, or decrease the running time.
7. Test periodically to determine improvement and to revise programs.

Suggestions for Teaching:
1. Have all students perform—some will be running, some walking back or resting, and others preparing to run.
2. Do the timing yourself (at least in early stages of program).
3. If rope jumping or bench stepping are used instead of running determine "distance" in jumps or steps. Otherwise the procedures are the same.

CIRCUIT TRAINING:

Objective: Physical fitness development—all or any aspect.

Equipment Needed: Depends on circuit stations—commonly used equipment includes ropes, weights, bars (chinning), balance beam, bench, etc.

Facts About Circuit Training:
1. Circuit training has the advantage of developing many aspects of fitness at the same time.
2. Circuit training is good in that it is highly individual in nature.
3. Circuit training, because of the variety of items, provides a change of scenery which helps to hold interest.

Procedure: Select the stations for the circuit allowing for physical fitness development of all body parts as well as development of the different aspects of physical fitness. There are many methods of conducting modified circuit programs. The following statements include a discussion of two simple methods:

Plan #1

A. Have the students run the circuit doing all items as many times as possible.
B. Have students perform the circuit two times daily at approximately $\frac{3}{4}$ maximal at each station.

Plan #2

A. Have the students run circuit performing set number of repetitions at each station usually 6 to 12 in number.
B. Time students on complete circuit.
C. Have the students run the circuit two times at $\frac{1}{2}$ to $\frac{3}{4}$ speed.

Suggestions for Teaching:

1. Have better students begin first so that they will not have to wait for the slow students at the various stations.
2. Retest frequently.
3. Change items periodically for variety.

Example Plan #1

Station 1 Chins	Station 2 Step the Bench
Station 4 Hanging Leg Lifts	Station 3 Sit Ups

Example Plan #2

(#1) Jump Rope (50 Times)	(#2) Run Around Chairs (2 Times)	(#3) Walk Balance Beam (One Time)
(#6) Bicycle Ride (50 Times)	(#5) Sit Ups (15 Times)	(#4) Chin Ups (3 Times)

OBSTACLE COURSE

Objective: Physical fitness—all aspects.

Equipment Needed: Permanent playground obstacles.

Grade Level: Any grade 1 to 6.

1. Have the children run from one obstacle to another, completing the course in as little time as possible.

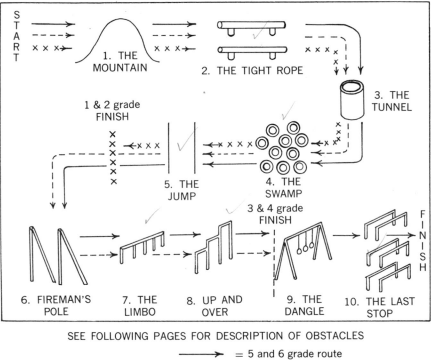

SEE FOLLOWING PAGES FOR DESCRIPTION OF OBSTACLES

⟶ = 5 and 6 grade route

----⟶ = 4 and 3 grade route

× × × ×⟶ = 1 and 2 grade route

Suggestions for Teaching:

1. When purchasing new playground equipment, place the equipment for maximal use in recreation and for maximal use in the obstacle course.
2. Give the obstacles a name. This adds to the motivation of the student. If possible, label all of the obstacles permanently.
   a. *The Mountain*—A large hill at least 8 to 10 feet above the playground with a gradual slope on all sides. *Task*—run over the hill.

b. *The Tight Rope*—Telephone poles supported by small lengths of sunken pole varying in height from 1 to 3 feet. *Task*—Walk the beam.

c. *The Tunnel*—A 3- to 4-foot diameter culvert—the length equals 10 to 20 feet. *Task*—Crawl through.

d. *The Swamp*—Old tires staggered to allow the student to step through the hole of one tire at a time. Tires should probably be stored in a bin that is built near the course—the tires can also be used for other activities. *Task*—jump from one hole to another.

e. *The Jump*—Two (or more) lines drawn on the ground comprise the obstacle. (Old fire hose nailed to the ground makes a good permanent obstacle.) *Task*—Jump from the first line to the next.

f. *Fireman's Pole*—10 to 15 foot poles with supporting diagonal poles comprise the obstacle. Use a minimum of 2 inch pipe. *Task*—Climb the diagonal pole, slide down the straight pole.

g. *The Limbo*—A pipe suspended 30 to 36 inches high is the obstacle. *Task*—Limbo or bend backwards while walking under the pipe.

h. *Up and Over*—Horizontal pipes suspended at 3, 5, and 7 foot heights. *Task*—Hip circle over the designated height.

i. *The Dangle*—Rings suspended by chain from a normal swing frame. *Task*—Walk with the hands from beginning to the end alternating hand placement from ring to ring.

j. *The Last Stop*—Pipe Parallel Bars. The bars are 4 feet high and from 15 to 20 inches apart. *Task*—Move from front to back of the bars supporting the weight with the arms and hands—alternately release one hand and move it ahead of the other.

3. Place obstacles so that several routes are available. Different routes should cater to the characteristics of different grade levels.

EXERCISES AND CALISTHENICS

ENDURANCE

Name of Exercise	Purpose	Description	Illustration
Pogo Jumps	All of these exercises develop the circulatory-respiratory systems of the body. In addition they require muscular endurance capacity of the legs and rib cage. Rope jump requires muscular endurance of the arms.	With the hands behind the head, with one foot ahead of the other, jump straight in the air alternately landing with the opposite foot forward—bend the knees between jumps to a half squat.	
Straddle Jump		Same as the above except the feet are spread to the side after each jump—*do not* bend the knees between jumps.	
Stride Jump		Same as Pogo Jump without bending the knees	
Rope Jumping		Jump Rope using one of three basic steps: 1. two foot step 2. skip step 3. hop step-one foot	
Bench Stepping		Use 10 to 20-inch bench. Step up with R-foot, bring L up also. Step down with R-foot, step down with the L foot. Repeat about once every 2 seconds.	
Running In Place		Run in place, lift knees high, touch the knees with the hands.	

ENDURANCE (CONTINUED)

Name of Exercise	Purpose	Description	Illustration
Sprinters Stride		From push-up position,* spring the feet off the ground bringing one foot forward with the other extended, spring the feet in the air again changing the position of the feet— the forward foot comes back and the back foot forward under the chest. The hands remain on the floor. Repeat.	
Burpee	see preceeding page!	The exercise is done by the count of six: 1. squat 2. lean to push up position. 3. bring the legs through or around the hands to a reverse push-up position. 4. turn over to push up position. 5. up to squat 6. stand up Repeat!	
Bicycle Ride		From supine position* roll back to the shoulders, press the feet and hips over the head. Swing the feet alternately forward and backward as if riding a bicycle.	

*Beginning Positions for Exercises

Push-up Position–The position normally assumed at the beginning of a push up. The face is pointed down with the body weight supported on the extended arms and the balls of the feet.

Supine Position–The position assumed when you are lying on your back.

Prone Position–The position assumed when you are lying on your stomach.

STRENGTH AND MUSCULAR ENDURANCE

Name of Exercise	Purpose	Description	Illustration
Bent Leg Sit Up	Stomach Muscles	Same as the above except the knees are bent at about 65°. Roll up lifting the head first, then the shoulders and finally the back.	
Hanging Front Leg Raises	Back muscles Stomach Muscles Hip Muscles	Hang from a bar. Lift the legs up to a 90° angle and then return to the hanging position. Keep the back straight as legs are lifted.	
Side Leg Raises	Hip Muscles Leg Muscles	Lying on the side lift one leg (top leg) up as high as possible and return to starting position. Repeat. Turn to the other side and repeat.	
Cork Screw	Leg Muscles Hip Muscles Stomach Muscles Side body Muscles	From the supine position lift one leg across the body touching the floor on the opposite side near the shoulder. Return. Repeat with the other leg.	
Back Hyperextension	Back Muscles	From the prone position and the hand behind the head, lift the shoulders off the floor keeping the head up—return—repeat.	
Toe Raises	Calf Muscles	From the standing position raise to the tip of the toes—return—repeat.	

FLEXIBILITY

Name of Exercise	Muscle Used	Description	Illustration
Arm Circles	Shoulder and Arm Muscles	Standing holding the arms extended at shoulder height, circle the hands first forward then backward in circles of 12-inch diameter.	
Stoop Stretch	Leg, Hip, Back, and Arm Muscles	Standing with the arms over the head with the feet spread, bend at the hips reach through the legs as far as the hands can reach—straighten to stand—repeat.	
Lift the Toe	Leg and Arm Muscles	From the standing position reach with one hand and grab the opposite toe, hold the toe and lift trying to touch the toe to the forehead—bend forward at the waist to aid attempt. Alternate feet.	

Name of Exercise	Description	Illustration
Stork Stand	From standing position, lift one leg off the floor placing the lifted foot on the knee of the other leg. Use the hands to help balance—hold this position for 10, 20 or 30 seconds—repeat with other foot.	
Diver's Balance	From the standing position, hold the arms straight in front—lift the body weight to the toes of both feet. Hold stance for 10, 20 or 30 seconds. Practice with eyes open or closed.	
Walk the Line	Students walk a line on the floor as if it were a tight rope. Use the hands for balance.	
Walk the Plank	Suspend a board on blocks several inches off the floor. Walk the board as if it were a tight rope.	
One Leg Swan Stand	From standing position lean forward at the hips—Lift the right foot off the floor behind you—Lift as high as possible—Balance on the left leg using the hands to stabilize. Repeat on the other foot.	
Toe to Head	From standing position, lift one foot to touch the head—allow the body to bend at the waist—hold the position while balanced on one foot.	
Knee Dip	Stand on one foot holding the other foot up behind the body. Bend the leg supporting the body until the knee of the lifted foot touches the ground. Return to the starting position by straightening the supporting leg—repeat with other leg.	
Indian Squat	From standing position, keep the feet in place-turn the body—when the legs are crossed sit down. Return to original position by standing up and facing original direction. Repeat turning the other direction.	

AGILITY

Name of Exercise	Description	Illustration
Jack Spring	From the standing position, jump in the air—spreading the legs while in the air touch the toes with the hands—immediately after landing jump into the air again and touch the toes in the same manner—repeat several times.	
Knee to Feet	From a kneeling position jump into the air landing on the feet—hold for 3 seconds. Student must leave the floor. Repeat. (Toes should be curled under in beginning position.)	
Six Count Burpee	Same as Six Count Burpee listed under endurance exercises.	
Figure Eight Run	Place two chairs on floor at distance of 10 to 50 feet. Student must run to the left of the first chair, to the right and around the second—back around the first. Continue as desired.	
Hop the Tires	Place regular tire carcasses on the play ground grouped closely. Students must run through the tires allowing only one foot to hit the ground in the center of each tire. Run the tires at random or in predetermined course.	
Tunnel Crawl	Several students stand in a line with their legs spread—other students crawl through the tunnel made by the legs.	
Stand Up	From the sitting position with the legs drawn close to the chest the student must stand up without letting the hands touch the floor.	

ISOMETRIC EXERCISES*

Name of Exercise	Description	Illustrations
The Press Together	Grasp the hands in front of the body keeping the elbows pointed out— press the hands together while squeezing the hands together.	
Neck Resistor	With a partner—grab behind his neck and him behind yours, interlocking the fingers of your hands behind the partners neck. Lever back with the head and pull with the hands so that both the arm and the neck are working.	
Curl the Arm	Stand straight up—loop a rope under your feet so that the elbows are flexed at 90°—curl the hands toward the chest while holding the rope in the hands.	
Sitting Arm lifts	From sitting position grab under the thighs with the hands. Keeping the back straight pull up with the arms and hands.	
V Sit	From the sitting position lean back lifting the feet off the floor keeping the legs straight—both the legs and the back are off the floor—hold in this position.	
Leg Straightener	Loop a rope under the feet while in a sitting position—draw the legs close to the body—hold the rope tight against the feet—try to straighten the legs.	
Leg Cross	From supine position cross the legs. Lift the feet a few inches off the floor —Try to lift the lower foot while trying to force the upper foot downward.	
Push the Wall	From standing position stand near a wall placing the hands on the wall at shoulder height—push against the wall with the hands.	

*All contractions should be held for 6 to 10 seconds. Each exercise should be repeated three times.

PHYSICAL FITNESS RECORDS

Record listings herein were those available as this book went to press. Readers are urged to acquire current catalogues to assure themselves up-to-date listings, catalogue designations, and price information.

Record Name	Number	Cost	Company
Postural Improvement Activities	Album 25 (4 records)	12.00	Educational Activities Inc. Freeport, L.I., N.Y.
Physical Fitness Activity			
Primary Grades	LP 14A	5.95	
Elementary-Jr. Hi	LP 15A	5.95	
Girls	LP 16A	5.95	
Fitness Fun for Everyone	Album 24 (4 records)	12.00	
Modern Dynamic Physical Fitness Activities Primary	Album 14 (4 records)	12.00	
Modern Dynamic Physical Fitness Activities-Elem.	Album 15 (4 records)	12.00	
Advanced Modern Dynamic Physical Fitness Activities for Girls	Album 16 (4 records)	12.00	
Music for Physical Fitness	Ch007	5.95	Children's Music Center 5373 W. Pico Blvd. Los Angeles, California
Fifteen for Fitness	Ch008	3.95	
Skip Rope Games	Ch009	4.25	
Fitness Fun for Everyone	Ch103A	12.00	
Physical Fitness for Boys	Ch005	6.98	
Physical Fitness for Girls	Ch006	6.98	
Chicken Fat	DS111	1.30	
Physical Fitness Activities			
Number 1	Ch108	12.00	
Number 2	Ch109	12.00	
Physical Fitness for Girls	Ch103B	12.00	
Exercises for the Classroom			
Number 1	Ch100	5.95	
Number 2	Ch101	5.95	
Physical Fitness for the Younger Set Grades 1-3	LP 1077	7.95	Kimbo Records Box 55 Deal, N.J. 07723
Rhythmical Activities and Physical Fitness Grades 1-3	LP 1088	7.95	
Physical Fitness for the Younger Set Grades 1-2	LP 1055	7.95	
15 Tunes for Fitness	LP 2080	7.95	
5 Minutes for Fitness	#235	1.30	
Physical Fitness Upper Elementary	LP 2020	7.95	
Chicken Fat	#209	1.30	
USA in Motion	LP 2010	7.95	
USA on the March	LP 2030	7.95	

Record Name	Number	Cost	Company
Graded Physical Fitness Exercises for Girls	LP 3010	7.95	Kimbo Records Box 55
Graded Physical Fitness Exercises for Boys	LP 3020	7.95	Deal, N.J. 07723
April Showers	Han 514	1.59	Hanf Records
Hi Neighbor	Han 540	1.59	Available from:
Don't Fence Me In	Han 514	1.59	
Let's Sing Like Bird's	Han 511	1.59	Loshin's
Drums	Han 519	1.59	215 E. 8th St.
Let's Do It Again	Han 511	1.59	Cincinnati, Ohio 45202
March Medley	Han 1008	1.59	
Pennsylvania Polka	Han 1007	1.25	
Wooden Soldier Jazz	Han 540	1.59	
Physical Fitness Novelties	Han 802	4.95	
Keep Fit	Sta 1009	5.95	Staler Records Available from: Loshin's
Exercises for the Classroom			Hoctor Dance Records
Volume I	CC-621	5.98	Waldwick, N.J. 07463
Volume II	CC-622	5.98	
Elementary School Exercises to Music	4008V	5.00	
Physical Fitness-Pop tunes	Set of 30	35.00	

Bibliography

Casady, D. R., Mapes, D. F. and Alley, L. E.: *Handbook of Physical Fitness Activities,* New York, The Macmillan Co., 1965.

President's Council on Physical Fitness, 414 G Street N.W., Washington, D.C.: 20548. *VIM—A Fitness Program For Girls. VIGOR—A Fitness Program For Boys. YOUTH PHYSICAL FITNESS.*

Bender, J. A. and Shea, E. J.: *Physical Fitness: Tests and Exercises,* New York, The Ronald Press, 1964.

Prudden, B.: *Is Your Child Really Fit,* New York, Harper & Brothers, 1956.

Dauer, V. P.: *Fitness for Elementary School Children,* Minneapolis, The Burgess Publishing Co., 1962, Chapters 2, 5, and 17.

Bucher, C. A. and Reade, E. M.: *Physical Education in The Modern Elementary School,* New York, The Macmillan Co., 1958, Chapters 4, 18 and Appendix.

Kirchner, G.: *Physical Education for Elementary Children,* Dubuque, Wm. Brown and Co., 1966, Chapters 12, 24, and 27.

19

Rhythms and Dance*

The following rhythms and dance activities are arranged in order from simple to complex. A specific grade level has not been recommended. Children of various ages can do different activities depending on their previous experience. The overlap is great and it is not unlikely that fifth and sixth grade children could do some of the activities listed in the early part of the chapter. Also second and third grade children might perform some of the more difficult activities. Like other activity chapters, only selected illustrative activities are presented. The reader is referred to the sources at the end of the chapter for other sources of rhythms and dance activities.

The rhythms and dance activities listed in this chapter would be used in a program of physical education to help children accomplish the following objectives:

1. To be able to perform rhythmic skills which could be used as a basis for rhythmical recreation activities outside the classroom or instructional situation.
2. To be able to perform the basic skills of walking, skipping, hop stepping, running, leaping and other movements to music.
3. To be able to perform folk dances of the American and other cultures.

*Each of the activities listed in this chapter is accompanied by a record number. The sources of these records are listed at the end of the chapter. Records listed herein were those available when this book went to press. Readers are urged to write to specific companies for more recent listings.

4. To learn specific skills of specific dances such as the alemende left in square dance.

5. To be able to work with other children in a rather complicated skill activity (example: square dance).

6. To participate in an activity with members of the opposite sex with confidence and to enjoy the experience.

7. To develop smoothness of body movement and a body movement style that is attractive.

8. To be able to follow specific directions (dance to a call).

9. To develop general agility, balance and general body coordination.

10. To develop appreciation for all forms of rhythms and dance.

11. To provide an opportunity to mix socially with many different children. To help overcome shyness through experience.

12. To provide a varied activity in which some children may excel even though they are poor in other physical endeavors.

TEN LITTLE INDIANS

Record: Stepping Tones 122 (Available from Loshins, see p. 329)

The children form one large circle. They are numbered from 1 through 10. If there are more than 10 children, start over again with the eleventh child numbering him 1, the twelfth child 2, etc. There may be several children with the same number. During the first verse the children indian dance (hop-step or slow skip, see fundamental skills Chapter 11) counter clockwise in a circle. The words are as follows:

One little, two little, three little indians,
four little, five little, six little indians,
seven little, eight little, nine little indians,
ten little indian boys.

On the second verse the children stoop down when their number is called. They do not move around the circle. As they sing, one little, the children with the number one stoop. This procedure continues through all ten numbers until every child is stooping.

On the third verse the song is sung as follows:

Ten little, nine little, eight little indians,
seven little, six little, five little indians,
four little, three little, two little indians,
one little indian boy.

As they sing this verse the children stand up from the stoop position as their number is called.

On the fourth verse the children again dance around the circle.

✖ HOKEY POKEY

> *Record:* Capital 6026
>
> The children form one large circle. As the record plays the children sing along. The verses are as follows:

> Verse 1:   You put your right hand in, you put your right hand out,
> You put your right hand in and you shake it all about,
> You do the Hokey Pokey and you turn yourself around,
> That's what its all about.
> Verse 2:   Put your left hand in, etc.
> Verse 3:   Put your right arm in, etc.
> Verse 4:   Put your left arm in, etc.
> Verse 5:   Put your right elbow in, etc.
> Verse 6:   Put your left elbow in, etc.
> Verse 7:   Put your head in, etc.
> Verse 8:   Put your right hip in, etc.
> Verse 9:   Put your left hip in, etc.
> Verse 10: Put your whole self in, etc.
> Verse 11: Put your back side in, etc.
> Finale: You do the Hokey Pokey, the Hokey Pokey,
> You do the Hokey Pokey, that's what its all about.

The children perform the appropriate action as the song calls for it. For "Hokey Pokey" the children put their hands above their heads and wiggle their hips as if they were "doing a Hawaiian Dance". After Hokey Pokey they merely turn themselves around by turning in place.

LOOBY LOO

> *Records:* Folkraft 1102 (Available from Herman Dance House, see p. 329)
>
> The children form a large circle. The children sing as they circle counter-clockwise to the music. The children sing the following chorus as they walk in the circle:

> Chorus: Here we go Looby Loo,
> Here we go Looby Light,
> Here we go Looby Loo,
> All on a Saturday.

During the singing of the six verses the children face the center of the circle and execute the maneuver dictated by the words. After each verse the chorus is repeated and the children walk or skip in a circle. The verses are as follows:

Verse 1: I put my right hand in,
        I put my right hand out,
        I give my right hand a shake, shake, shake,
        And turn myself about.
Verse 2: I put my left hand in, repeat as above.
Verse 3: I put my right foot in, repeat as above.
Verse 4: I put my left foot in, repeat as above.
Verse 5: I put my head in, repeat as above.
Verse 6: I put my whole self in, repeat as above.

Example: When the words call for the child to put his right arm in he extends it toward the center of the circle, when the words tell him to put his right hand out he extends the arm to the outside of the circle, and on shake, shake, shake the child vigorously shakes his arm three times. The last line of the verse calls for the child to turn about. The child merely turns around in place. Repeat for all verses in a similar manner.

PAW PAW PATCH

Record: Folkraft 1181.

The children form two lines. One line of 4 to 8 boys and a line of 4 to 8 girls who line up on the right of the boys. The first girl in the line of girls is "Nellie". "Nellie" begins to skip as the children sing the first verse. She leads out to her right and skips in a circle around all of the children. The first verse is sung as follows:

Verse 1: Where, Oh where is sweet little Nellie,
        Where, Oh where is sweet little Nellie,
        Where, Oh where is sweet little Nellie,
        Way down yonder in the Paw Paw Patch.

The children sing the second verse as Nellie skips around in a circle this time followed by all of the boys in a single file line. The second verse is sung as follows:

Verse 2: Come on boys, lets go find her,
        Come on boys, lets go find her,
        Come on boys, lets go find her,
        Way down yonder in the Paw Paw Patch.

As the children sing the third verse the leader of each line, one boy and one girl, turn to the outside and skip in a circle. The other boys and girls follow the leader of their line. As the lead boy and girl finish skipping in a large circle they join hands. The other boys and girls duck under the arch formed by the hands of the leaders. As they duck under they join hands with a partner and skip back to their starting places. The boy and girl at the end of each line become the new leaders. The third verse is sung as follows:

> Verse 3: Picken' up Paw Paws, putten' em in your basket,
> Picken' up Paw Paws, putten' em in your basket,
> Picken' up Paw Paws, putten' em in your basket,
> Way down yonder in the Paw Paw Patch.

Repeat several times allowing each child to lead his line one time.

Teaching Suggestions:
1. Have the children bend over as they skip as if they were picking up Paw Paws. Also they can give other motions as they skip such as swinging the arm to indicate "come on boys".
2. Substitute the name of the girl who is the leader of the line for Nellie as you sing the song.
3. Make sure children can skip without music before they attempt to perform the skip to music (see Chapter 11).

MULBERRY BUSH

Record: Victor 20806.

All children stand in a circle facing clockwise. During the chorus the children skip in a circle singing the following words:

> Here we go round the Mulberry Bush,
> The Mulberry Bush, the Mulberry Bush,
> Here we go round the Mulberry Bush,
> So early in the morning.

During the verses of the song the children stand in place and act out the verses. The verses are as follows:

> Verse 1: This is the way we wash our clothes,
> We wash our clothes, we wash our clothes;
> This is the way we wash our clothes
> So early in the morning.
> Verse 2: This is the way we iron our clothes.
> Verse 3: This is the way we scrub the floors.
> Verse 4: This is the way we mend our clothes.
> Verse 5: This is the way we sweep the house.
> Verse 6: This is the way our work is done.

BINGO* (*Scotland-America*)

Records: RCA Victor, LPM 1623 (33⅓ RPM), 41-6172 (45 RPM), 45-6172 (78 RPM).

This is one of America's favorite party games, enjoyed by young and old. The singing does not have to be good, but it should be loud! This recording changes key so there's opportunity for everyone to sing at some time of the dance.

Opening Formation: Double circle (of any number of couples), partners side-by-side and arm-in-arm, girl on the right.

Part 1: All walk counterclockwise around the circle, singing,

"A big black dog sat on the back porch
And Bingo was his name.
A big black dog sat on the back porch
And Bingo was his name."

Part 2: All join hands to form one large, single circle, girls on partners' right and still walking counterclockwise. Sing (spelling name),

"B-I-N-G-O; B-I-N-G-O; B-I-N-G-O
And Bingo was his name."

Part 3: Partners face each other and clasp right hands, calling out "B!" on the first chord.

All pass on to a new person with a *left*-hand hold, calling "I!" on the next chord.

Continue to a third person for a right-hand hold and shout "N!".

On to a fourth person with the left-hand, shouting "G!".

Instead of a right-hand to the fifth person, shout "O!" and hug your new partner vigorously! (Or you may swing this partner once around.)

Repeat dance from beginning, with new partners, each time moving forward until orginal couples are together.

SEVEN JUMPS (*Denmark*)

Records: RCA Victor, LPM 1623 (33⅓ RPM), 41-6172 (45 RPM), 45-6172 (78 RPM).

Originally danced only by men, any number of people may participate in this dance-game. Notice that the sustained notes are of varying duration to cause teasing suspense, since dancers must hold position for the duration of the note.

Opening Formation: Single circle, all hands joined. If preferred, in couple

---

*Dances pp. 308 to 318 taken from the RCA Victor instruction manual by permission of the company. Instruction manuals accompany the purchase of all records from the company. © *by Radio Corporation of America, 1958.*

formation, with partners joining both hands for CHORUS, facing each other for Figures.

Chorus: Begin the dance with the CHORUS and return to it after *each* of the 7 Figures below. CHORUS consists of 7 step-hops to the left with a jump on the 8th. Repeat step-hops and jump to the right. Step-hop by stepping, then hopping on one foot as the opposite leg swings forward and across. (The jump may be left out for general use and dancers may do 8 step-hops to the left, then 8 to the right.)

Figures: 1. Right Foot—On first sustained note, place hands on hips and raise right knee. Do not lower knee until the *second* note and stand motionless throughout the *third* note.

Repeat CHORUS.

Note: Stand motionless each time only on the last sustained note of music in each Figure.

2. Left Foot—Repeat Figure No. 1, adding identical figure with *left* knee.
Repeat CHORUS.

3. Right Knee—Repeat Figures No. 1 and 2, then kneel on right knee.
Repeat CHORUS.

4. Left Knee—Repeat Figures No. 1, 2 and 3, add kneel on left knee.
Repeat CHORUS.

5. Right Elbow—Repeat Figures No. 1, 2, 3 and 4, then kneel and place right elbow on floor.
Repeat CHORUS.

6. Left Elbow—Repeat Figures No. 1, 2, 3, 4 and 5, placing left elbow on floor.
Repeat CHORUS.

7. Head—Repeat Figures No. 1, 2, 3, 4, 5 and 6, then place head on floor.

Finish dance with a final CHORUS.

★ POLLY WOLLY DOODLE (*America*)

Records: RCA Victor, LPM 1625 (33⅓ RPM), EPA 4145 (45 RPM).

This merry tune has had many a dance set to it—both couple and square dances. Here is a little mixer usable with any age. Since nearly everyone knows at least some of the words, it is fun to do and easy to teach.

Opening Formation: Double circle of dancers, partners facing one another, both hands joined, man with back to center of ring.

Part 1: Words: "Oh, I went down south for to see my Sal,"

Action: All slide four steps—men to the left, ladies to the right, counterclockwise.

Words: "Sing polly wolly doodle all the day."

Action: Drop hands and all turn solo, men to left, ladies to right, with 5 stamps in this rhythm: 1—2—1,2,3. (Stamp on the word "polly," stamp on the other foot on the word "doodle" and take 3 quick stamps on the word "day.")

Words: "My Sally am a spunky gal, Sing polly wolly doodle all the day."

Action: Same as above but in opposite direction, with men moving to right and ladies to left, and men turning right, girls left, at end.

Part 2: Words: "Fare thee well, fare thee well."

Action: Both bow to each other, men with hands on hips, girls holding skirts.

Words: "Fare thee well, my fairy fay."

Action: Both move backward, away from each other, either with 4 walking steps, or skipping steps.

Words: "For I'm off to Louisiana for to see my Susyanna."

Action: Both dancers move diagonally forward to own left to meet a new partner.

Words: "Singing polly wolly doodle all the day."

Action: (Swing in place, or skip around with two-hand hold.)

Repeat dance from beginning with a new partner.

✠ DANCE OF GREETING (*Denmark*)

Record: RCA Victor, LPM 1625, or 41-6183, (45 RPM), or 45-6183 (78 RPM).

Opening Formation: Single circle, girls on partners' right. All face center.

Part 1: Meas. 1: All clap own hands twice, face partners and bow (girls curtsy).

Meas. 2: Facing center, clap hands twice and bow (or curtsy) to *neighbor*.

Meas. 3: Facing center again, all stamp twice in place (right, left).

Meas. 4: Turn in place with four light running steps.

(Meas. 1-4): Repeat PART 1.

Part 2: Meas. 5-8: All join hands and run, lightly, 16 steps left.

(Meas. 5-8): Repeat 16 running steps to the *right*.

Note: Older groups may prefer the following variation:

Part 1: Meas. 1: Clap hands twice, on the beat.

Meas. 2: All turn in place with four light running steps.

Meas. 3-4: Bow (and curtsy) slowly to partner, holding for two full measures.

Meas. 5-8: Repeat PART 1.

Part 2: Meas. 9-16: In shoulder-waist position, couples move counterclockwise around the circle with 16 step-hops. (Step-hop by stepping, then hopping, on one foot as the other foot swings forward and across.)

Part 3: Meas. 1-8: Repeat PART 1 (twice through).

Part 4: Meas. 9-16: All step-hop around the circle in a "grand right and left": facing each other, partners grasp right hands and pass on to the next person with a *left*-hand hold. Continue around the circle in this fashion, alternating right and left-hand holds, for 16 step-hops.

If the 16 step-hops do not bring original partners together, each repeats the dance from the beginning with a new partner—that person with whom hands are clasped at the end of the 8 measures.

✗ KINDERPOLKA (*"Children's Polka"*) (*Germany*)

Records: RCA Victor, LPM 1625 (33⅓ RPM), 41-6179 (45 RPM), 45-6179 (78 RPM).

Opening Formation: Single circle, partners facing, with hands joined. Arms extended sideward, shoulder high.

Part 1: Meas. 1–2: Couples take two step-draws toward center of circle (step-close, step-close), and three steps in place.

Meas. 3–4: Then two step-draws back to place and three more steps.

Meas. 5–8: Repeat all PART 1.

Part 2: Meas. 9–10: Slap thighs with both hands, clap own hands, then clap partner's hands three times.

Meas. 11–12: Repeat PART 2.

Part 3: Meas. 13–14: Place right heel forward and shake right forefinger at partner three times.

Repeat, with *left* heel and forefinger.

Meas. 15–16: Turn about in place with four running steps, face partner and stamp three times.

KINDERPOLKA can be a good "mixer" if the boy moves forward to a new partner for each repetition of the dance. Children may enjoy jumping as they turn about, rather than running (PART 3).

THE WHEAT (*Czechoslovakia*)

Records: RCA Victor, LPM 1625 (33⅓ RPM), 41-6182 (45 RPM), 45-6182 (78 RPM).

Opening Formation: Sets of three, preferably one boy and two girls, or one girl and two boys. All face counterclockwise, inside hands joined.

Part 1: All walk forward 16 steps.

Part 2: Center dancer hooks right elbow with right hand partner and turns twice around with 8 skipping steps. Repeat with partner on left.

Repeat from beginning as often as desired. Center dancer may move forward to dance with a new set of partners each time dance is repeated.

NORWEGIAN MOUNTAIN MARCH (*Norway*)

Records: RCA Victor, LPM 1622 (33⅓ RPM), EPA 4137 (45 RPM).

Opening Formation: Groups of three: preferably, but not necessarily, one boy and two girls. The boy (or middle dancer) stands in front, holding a handkerchief by the corner in each hand. His two partners stand behind him, each holding the other corner of the nearer handkerchief. They, in turn, are connected by a handkerchief held in their inside hands.

The Step: A waltz-step is preferable for this dance, but a step-hop may be substituted: ordinarily in 2/4 time, the 3/4 step-hop is done slowly, stepping forward on the count of 1, swinging the free foot forward and across on count 2, and hopping on the first foot for count 3.

Part 1: Meas. 1–8: Take 8 step-hops forward, beginning with the right foot and accenting slightly the first beat of each measure. As the group moves, the boy turns to his right and left, looking at the girls behind him.

Part 2: Meas. 9–10: Girls form an arch with their inside hands, the boy continuing the waltz-step (or step-hop) backward under the arch.

Meas. 11–12: Girl on the left, moving clockwise, dances across and under the boy's right arm.

Meas. 13–14: Girl on the right turns left about under boy's right arm.

Meas. 15–16: Boy turns right about and under his own right arm, so that group is in original position.

Meas. 17–24: Repeat PART 2.

Note: This dance represents a guide leading climbers up and down the mountain and should be performed with this impersonation in mind. Most important to the fun, of course, is keeping the chain unbroken and untangled.

ACE OF DIAMONDS (*Denmark*)

Records: RCA Victor, LPM-1622 (33⅓ RPM), EPA-4137 (45 RPM).

Opening Formation: Double circle with boys on inside, facing partners.

Part 1: Meas. 1: All clap hands and, at the same time, place right heel forward on floor (on the count of 1).

Return right foot to original position and, at the same time, place both hands on own hips (on the count of 2).

Meas. 2–4: Hook right elbow with partner, walk around and back to place with 6 steps.

Meas. 5–8: Repeat all above, but extend *left* foot and hook *left* elbow instead of right.

Part 2: Meas. 9–16: Hop on left foot, placing right heel forward. Hop on *right* foot, placing *left* heel forward.

Then do 4 of these "Change-Steps" rapidly by placing right, then left, then right, then left heel forward.

Repeat all of PART 2.

Part 3: Meas. 17–24: In shoulder-waist position, polka around the floor for 8 measures until PART 1 theme returns.

Repeat dance from beginning as often as desired.

COME LET US BE JOYFUL (*Germany*)

Records: RCA Victor, LPM 1622 (33⅓ RPM), 41-6177 (45 RPM), 45-6177 (78 RPM).

Opening Formation: Sets of three (preferably one boy and two girls), side-by-side with inside hands joined. Groups of two sets, facing, spaced around the circle.

Part 1: Meas. 1–2: Facing sets walk forward 3 steps and bow to opposite set on 4th step.

Meas. 3–4: Walk backward 3 steps, bringing feet together on 4th.

Meas. 5–8: Repeat all PART 1.

Part 2: Meas. 9–12: The boy (or center person) turns his right-hand partner with a right-elbow turn 4 steps, then the left-hand partner with a *left*-elbow turn for 4 steps.

Meas. 13–16: Repeat all PART 2.

Part 3: Meas. 1–4: Facing sets again walk forward 3 steps and bow, then backward 4 steps.

Meas. 5–8: Instead of repeating, as in PART 1, each set walks forward and *through* the opposite set, dropping hands and passing right shoulder to right shoulder, to face a new set for the next repetition of the dance.

Repeat from the beginning as often as desired.

BLEKING (*Sweden*)

Records: RCA Victor, LPM 1622 (33⅓ RPM), EPA 4137 (45 RPM).

Opening Formation: Single circle, partners facing each other with both hands joined.

Part 1: Meas. 1: Thrust right arm forward and extend right heel (on the count of 1). Thrust *left* arm forward and extend *left* heel (on the count of 2).

Meas. 2: Perform the same step 3 times rapidly, right, left, right. (This is the "Bleking Step.")

Meas. 3–4: Repeat entire sequence from beginning, starting with *left* heel and arm.

Meas. 5–8: Repeat all of PART 1, both "left" and "right" sequences.

Part 2: Meas. 9–16: In ballroom position, step-hop around the circle for 8 measures, moving joined hands vigorously up and down in windmill fashion. Step-hop by stepping, then hopping on each foot.

Do 16 step-hops in all (that is, 8 on each foot).

(Children may prefer to do PART 2 by extending and joining hands at shoulder height.)

Repeat entire dance as often as desired.

Note: This record may also be used to dance a plain schottische: partners stand side by side, girl on the right.

Holding inside hands and starting with outside foot, take 3 steps forward and hop on the 4th (for the boy: left, right, left, left—counting one-and-two-and). Beginning with the *inside* foot, repeat the 3 steps and hop (right, left, right, right).

Take 4 step-hops (see above) forward, in same position or, if preferred, shoulder-waist position.

Repeat from beginning as often as desired.

TANTOLI (*Sweden*)

Records: RCA Victor, LPM 1621 (33⅓ RPM), EPA 4133 (45 RPM).

Each of the Scandinavian countries has its own version of the *Tantoli*, any of which may be danced to this recording.

It would be helpful to familiarize participants with these three basic steps, before beginning the dance.

Step-hop: (one beat)—Step ("1"), then hop on same foot ("and").

Schottische: (two beats)—Step left ("1"), right ("and"), left ("2"), *hop* on left ("and")—or similar sequence beginning with right foot.

Step-draw: (one beat)—Step sideward ("1") and close ("and").

Opening Formation: Double circle, all facing counterclockwise. Girl on partner's right with her left hand on his right shoulder. Boy's right arm around her waist. Free hands on hips.

Part 1: Meas. 1–2: Beginning with outside foot, all take two step-hops forward. Face partner and turn to right, in place, with two more step-hops.

Meas. 3–8: Repeat PART 1 *three more* times.

Part 2: Meas. 1–2: Facing forward again, couples take one schottische step forward and one back again.

Meas. 3–4: Couples turn to right, twice around in place, with four step-hops.

Meas. 5–8: Repeat PART 2.

Part 3: Meas. 1: In open (original) position, all place outside heel forward, then touch toe of same outside foot to the floor behind.

Meas. 2: Take three steps forward, beginning with outside foot.

Meas. 3–4: Repeat beginning with inside foot.

Meas. 5–8: Repeat PART 3, measures 1–4.

Meas. 9–16: Chorus: In ballroom position, couples take 16 step-hops, turning to right and around the circle. Raise and lower joined hands with each step.

On last step-hop, couples separate to form double circle with partners facing, girls in outside circle. Both hands on hips.

Part 4: Meas. 1–2: All take four step-draws, boy stepping left and girl right. Stamp on the fourth step. (Swing the leading foot in a sharp arc each time, rather than just stepping to the side. On the fourth, or stamping, step, the *free* foot should swing sharply in front of the other.)

Meas. 3–4: Repeat the four step-draws back to place, leading with the *other* foot.

Meas. 5–8: Repeat PART 4.

Meas. 9–16: Chorus: Repeat the 16 step-hops around the circle.

Part 5: Meas. 1–2: In open (original) position, all take one schottische forward, beginning with outside foot, and one back.

Meas. 3–4: Brush the outside foot twice from front to back and tap that toe behind, three times.

Meas. 5–8: Repeat PART 5.

Meas. 9–16: Chorus: Repeat the 16 step-hops around the circle.

Traditionally, at the last step-hop, the boy lifts his partner high off the floor—if he can!

HIGHLAND SCHOTTISCHE (*Scotland*)

Records: RCA Victor, LPM 1621 (33⅓ RPM), 41-6179 (45 RPM), 45-6179 (78 RPM).

Unlike most of the Scottish folk dances, which are group activities, the popular Schottische is intended for couple dancing. Of the several versions, this is one of the easier ones.

Opening Formation: Double circle of couples side-by-side, *in ballroom position,* facing counterclockwise, girl to right of man.

Part 1: Meas. 1: All hop on inside foot—boy's right, girl's left—(pointing outside toe forward and to the side).

Hop again on inside foot (bringing outside toe behind other ankle).

Hop again on inside foot (again pointing outside toe forward).

Hop once more on inside foot (bringing outside toe in *front* of other ankle).

Meas. 2: Beginning with the *outside* foot, take a schottische step forward: step, step, step, hop (for the boy: left, right, left, left).

At the end of the schottische step, couples turn to face opposite direction.

Meas. 3–4: Repeat the four hops (this time on the new *inside* foot), the schottische step (beginning with the new *outside* foot), and turn.

Meas. 5–8: Repeat all PART 1, *i.e.,* two complete sequences.

Part 2: Meas. 1–8: Facing original direction (counterclockwise), couples dance around the circle with step-hops or quick polka steps. (Step-hop by stepping, then hopping on the same foot.)

Note: Couples may prefer to do PART 1 in open position: girl on boy's right with her left hand on his right shoulder, his right arm around her waist. In changing directions from open position, partners separate, turn, then rejoin hands.

PART 1 may also be done with partners facing, one hand high in the air, the other on the hip. In this case, dance PART 2 holding right, then left hands, rather than in ballroom position.

To make the dance a "mixer," you may prefer a "grand right and left" in PART 2: boys moving counterclockwise and girls clockwise, passing each other with right and left-hand holds.

ALL-PURPOSE POLKA (*International*)

Records: RCA Victor, LPM 1619 (33⅓ RPM), EPA 4128 (45 RPM).

The polka is truly an international dance step. Basically a "two-step," it changes style in each country, acquiring a variety of different characteristics. In Scotland it is called a "skip-change-step." The Polish people do it with very light hops and running steps. The Germans do it as a heavy two-step, the Slavs do it without any hops at all and the Norwegians do not even use a polka step of any kind in the dance they call *Norwegian Polka.* This music captures the quality of almost any polka style. Here are some of the dances that can be done to it:

Scandinavian or Norwegian Polka: Couples start side by side, lady to right of man, holding inside hands. Man starting on left, lady on right foot, walk 3 steps forward and kick inside foot forward. Change hands, turn inwards and face opposite direction. Man now starts on right, lady on left (the foot that was just swung). Take 3 steps forward in other direction and kick the inside foot forward. Change hands, turn inwards and face original direction (counterclockwise). Walk forward 3 steps, man starting on left, lady on right, and DO NOT KICK. Instead, take the 4th step towards partner, assuming ballroom position, and finish the dance with a 4-step pivot. Repeat dance from beginning. This is an easy version, often used as an intermission dance by American folk dance groups. It is extremely popular and not as strenuous as other forms of the polka.

Polish Polka: Couples in ballroom position do a very light running step— 1, 2, 3; 1, 2, 3—with relaxed knees and a slight pause on count 3. A hop may precede the running step, but it should be like a grace note in music— barely perceptible. Occasionally there may be a stamp at the end of the 8-measure phrase. Couples turn at will in any direction. The Poles do the dance only in ballroom position, but many younger-generation American Slavs and Poles do the dance with other figures, adding a side-by-side position, or a lady-twirling position.

American Heel-and-Toe Polka: Couples in Varsovienne position, lady to right of man. Do a heel-and-toe, both starting on left foot while hopping on right. Take 3 steps, the lady moving over to the man's left in a sidewards movement. Do a heel-and-toe with the right foot while hopping on left. Take 3 steps as lady moves back to original position. Both now move forward with 4 two-steps or a hop-polka step.

GLOW WORM (*America*)

Records: RCA Victor, LPM 1623 (33⅓ RPM), EPA 4139 (45 RPM).

There are many versions of this American dance, the real origin of which is unknown. Jane Farwell, well-known recreation leader, has one she calls the *Maine Mixer,* which is accompanied by singing. This version follows.

Opening Formation: Couples in a double circle, side by side, with ladies to right of men, holding inside hands or crossed hands in front (skater's position).

The Dance: Words: "Everybody goes to town, pick them up and lay them down."

Action: All promenade with a walking step around the circle (8 steps).

Words: "Back away and say adieu."

Action: Drop hands and walk away from partner (4 steps).

Words: "Balance to the right of you."

Action: All step towards new partner on the right, by stepping on the right foot, swinging left foot forward. Then step on left foot, swinging right foot forward. This should bring each dancer directly in front of new partner.

Words: "Do-si-do and watch her smile."

Action: Do a do-si-do with new partner by passing right shoulders. Without turning around, move back-to-back and return to place, passing left shoulders. (8 walking steps.)

Words: "Step right up and swing awhile."

Action: Face partner again and swing for the remainder of the phrase (8 counts).

Repeat dance from beginning.

Another version of this dance:

Opening Formation: Double circle of dancers, ladies stand to right of men, inside hands joined, free hand on skirt for lady or on hip for man.

Part 1: Man starts on left foot, lady on right. Walk forward 3 steps and point inside toe. Start on inside foot, walk forward 3 steps and point outside toe.

Part 2: Grapevine step for man: Step on left foot to left. Step on right foot behind left. Step to left on left foot and swing right foot forward.

Grapevine step for lady: Step to right on right foot. Step on left foot behind right. Step to right on right foot and swing left foot forward.

Face partner, join both hands and do the above grapevine step, first to the man's left, lady's right as described; then in the opposite direction, starting on the foot you have just swung.

Part 3: Partners now exchange places, man's right hand holding lady's left hand, with 3 walking steps; point toe on 4th count. Lady may do a twirl under joined hands in cross-over. Now cross back into original places in the same manner with 3 steps, and point.

Part 4: Take ballroom position and do four "two-steps" around the circle.

Variation: Swing in place for 8 counts.

This record will fit many other forms of the dance.

LA RASPA (*Mexico*)

Records: RCA Victor, LPM 1623 (33⅓ RPM), EPA 4139 (45 RPM).

La Raspa is a novelty dance, rather than one of Mexico's traditional dances. In the United States it is quite often called the *Mexican Hat Dance,* which is confusing for there is a traditional dance by that name that is quite different from *La Raspa.* Other names for *La Raspa* include *Shuffle Dance, Scissors Dance* and *The File.* Note that the step is known as the "bleking" step in folk dance circles and is similar to that found in the Danish *Ace of*

Diamonds, Swedish *Bleking,* Lithuanian *Noriu Miego* and German *Herr Schmidt.*

Opening Formation: Couples scattered around the room, partners facing each other.

Chorus: Hold two hands. Spring on left foot and send right foot forward, heel down, toe up. Spring on right foot and send left foot forward, heel down, toe up. Spring on left foot and send right foot forward, heel down, toe up. Pause.

Repeat above but start on right foot. Repeat again starting on left foot. Repeat again starting on right foot.

Figure: Variation 1: Clap hands once, hook right elbows with partner and skip around 8 steps. Clap hands again, hook left elbows and skip around 8 steps. Repeat all of this.

Repeat the whole dance from beginning.

Variation 2: Skip 16 steps, linking right elbows, and 16, linking left elbows. Do not repeat.

Variation 3: Take ballroom position and do a polka around the ring for 16 polka steps.

Variation 4: Face partner (all should be in a single-circle formation for this version) and do a grand right-and-left around the circle; then repeat the chorus with a new partner.

Variation 5: Instead of a two-hand hold for the CHORUS, all face center or partner and do the "bleking" or "raspa" step. On each pause, clap own hands twice.

Variation 6: For sessions with boys only: during the CHORUS, boys may do the "raspa" step, gradually going down into a crouching position, holding on to two hands for support.

VIRGINIA REEL (*America*)

Records: RCA Victor, LPM 1623 (33⅓ RPM), 41-6180 (45 RPM), 45-6180 (78 RPM).

Probably the most popular of the "contra" or "longway" dances, the Virginia Reel is most often done in "family style," with all participants active throughout. It is done to many tunes; this recording uses a medley of familiar tunes to encourage group singing in PART 3.

Opening Formation: A "longways" set of six couples—two parallel, facing lines, "ladies" on the left and "gents" on the right (from the head couple).

Part 1: "Forward and back"—both lines take 4 steps to center, bow (or curtsy) to partner and 4 steps back to place.

"Right hand around"—partners meet, join right hands, swing once around, clockwise, and return to place.

"Left hand around"—repeat, using *left* hand and swinging *counter*-clockwise.

"Both hands around"—repeat, using both hands and turning clockwise.

"Do-si-do"—lines walk forward, pass partners by the right shoulder, slide back-to-back and return to place, passing left shoulders.

Part 2: "Head couple down and back"—head couple joins both hands and "sashays" down the set and back to head position. ("Sashay" with quick—but smooth—sliding side-steps.)

"Reel the set"—head couple hooks right elbows, turns once and a half around, then separates and goes to opposite line. Head gent turns second lady once around with a left elbow turn, as head *lady* does the same with the second *gent.*

Head couple meets in center for a *right* elbow turn and continues to the *third* lady and gent for a left elbow turn.

Head couple continues down the set in this fashion—left elbow turns to the set, right elbow turns in the center—until it has "reeled" the entire set.

At the foot of the set, head couple swings half-way around so that gent and lady are on correct side, joins hands, and "sashays" back to places.

Part 3: "Cast off to the foot"—at the change of music, head couple leads to the outside (gent to his left, lady to her right) and, followed by the lines, marches to the foot of the set.

"Form the arch"—upon reaching the foot of the set, head couple joins hands to form an arch. The others, now led by the *second* couple, join hands and "sashay" through the arch. Second couple leads to the head of the set where it now stands as *head* couple for the next figure.

When all couples have gone through the arch, head couple drops hands and steps back to become the *foot* couple.

In this manner, after six changes, each couple will have had its turn as head couple.

Note: Playing this record through once will provide music for three changes. Replaying the record will complete the Reel for all six couples.

✂ COMIN' ROUND THE MOUNTAIN*

Record: "Comin' Round the Mountain", MacGregor #004-4A.

Figure:

Oh, the head couples ladies chain, side couples swing: Couples #1 and #3 are the head couples. Couples #2 and #4 are the side couples. #1 and #3 ladies cross to the opposite side of the set touching right hands as they pass, extending left hand to opposite gentleman. The gentleman turn the ladies half around (CCW) and send them back across the set, the ladies touching right hands as they cross over extending left hands to their partner's. The gentlemen turn them half around (CCW) into place. While the head couples are executing the ladies chain the two side couples are swinging.

Now the side couple's ladies chain, head couples swing chain them round the

---

*Dances pp. 319 to 322 taken from the MacGregor instruction sheets by permission of the company. Instruction sheets accompany the purchase of all records from the company.

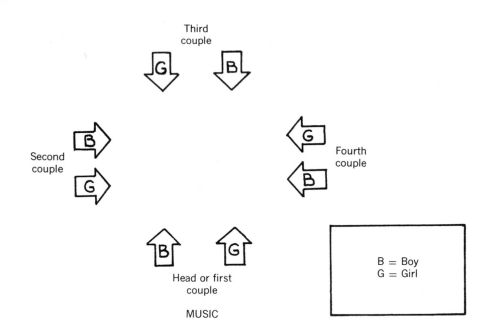

Third
couple

Second
couple

Fourth
couple

Head or first
couple

MUSIC

B = Boy
G = Girl

mountain, chain them home: Side couples repeat the ladies chain while the head couples swing as explained above.

Allemande left to your corner, right hand your own: Gents face left hand lady, extend left hand to her left hand walk around her (CCW) give partner right hand as you pass by.

Swing the next lady on your right, swing her high, swing her low: Swing the next lady beyond your partner.

Promenade the mountain, promenade: Promenade the lady you have just swung back to gent's home position.

Repeat the figure three times until the gentlemen get their own partners back.

Note: Left hand lady is also referred to as corner lady. The lady across the hall is your opposite lady.

HOT TIME IN THE OLD TOWN TONIGHT

Record: "Hot Time In The Old Town Tonight", MacGregor #004-B.
Figure:
First couple out and circle four hands round: #1 couple walks to #2 couple, they join hands and circle to the left once around.

Pick up two and circle six hands round: #1 gent drops #2 lady's hand and joins with #3 lady. #2 lady joins hands with #3 gent and they circle to the left, once around.

Pick up two and circle eight hands round: Couples let go of hands. Gents face their left hand ladies, extend their left hand to the lady's left hand. They walk past them, turn, face them again and balance (left foot on floor, right foot up) walking CCW around the ring, passing their partners.

Allemande right with the lady on your right: Gents face their right hand ladies, extend their right hand to the lady's right hand, they walk past them, turn, face them again and balance, gents walking CW passing partner again and repeat the Allemande left with the lady on the left.

A Grand old right and left around the ring: Gents give partner right hands, the next lady left hand, alternating around the ring until he meets his own partner.

Meet your little honey with a do-sa-do: Gents pass partner's right shoulders back to back and face them.

Take her in your arms and around and around you go: Gents swing partners with a waist type swing.

Promenade with the sweetest gal in town: Gents cross hands with partners and promenade back to home position. Repeat with #2, #3 and #4 couples.

POP GOES THE WEASEL

Record: "Pop Goes The Weasel", MacGregor #004-3B

Figure:

The first lady leads to the right and don't you dare to blunder you circle three hands 'round and 'round and pop the lady under: The #1 lady walks to #2 couple and joins hands and circles to the left. At the call, "Pop The Lady Under", #2 couple passes #1 lady between them under their upraised arms to couple #3.

Lead to the next, the gentlemen bow and don't you dare to blunder you circle three hands 'round and 'round and pop them all the way under: #1 lady joins hands with couple #3, #1 gent joins hands with couple #2, and they form two circles of three, circling to the left, At the call, "Pop Them All The Way Under", the #2 and #3 couples pass them under their arched arms and they meet and swing once around in the center of the set.

Lead to the next, the gentlemen bow and don't you dare to blunder: #1 lady joins hands with couple #4. #1 gent joins hands with couple #3. They circle to the left and repeat the same as in above paragraph.

The lady come back, the gent come on and don't you dare to blunder circle four hands 'round and 'round and pop them all the way under: #1 couple joins hands with couple #4 and circles once around to the left. #4 couple passes #1 couple thru the arch and back to #1 couple's home position.

Repeat the figure with #2, #3, and #4 couples.

Note: The working couple must remember to swing in the center of the set (once around) each time, after passing thru the arch, before going on to the next couples.

The word "Bow" means to follow up in this dance.

OH, JOHNNY

Record: "Oh, Johnny, MacGregor #007-3B
Figure:
All join hands and circle the ring: Couples join hands and circle to the right.
Stop where you are and give her a swing: The gents swing their partners once and a half around. (Using waist swing.)
Swing that little gal behind you: The gents swing their left hand or corner lady.
Swing your own if you have found that she's not flown: Gents swing their own partners again.
Allemande left with the corner gal: The gents execute the allemande left.
Do-sa-do your own: The gents walk around their partners, passing right shoulders back to back.
Now you all promenade with that sweet corner maid singing Oh, Johnny, Oh, Johnny, Oh: The gents promenade their left hand or corner ladies around the ring. The gents now have a new partner and figure can be continued as often as desired.
Note: This dance is a wonderful mixer and can also be a great deal of fun danced in a large circle around the entire hall.

OH, SUSANNA

Record: "Oh, Susanna", MacGregor #007 4-B
Figure:
Oh, the first couple lead out to the right, change partners there and swing: No. 1 couple walks to couple #2, they change partners and swing about once and a half around.
Take that lady on to the next and do it once again: No. 1 gents takes #2 lady and walks to couple #3. They change partners and sing again about once and a half around.
Take that lady on to the next and do it once again: No. 1 gent takes #3 lady and walks to couple #4. They change partners and swing once again.
Take that gal and home you go and everybody swing: No. 1 gent takes #4 lady to his original or home position and all four couples swing with their new or temporary partners.
Honors to your partners: The gents bow to their partners, the ladies curtsey.
To your corners all: The gents bow to their left hand or corner ladies, the ladies curtsey.
Swing around with the corner gal and promenade the hall: The gents swing their corner ladies and promenade around the set back to the gents' original home position. No. 2, No. 3, and No. 4 couples now take turns leading the figure.

TINIKILING (*Bamboo Hop Dance*)

Records:

Tinikiling—RCA Victor LPM 1619 (33⅓ RPM) or RCA Victor EPA 4126 (45 RPM)

Carinosa—RCA Victor LPM 1619 (33⅓ RPM) or RCA Victor EPA 4126 (45 RPM)

Neapolitan Tarantella—RCA Victor LPM 1619 (33⅓ RPM) or RCA Victor EPA 4126 (45 RPM)

Czardas-Vengerka—RCA Victor LPM 1619 (33⅓ RPM) or RCA Victor EPA 4126 (45 RPM)

No Matter What the Shape—Liberty 55836 (45 RPM)

Alley Cat—ATCO 45-6226 (45 RPM)

Equipment Necessary: Records, Record Player, 2 Bamboo Poles for every four children (9–10 feet x 1–1½ inches).

Source of Poles: Charles H. Demarest, 215 Water St., New York, New York 10038

General Information: This dance was developed as an imitation of the Tikling bird, a long legged, long necked fowl. This rhythmical activity is a simplification of a difficult Philippine folk game.

Procedures: Manipulating the Poles. The children work in groups of 4. Two children manipulate the poles while the other two children dance. In manipulating the poles the children kneel, one at each end of the two 10 foot poles. The poles are lined up parallel on the floor two feet apart. The pole manipulators work the poles to the three count rhythm of the music; first, two beats (hit against the floor) and then one beat (hit sticks together in the air). The pole manipulators continue this regular rhythm, DOWN, DOWN, TOGETHER through the dance.

BASIC TINIKILING STEP

The dancers perform the following step with the regular 3 count rhythm, hopping in and out of the poles. The children should allow the music to start and the poles to start beating before they begin dancing. Most of the beginning Tinikiling records have an introduction. The dancers begin by standing on the right of the poles with their left side near the poles. On the third beat of any measure of music, prepare to dance. The dancer begins on the first beat of the measure, immediately after the third beat of the previous measure (third beat is when the poles hit together in the air).

Starting position

Measure 1

Beat 1: Poles hit the floor two feet apart. Step between the poles with the left foot.

Beat 2: Poles hit the floor again. Shift the weight from the left foot to the right foot, between the poles, lifting the left foot off the floor.

Beat 3: Poles hit together in the air. Step out on the opposite side of the poles placing the weight on the left foot.

Measure 2

Beat 1: Poles hit the floor. Step between the poles with the right foot.

Beat 2: Poles hit the floor again. Shift the weight from the right foot to the left foot (between poles), lifting the right foot off the floor.

Beat 3: Poles hit together in the air. Step out on the opposite side (beginning position) of the poles placing the weight on the right foot.

Continue to perform the same step.

Caution: Be ready to step back immediately after stepping out side the poles on beat three. The foot must step in again on beat one of the next measure.

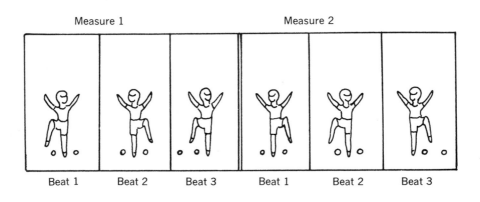

Measure 1			Measure 2		
Beat 1	Beat 2	Beat 3	Beat 1	Beat 2	Beat 3

The music is the same as for the basic step. The pole manipulation is the same also.

Measure 1

Beat 1: Stand straddling the poles. On the first beat, jump between the poles with both feet touching the floor.

Beat 2: Hop up in the air, landing again between the poles on both feet.

Beat 3: Hop in the air again straddling the legs so that the performer lands outside the poles with one leg on either side of the poles.

Repeat!

Measure 1

| Starting position | Beat 1 | Beat 2 | Beat 3 |

TURN STEP

Measure 1

Beat 1: Step between the poles with the left foot as in the basic step.

Beat 2: Hop in the air, doing a ½ turn, landing again on the left foot.

Beat 3: Step out from between the poles on the right foot (on opposite side of the poles).

Measure 2

Beat 1: Step between the poles with the left foot.

Beat 2: Hop in the air, doing a ½ turn, land again on the left foot.

Beat 3: Step out from between the poles on the right foot (beginning position).

Repeat!

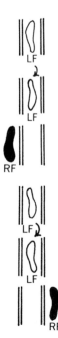

Measure 1 Measure 2

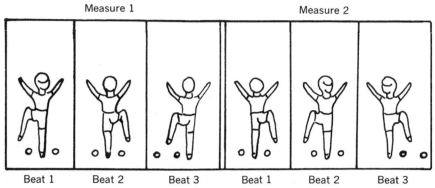

Beat 1 Beat 2 Beat 3 Beat 1 Beat 2 Beat 3

CROSS OVER STEP

Measure 1

Beat 1: Step in with the left foot as in the basic step.

Beat 2: Hop on the left foot landing again on the left foot, between the poles.

Beat 3: Step across in front of the left foot, stepping outside the poles on the far side with the right foot.

Measure 2

Beat 1: Step in with the left foot.

Beat 2: Shift the weight to the right foot lifting the left foot off the floor.

Beat 3: Step across in front of the right foot, stepping outside the poles with the left foot.

Measure 3

Beat 1: Step in with the right foot.

Beat 2: Shift the weight from the right to the left foot.

Beat 3: Step over the left foot with the right, stepping outside the poles with the right foot.

Measure 4

    Beat 1: Repeat measure 2.

Continue to perform as in Measures 2 and 3.

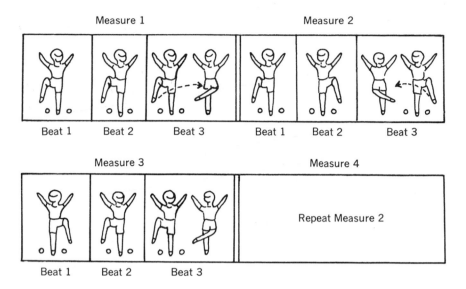

Measure 1			Measure 2		
Beat 1	Beat 2	Beat 3	Beat 1	Beat 2	Beat 3

Measure 3			Measure 4
Beat 1	Beat 2	Beat 3	Repeat Measure 2

POLES VARIATIONS

    Single File: Have several pairs of poles lined up next to each other. The children perform the basic step progressing from one set of poles to the next.

    Proceed from one end of the single file row of poles to the other.

    Doubles: Perform as in single file, except the dancer goes down one row and back the other.

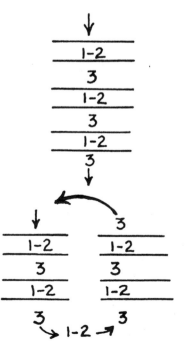

Cris Cross Variation 1: Dance the basic step around the outside rim of the crossed poles. Dance in a circle.

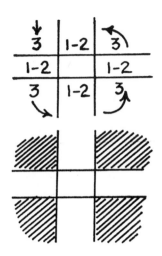

Cris Cross Variation 2: One dancer may dance any pattern between the crossed poles. Beats 1 and 2 may be danced in any of the non shaded areas. Beat 3 must be danced in one of the shaded areas.

References

On the following pages of this text is a list of the companies dealing almost entirely with the sales of educational records. Most of these companies include written teaching instructions with their rhythms and dance records. Such instruction sheets are excellent aids for teachers interested in discovering new rhythmical activities. Most companies supply these instruction sheets free of charge with the purchase of records.

Latchaw and Pyatt: *A Pocket Guide of Dance Activities,* Englewood Cliffs, N.J., Prentice-Hall Inc., 1958.

Andrews: *Creative Rhythmic Movement for Children,* Englewood Cliffs, N.J., Prentice-Hall Inc., 1954.

Hall, T.: *Dance,* Belmont, Calif., Wadsworth, 1963.

Stuart and Gibson: *Rhythmical Activities,* Minneapolis, Burgess.

ADDITIONAL OUTSTANDING RHYTHMICAL ACTIVITIES AVAILABLE ON ALBUMS PREVIOUSLY LISTED IN THIS CHAPTER

RCA Album 1623—All Purpose Folk Dances
- The Irish Washerwomen
- Chestnut Tree
- Cherkassiya
- Oh Susanna
- Pop Goes the Weasel
- Hora

RCA Album 1621—Festival Folk Dances
- Ribbon Dance
- La Cucaracha

Sailor's Hornpipe
Sellenger's Round
Gatherin Peascods
Maypole Dance
Highland Fling
Minuet
Cotten Eyed Joe
Sicilian Tarantella
Sudmalinas

RCA Album 1619—Special Folk Dances
Carinosa

Dashing White Sergeant
Neopolitan Tarantella
Krakowiak
Czardas-Vengerka
Tivoli Hambo
El Jarabe Tapatico
Mexican Mixer
Bavarian Länder
Kiigidi Kaagadi

MacGregor Album 7—Square Dances
Darling Nellie Gray
El Rancho Grande
Wabash Cannon Ball
Jingle Bells
Spanish Cavalier
Solomon Levi

RCA Album 1625—First Folk Dances
How Do You Do My Partner
I See You
Bridge of Avignon
Nigarepolska

Jump Jim Jo
Gay Musicians
Carrousel
Round and Round the Village

RCA Album 1622—Folk Dances for All Ages
Brummel Schottische
Tra la la Ja Saa
Lott' Ist Tod
Shiboleth Basadeh
Joy for Two
Gustaf's Skoal
French Reel
Moskrosser

MacGregor Album 4—Square Dance
Old Pine Tree
Parle Vous
Pistol Packin Mama
Marchin Through Georgia
Indian Style

ADDRESSES OF RECORD COMPANIES

Bomar Records
10515 Burbank Blvd.
North Hollywood, Calif. 91601

Children's Music Center Inc.
5373 W. Pico Blvd.
Los Angeles, California 90019

Educational Activities Inc.
P.O. Box 392
Freeport, New York 11520

Educational Record Sales
157 Chambers St.
New York, New York

Hoctor Dance Records Inc.
Waldwick, New Jersey 07463

Kimbo Records
Box 55
Deal, New Jersey 07723

Loshin's
215 E. 8th Street
Cincinnati, Ohio 45202

MacGregor Records Available from:
Children's Music Center Inc.
5373 W. Pico Blvd.
Los Angeles, California 90019

Michael Herman Folk Dance House
108 West 16th Street
New York, New York 10011

RCA Victor Educational Sales
155 E. 24th St.
New York, N.Y. 10010

20

Evaluation

Evaluation is a continuing process. Like the good teaching process, of which it is a part, evaluation is a never ending process which is essential if children are to become physically educated as a result of programs established for this purpose.

Evaluation is important as an early step in planning a sound program of physical education in that student needs and interests are fundamental considerations in building such a program. Continuing evaluation is, then, important because it is through constant evaluation that the teacher determines if the child is progressing toward the predetermined outcomes of the physical education program. The ongoing evaluation process provides a yardstick for both teacher and student in determining whether the child is becoming physically educated.

What is Evaluation?

Evaluation is more than measurement. While measurement is the quantitative assessment of what is, evaluation is the qualitative assessment or judgment of what is. Measurements precede evaluation. A teacher may measure the distance of a broad jump without evaluating the quality of the jump. It is only when the teacher labels or judges the jump as "excellent", "poor", etc, that an evaluation is made. Raw measurements are frequently meaningless in assessing student performance. For this reason the teacher must have some basis for judging a measurement. How do you know what is good? What performance merits an A? Evaluation provides the answer, but only when judgments are based on information pertinent to the evaluation being made.

OBJECTIVITY VS. SUBJECTIVITY

Objectivity refers to measurements or evaluations which are made with as little references as possible to personal prejudices or bias. Thus measurements and evaluation should be as objective as possible. However, since evaluations are judgments, they are more likely to be subjective than measurements. Evaluation can in some instances be quite objective. By the same token some measurements are quite subjective.

Example of subjective measurements would be measuring height with a rubber band or measuring softball throwing distance by stepping off the distance. Assigning a grade of A for a measured score of 92 (between 90 and 100) is an example of an objective evaluation.

It should be every teachers goal to be as objective as possible in evaluating students. Since all evaluation is based on measurement, it is also essential that measurements be objective.

One way of increasing objectivity is through *standardizing* measurements and evaluations. Standardization refers to any technique used to make measurement evaluation more consistant. That is, developing procedures of measuring and evaluating which require all persons being measured to perform in a like manner and which require repetitions of measurements and evaluations to be given in a like manner. An example of standardization of measurement would be as follows: In measuring standing broad jump ability all individuals being tested must jump with their toes behind a given line, must wear rubber sole shoes, must always be tested on the same type floor surface, must be measured from the closest point to the jumping line and must be allowed three attempts at jumping. If all of the above conditions are met in measuring standing broad jump performance, the chances of similar measurements from test to test and from student to student are improved.

THE PURPOSES OF EVALUATION

Why evaluate? Before selecting measurements and determining standards for evaluation it is most important that the teacher understand the purposes of measuring and evaluating students. The following is a list of the basic reasons for measuring and evaluating in elementary school physical education:

1. To determine the needs and interests of specific children and groups of children.
2. To determine whether the program objectives have been met. (Did students accomplish what you hoped they would accomplish?)
   a. To help students determine progress toward program objectives.
   b. To help the teacher determine student progress toward program objectives.
3. To determine areas of need for program change.

If these three basic purposes have been accomplished the program of evaluation has been successful.

DETERMINING STUDENT NEEDS AND INTERESTS

As previously mentioned, evaluation is and should be the first step in the "Good Teaching Process". It is in using evaluation as the first step of the process that student needs and interests are determined. For the purposes of this text the general objective of physical education have been defined as: physical fitness, social emotional objective, skill objective, weight control objective, cognitive-affective objective and the carry over objective. In determining student needs it is important that the teacher limit evaluation to needs and interests within the realm of these objectives. If this were not done, unlimited time could be wasted in programs of evaluation. The question then becomes what do children need within these six objectives? Do they need strength as a part of physical fitness? The only way to find out is to measure and evaluate students in each of the six areas.

DETERMINING THE NEED FOR PHYSICAL FITNESS

The teacher can choose several methods of evaluating the needs of students in the area of physical fitness. He can choose a national test battery such as the AAHPER test or the Kraus Weber test. However, a teacher may decide to select a test of his own construction.

1. *The AAHPER Test.* (see appendix F for test and instructions). This test is a total test of motor fitness. The test is the only test with nationally standardized norms. The test norms have been revised as recently as 1965 and include tests designed to test agility (shuttle run), power (softball throw, 50 yard run, soft ball throw), strength, and muscular endurance (sit-ups and chin-ups) and endurance (600 yard run walk). One of the main advantages of the test is that it measures many aspects of fitness. The major drawback is the large amount of time necessary for test administration. Since the test was developed in the late 1950's, several states have developed state wide fitness testing programs using the AAHPER test.

2. *The Kraus-Weber Test.* (see appendix A for administration and scoring). This test of minimum muscular strength and flexibility is a collection of 6 test items selected from a test battery originally designed as a diagnostic test for persons with potential low back problems. It has since been used to measure the fitness of the youth of many countries. Since the test only measures *minimal* muscular strength and flexibility, its primary values would be as a *screening* test at the lower elementary school levels. Children failing this minimal test would be in need of special programs of fitness development prior to their inclusion in the regular program of physical education. The test items are not neces-

sarily good items to be used to develop strength and flexibility in children.

3. *Self-Constructed Physical Fitness Tests.* A wealth of test items are available to measure the physical fitness of elementary school children. Of greatest importance in constructing a test is that the test measure: (*a*) all aspects of fitness and (*b*) fitness of all body parts. Table 20-1 includes a list of several test items, not included in the above tests. These items as well as those used in standardized tests may be used in constructing test batteries.

TABLE 20-1. Tests of Physical Fitness

Item Name	Purpose	Description	Illustration
Medicine Ball Put	*Fitness Aspect:* Explosive strength *Body Part:* Upper arms & shoulders	Place the foot of the same side of the throwing hand, in an 18-inch circle. With one hand, put (push) the ball as far as possible. The feet must not move. Measure the distance of the put.	
Lower the Legs	*Fitness Aspect:* Strength *Body Part:* Abdominal	Lie supine on the floor. Lift the legs to a 90° angle. Slowly lower the legs until the lower back arches off the floor. Measure the angle formed by the legs and the floor. The smaller the angle the better the score.	
Back Hyper-extension	*Fitness Aspect:* Strength & flexibility *Body part:* Legs	Lie prone on the floor with the hands behind the head. A partner holds the legs above the knee. Lift the chin and the chest off the floor as high as possible. Measure the height of the chin from the floor.	
Vertical Jump	*Fitness Aspect:* Explosive strength *Body Part:* Legs	A tape measure is taped to the wall. Students stand with the side to the wall. Squat, then jump into the air. Touch the wall at the height of the jump. Determine the height of the jump subtracting the standing reaching height.	

TABLE 20-1. Tests of Physical Fitness (Continued)

Item Name	Purpose	Description	Illustration
Leg Hyper-extension	*Fitness Aspect:* Strength & flexibility *Body Part:* Legs & Back	Lie prone on the floor. A partner holds the back below the shoulder blades lift the legs off the floor as high as possible. The score is the number of seconds the feet are held off the floor.	Measures
20 Second Beam Stand	*Fitness Aspect:* Balance *Body Part:* Total	Stand on a ¾-inch board supported with a 24-inch base. Hold the balance on one foot for 20 seconds. Pass or Fail.	
Bench Step	*Fitness Aspect:* Cardiorespiratory Endurance *Body Part:* Total	Step up and down on a 15-inch bench. Right foot up, left foot up, right foot down, and left foot down. Repeat once every 2 seconds for 2 minutes. Take the pulse for 30 seconds beginning 1 minute after exercise. The lower the heart rate, the better the score.	1 2 3 4

DETERMINING THE NEED FOR SKILL DEVELOPMENT

Before the teacher can determine what skills should be taught to a specific group of children, he must determine what they are currently capable of performing. As with physical fitness, the teacher may choose to administer a standardized test battery or administer a test of his own construction.

1. *The Iowa Brace Test.* (see appendix B). This test was first developed as the Brace test of general motor educability. Later revised at the University of Iowa, the Iowa Brace test is used to measure the general "skill I.Q." of children. The test is to be used for children from 4th to 12th grades. Practice effects students performance and should not be allowed. Results of the test would give general information

concerning the skill ability of a group of children and the skill needs of these children.

2. *Self-Constructed Skills Test Items.* (see Table 20-2). Many types of test items have been developed for use in testing motor skills. Table 20-2 includes four general types of tests which can be used to assess motor skill. Any motor skill may be evaluated using one or more of these tests. Self-constructed skill tests might include a combination of several of these types of tests.

DETERMINING NEEDS FOR CONTROLLING WEIGHT

Several methods are frequently used in determining the needs of specific students in controlling weight. Any or all of these techniques may be used by the elementary physical education teacher in cooperation with the school nurse and physician.

1. *The Meredith Height Weight Charts* (see appendix C and D). The height-weight chart is useful because it is the simplest and most readily accessible measure for use by the teacher. The only measurements necessary are the height, weight and age of the child. Although there is evidence that the height-weight chart has weaknesses in determining desirable weights of children, the teacher can get some general indication of the overweightness of children with the charts. The Meredith charts are particularly simple to use in that the teacher merely plots the height and weight of the child on the chart in the proper age column. Normally children fall in similar weight and height zones (tall-heavy, average-average, short-light). However, when a child falls in unlike zones (average height-heavy weight) this may indicate an overweight condition.

2. *Wetzel Grid* (see appendix E). The Wetzel Grid is another method of understanding the growth, development and physique of children. The Wetzel Grid goes one step beyond the height-weight table in that it provides a longitudinal picture of the childs height and weight development which reflects deviations from normal which may occur during the school years.

DETERMINING THE SOCIAL-EMOTIONAL NEEDS OF CHILDREN

Since the teacher is specifically concerned with those social and emotional needs which related to children in physical education classes, specific checklists can be used to determine student needs in these areas. Such a checklist is included in the following section of this book (Table 20-3). However, this or any other checklist would have to be modified for the age and grade levels of the student being evaluated.

TABLE 20-2. Tests of Skill

Test Item & Purpose	Description	Illustration
DISTANCE TEST ITEMS To determine skill in throwing, kicking or striking where performance involves a need for projecting an object a long distance.	The performer throws, kicks or strikes an object (basketball, softball, soccer ball, etc.) attempting to propel it a great distance. The score equals the distance the object travels from the line. Test skills which are being developed in class.	Distance equals score
ACCURACY TEST ITEMS To determine skill in throwing, kicking or striking when performance involves accuracy in hitting a target or goal, (passing a football, etc.)	The performer throws, kicks or strikes an object (softball, rubber ball, etc.) at a target. The target might be several circles drawn on the wall, a goal (basketball or soccer) or some other mark. Score successful hits on target.	
TIME TEST ITEMS To determine the length of time required to perform a specific skill.	The student attempts to perform a specific skill task in the shortest possible time. The score is the time required to perform the skill. Example: Dribble a basketball around a marker and back to the starting line.	
SPECIFIC TASK TESTS To determine whether children can perform specific skill tasks (catch a ball, skip, hop, etc.)	The student is asked to perform a specific skill. A score is assigned as follows: 0 points for failure to perform the task, 1 point for a crude but non failing performance, and 2 points for proper performance of the skill. Several specific skill tasks may be combined to make up a test.	Zero points for a missed attempt One point for a success (crude) Two points for a proper jump Example: jump the bar

TABLE 20-3. Checklist of Social-Emotional Needs

Evaluating Social Emotional Needs of Children in Physical Education — Students's Name	Group Cooperation			Participation			Social Attitude			Responsibility		
	Accepts Decisions	Gets along in Group	Follows Rules	Shows Interest	Never Wastes Time	Never Quits	Shares Equipment	Takes Proper Turn	Adapts to Limitations of Self and Others	Controls Temper	Helps Enforce Rules	Follows Moral Rule as Well as Game Rule
				+ = Attainment of expected level								
				0 = Progress toward expected level								
				− = Needs help								

DETERMINING NEEDS FOR KNOWLEDGE AND UNDERSTANDING

As in any other subject matter in the curriculum, it is desirable to determine the amount of knowledge and understanding a child has prior to this entry into a specific program. Written or oral examinations may be used for this purpose. Such tests are usually teacher constructed. It is beyond the scope of this text to cover material concerning cognitive test construction, but the methods for written test construction used in other subject matter areas are identical to those used to determine needs of elementary school children in the areas of knowledge and understanding.

EVALUATING THE ACCOMPLISHMENT OF OBJECTIVES

Perhaps the most important phase of evaluation is determining whether the children accomplished what the program was supposed to help them accomplish. This is the key to the future improvement of the program.

Since the general purpose of physical education is to produce or contribute to the development of the "Fully Functioning Healthy Individual", evaluation is done to see if students are progressing toward this end. This can be more specifically evaluated by determining whether students have met the specific objectives as outlined prior to the beginning of the program.

The specific objective within each of the six major objectives must be evaluated if the teacher is to determine if students truely have accomplished what they should accomplish. Thus, if the teacher has ten objectives for fourth graders, all classified under physical fitness objectives, he must develop a test or test items to see if the ten specific objectives have been accomplished. He may use the tests already discussed or he may develop tests specifically to measure and evaluate the outlined objectives. At any rate he does not need to give lengthy standardized tests each evaluation period, rather the teacher must test the specific objectives which were to be accomplished during that evaluation period. Since different objectives are emphasized during different evaluation periods, it is quite likely that different measurement devices will be used each grading period. An attempt should be made to evaluate *all* of the claimed program objectives during each evaluation period, even if the evaluation is relatively informal.

DETERMINING NEED FOR PROGRAM CHANGE

A special evaluation is not necessary in determining the need for program change. If the teacher has effectively evaluated whether students have accomplished the program objectives, he will have a good basis for determining the need for program change. If the children have *not* met the objectives, it means either the program is ineffective in meeting the outlined objectives, the teachers method of teaching is inadequate, or the evaluation is inaccurate. In any case the teacher is obligated to locate the source of the problem and correct the situation so that future students will better meet the objectives outlined for the program.

EVALUATING THE CARRY OVER OBJECTIVE

The "carry over" objective is one of great importance but also an objective which is very difficult to measure and evaluate. Determining whether children attempt to become fit during leisure time or whether they use the skills of physical education for recreational purposes is a difficult task. Perhaps the only real evaluation of the attainment of this objective would be a result of a longitudinal evaluation in which follow up case studies are made on students completing the program of physical education.

The teacher can, however, determine something about the accomplishment of this objective by observing the behavior of children during play periods and intramural programs. Gross evaluation of the accomplishment of this objective could be made through observing the play habits of the children near their homes and in the parks. Considerably more research needs to be done to identify the best techniques for measuring and evaluating this objective, but difficult as it may be, each teacher must make some attempt to find out if "carry over" is occuring.

REPORTING TO PARENTS (GRADING)

Although the primary purpose of evaluation is to provide information for the student and for the teacher, evaluation is and should be for the parent as well. The parent is concerned with the educational progress of the child and this is as it should be. However, the evaluation report to the parents should be much the same as the evaluation done for the student or the teacher. The parent would want to know to what extent his child has progressed toward the objectives of the physical education program. For the above reason, special evaluations made strictly for reporting or grading are not desirable. Rather parents should receive an accurate report of the evaluation that is done as part of the regular evaluation process.

If the report to the parent is to truly be a report of the evaluation of student accomplishment, a letter grade is not adequate, especially in an area with such diversified objectives as physical education. In reporting student progress in physical education, the most logical alternative is to have a parent-teacher conference during which the results of the evaluation of the accomplishment of each objective is discussed. Since the parents and the teacher are both concerned about the fulfillment of student potential, the teacher would report the progress of the student not only in terms of test score, but also concerning the extent to which this score represents achievement of the child's potential.

In cases where the parent-teacher conference is impossible, a written report may be distributed to the parents. In such a report the objectives of

TABLE 20-4. Physical Education Evaluation Report

Name _Johnny Jones_ Grade _5_

Height _____ Weight _____

PRE-SCHOOL RESULTS

Measurements	Test Score	Evaluation	Comments
Sit Ups	35	average	Johnny shows a need for improvement in physical fitness. He has tremendous potential for physical performance and his fitness level is improving. His attitude is good. His skill is not as good as it could be for his levels of natural ability.
600 Yard Run	2:35	average	
Chins	1	average	
Physical Education Social Evaluation		very good	
Iowa Brace Skills Test	15	very good	
Tricep Skinfold Measure	9	normal fatness	

EVALUATION PERIOD #1

Objective Evaluated	Test Score	Evaluation	Comments
CardioRespiratory Endurance (2 minute-Step Test)	50 heart beats per min. after exercise	very good	John has shown excellent improvement from the beginning of the year. He is working to the fullest of his potential in all areas including his knowledge of games and knowledge of the value of exercise.
Strength (Chins)	3	excellent	
Ball Skills (Skills Test)	25	excellent	
Group Cooperation		excellent	
Responsibility		excellent	
Physical Education Knowledge Test	96	excellent	

EVALUATION PERIOD #2

Objective Evaluated	Test Score	Evaluation	Comments

Robert T. Smith
Robert T. Smith, Instructor

the grading period would be outlined and an evaluation would be made as to the level of accomplishment of the objective (considering student's potential) (Table 20-4).

The teacher could prepare a standard form and fill in the objectives for each particular grading period just prior to reporting to the parents.

SOME GUIDELINES FOR EVALUATION AND REPORTING EVALUATIONS

1. Evaluation need not be done at every grading period in the elementary school. Physical education reports could be sent out at any time after the normal evaluation by the teacher providing the parent receives at least two reports per school year. However, school policy may be the determining factor in frequency of evaluation reports.
2. One problem with evaluation is that it is time consuming and may not contribute to the accomplishment of any specific objectives. For this reason it may be desirable to reduce the precision of some measurement in order to keep evaluation time to a minimum.
3. Many measurements can be speeded up through the use of estimation procedures, as long as these procedures are standard with each test administration.
4. If a letter grade must be assigned, it should be based on the total assessment of whether the student met all the objectives of the program *within his performance potential.*

SUMMARY

The good teacher is one who determines student needs, works to fulfill them, and perhaps most important of all, strives to improve on his ability to accomplish these purposes. Such a program of evaluation will help the teacher in really becoming the "good teacher" and will help the student in becoming the "fully functioning healthy individual."

Appendixes

Kraus-Weber Tests*

Test 1: Abdominal Plus Psoas Muscle Strength.

From a supine-lying position, neck firm, with feet held down by examiner, the testee rolls up into a sitting position.

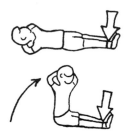

Abdominal plus. PSOAS.

Test 2: Abdominal Muscle Strength Minus Psoas.

From a supine-lying position, neck firm, knees flexed, heels close to buttocks, and feet held down by examiner, the testee rolls up into a sitting position.

Abdominal minus. PSOAS.

Test 3: Psoas and Lower Abdominal Muscle Strength.

From a supine-lying position with neck firm, the testee flexes both hips to raise the heels 10 inches and holds for 10 seconds while the examiner counts.

Psoas and lower abdomen.

Test 4: Upper Back Muscle Strength.

From a prone-lying position, neck firm, with pillow under hips and lower abdomen, and examiner holding the feet down, the testee raises chest, head, and shoulders and holds this raised position for 10 seconds while the examiner counts.

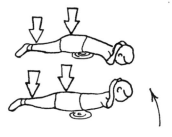

Upper back.

*Kraus, Hans and Hirschland, Ruth P.: Minimum Muscular Fitness in School Children, *Research Quarterly,* 25, 178 (May, 1954).

Test 5: Lower Back Muscle Strength.

From a prone-lying position, arms on table with head resting on them, examiner holding chest down, the testee raises his legs off the table with knees straight for 10 seconds while the examiner counts.

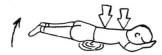

Lower back.

Test 6: Back and Hamstring Muscle Strength.

From an erect standing position without shoes, the testee bends slowly downward to touch the floor with the finger tips, holding contact for 3 seconds. The examiner should hold the knees of testee to prevent or detect any bend. Bouncing is not permitted.

Back and hamstrings.

APPENDIX B
Iowa Brace and Carpenter Skills Tests*

DIRECTIONS

Select the proper stunts for each test and each sex from Table A-1. The Iowa-Brace test consists of ten items for boys and ten items for girls. The Carpenter test consists of six items.

Allow no practice. Demonstrate the item. Score 2 points for an acceptable first try, 1 point for an acceptable second try and 0 for those failing both attempts. On stunts requiring a count, the count should be one thousand one, one thousand two, one thousand three as opposed to 1, 2, 3.

The maximum score is 20 for the Iowa-Brace test and 12 for the Carpenter test. Add the total test score and determine the students rating from Tables A-2 and A-3. Items on the Carpenter test must be given in the listed order.

1. *Hop-backward test.* Stand on either foot. Close eyes, and take five hops backward. Failure: (*a*) to open eyes; (*b*) to touch the floor with foot not supporting the weight of body.

*McCloy, C. H. and Young, N. D.: *Tests and Measurements in Health and Physical Education,* New York, Appleton-Century-Crofts, 1954.

2. *One-knee-balance test.* Right face. Kneel on one knee, with other leg raised from the floor and with arms raised sideward to the level of shoulders. Hold the position for five counts. Failure: (*a*) to touch the floor with any other part of body than one lower leg; (*b*) to fall over.

3. *Half-turn-jump-left-foot test.* Stand on left foot, and jumping, make a one-half turn to the left. Keep the balance. Failure: (*a*) to lose the balance; (*b*) to fail to complete the half turn; (*c*) to touch the floor with right foot.

4. *Forward-hand-kick test.* Jump upward, swinging legs forward. Bend trunk forward, and touch toes with both hands before landing. Keep lower legs in as straight a line as possible with upper legs. Failure: (*a*) not to touch toes with both hands before landing; (*b*) to bend lower legs more than 45 degrees.

5. *Full-left-turn test.* Stand with feet together. Jump upward, making a full turn to the left. Land at approximately the same place from which the test was started. (Feet may be separated when landing.) Do not lose the balance, or move feet after they have touched the floor. Failure: (*a*) not to make a full turn to the left; (*b*) to move feet after they have returned to the floor; (*c*) to lose the balance.

6. *Side-leaning-rest test.* Sit on the floor, with lower legs extended, and feet together. Put right hand on the floor behind body. Turn to the right, and take a side leaning-rest position, resting the body on right hand and right foot. Raise left arm and left leg, and hold this position for five counts. Failure: (*a*) not to take the proper position; (*b*) not to hold the position for five counts.

7. *Grapevine test.* Stand with heels together. Bend trunk forward, extend both arms down between legs and behind ankles, and hold fingers of hands together in front of ankles. Hold this position for 5 seconds. Failure: (*a*) to lose the balance; (*b*) not to hold fingers of both hands together; (*c*) not to hold the position for 5 seconds.

8. *Cross-leg-squat test.* Fold arms across chest. Cross feet and sit down. Get up without unfolding arms and without moving feet about to regain the balance. Failure: (*a*) to unfold arms; (*b*) to lose the balance; (*c*) not to get up.

9. *Kneel-jump-to-feet test.* Kneel on both knees. Rest backs of toes on the floor. Swing arms, and jump to the standing position. Do not rock backward on toes, or lose the balance. Failure: (*a*) to curl toes and to rock backward on them; (*b*) not to execute the jump, and not to stand still after the standing position has been reached.

10. *Russian-dance test.* Squat. Raise one leg forward. Perform a Russian-dance step by extending legs alternately while in a squat position. Perform four such steps, that is, two with each leg. Heel of forward foot may touch the floor. Heel of rear foot should strike hip on that side. Failure: (*a*) to lose the balance; (*b*) not to do the stunt twice with each leg.

11. *Full-right-turn test.* Stand with feet together. Jump upward, making a full turn to the right. Land at approximately the same place from which the test was started. (Feet may be separated when landing.) Do not lose the balance or move feet after they have touched the floor. Failure: (*a*) not to make a full turn to the right; (*b*) to move feet after they have returned to the floor; (*c*) to lose the balance.

12. *Top test.* Sit, with lower legs flexed, on the floor. Put arms between legs, and under and behind knees, and grasp ankles. Roll rapidly around to the right, with the weight first over right knee, then over right shoulder, then on back, then on left shoulder, and then on left knee. Sit up, facing in the opposite direction from which the test was started. Repeat the movements from this position, and finish facing in the same direction from which the test was started. Failure: (*a*) to release hold on ankle; (*b*) not to complete circle.

13. *One-foot-touch-head test.* Stand on left foot. Bend trunk forward, and place both hands on the floor. Raise right leg, and extend it backward. Touch head to the floor, and return to the standing position without losing the balance. Failure: (*a*) not to touch head to the floor; (*b*) to lose the balance.

14. *Double-heel-click test.* Jump upward, clap feet together twice, and land with feet apart (any distance). Failure: (*a*) not to clap feet together twice; (*b*) to land with feet touching each other.

15. *Side Kick test.* Swing left leg sideways to the left, jumping upward with the right leg. Strike feet together in the air, and land with feet apart. Feet should strike together in a line that would go to the left of left shoulder. Failure: (*a*) not to swing leg enough to side; (*b*) not to strike feet together in the air, to the left of the line of the left shoulder; (*c*) not to land with feet apart.

TABLE A-1. Stunt Selections for the Iowa-Brace
and the Carpenter Tests.

I-B Test for Boys	I-B Test for Girls	Carpenter Test
1	1	7
2	11	2
3	5	8
4	12	5
5	4	1
6	13	9
7	7	
8	9	
9	14	
10	15	

TABLE A-2. Iowa-Brace Test Scoring Table

Boys			Girls		
Score	Rating		Score	Rating	
20	Excellent		20	Excellent	
19			19		
18			18		
17	Very Good		17	Very Good	
16			16		
15			15		
			14		
14	Average		13	Average	
13			12		
			11		
12	Poor				
11			10	Poor	
10			9		
9	Very Poor		8	Very Poor	
8			7		
7			6		
6			5		
5			4		
4			3		
3			2		
2			1		
1					

TABLE A-3. Carpenter Stunt Test Scoring Table (Grades 1–3)

Test Score	Rating
12	Excellent
11	
10	Very Good
9	
8	Average
7	
6	Poor
5	
4	Very Poor
3	
2	
1	

The Meredith Height-Weight Chart for Boys*

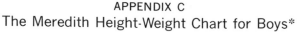

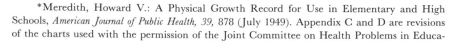

*Meredith, Howard V.: A Physical Growth Record for Use in Elementary and High Schools, *American Journal of Public Health,* *39,* 878 (July 1949). Appendix C and D are revisions of the charts used with the permission of the Joint Committee on Health Problems in Educa-

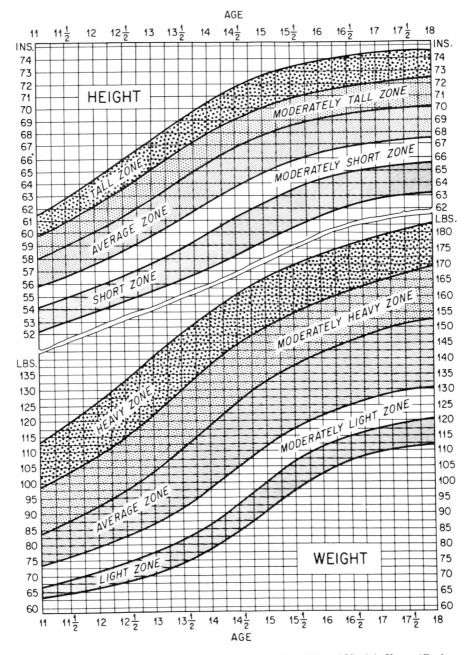

tion of the NEA and AMA with the consent of Howard Meredith and Virginia Knott. (Copies may be obtained from the American Medical Association, 535 N. Dearborn Street, Chicago, Illinois.)

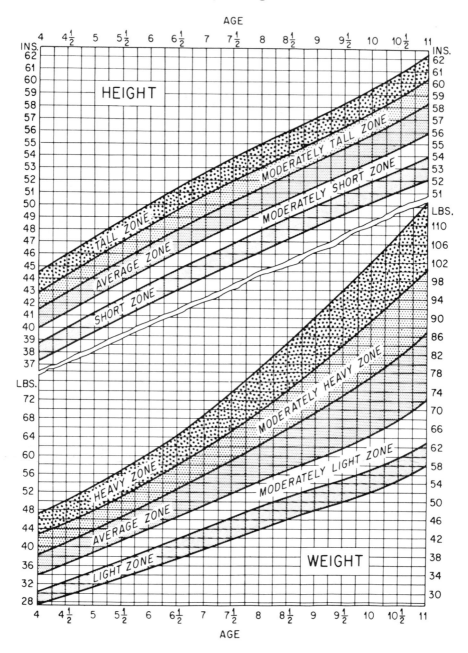

APPENDIX D
The Meredith Height-Weight Chart for Girls

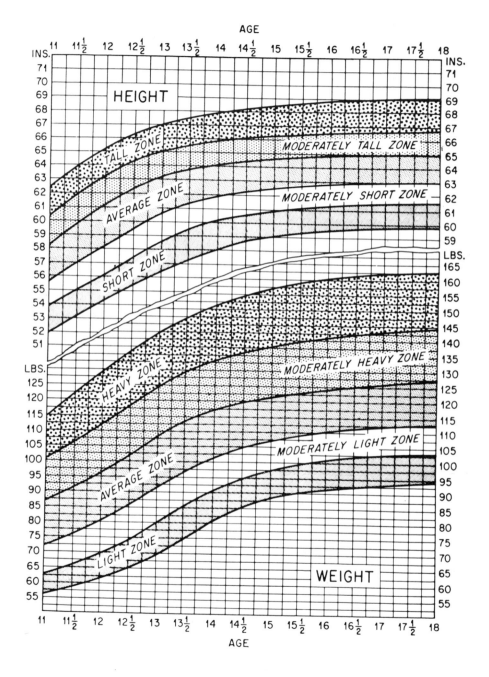

APPENDIX E
The Wetzel Grid*

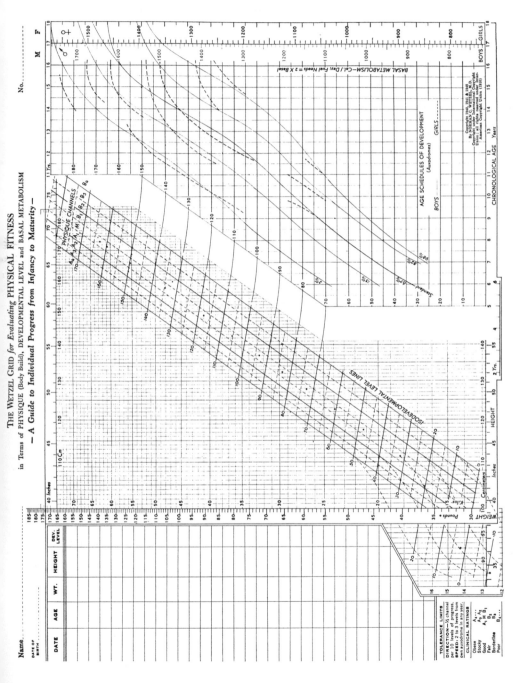

*Wetzel, Norman C.: *The Treatment of Growth Failures In Children,* Cleveland: NEA Service Inc., 1948. Grids may be obtained from the NEA Service.

APPENDIX F

The American Association of Health, Physical Education and Recreation Physical Fitness Test*

Directions and norms for the AAHPER Tests are included on the following pages. Boys take tests 1, 3, 4, 5, 6, 7, and 8. Girls take tests 2, 3, 4, 5, 6, 7, and 8.

TEST 1—PULL UPS FOR BOYS

Equipment: A metal or wooden bar approximately $1\frac{1}{2}$ inches in diameter is preferred. A doorway gym bar can be used, and, if no regular equipment is available, a piece of pipe or even the rungs of a ladder can also serve the purpose.

Description: The bar should be high enough so that the pupil can hang with his arms and legs fully extended and his feet free of the floor. He should use the overhand grasp. After assuming the hanging position, the pupil raises his body by his arms until his chin can be placed over the bar and then lowers his body to a full hang as in the starting position. The exercise is repeated as many times as possible.

Rules: 1. Allow one trial unless it is obvious that the pupil has not had a fair chance.

2. The body must not swing during the execution of the movement. The pull must in no way be a snap movement. If the pupil starts swinging, check this by holding your extended arm across the front of the thighs.

3. The knees must not be raised and kicking of the legs is not permitted.

Improvised equipment for pull-up—
doorway gym bar in background,
ladder in foreground.

Starting position for pull-up.

*American Association of Health, Physical Education and Recreation, *AAHPER Youth Fitness Test Manual.* Washington, D.C.: AAHPER, 1965. (Revised edition.) Reprinted by permission.

Scoring: Record the number of completed pull-ups to the nearest whole number.

TEST 2—FLEXED-ARM HANG FOR GIRLS

Equipment: A horizontal bar approximately 1½ inches in diameter is preferred. A doorway gym bar can be used; if no regular equipment is available, a piece of pipe can serve the purpose. A stop watch is needed.

Description: The height of the bar should be adjusted so it is approximately equal to the pupil's standing height. The pupil should use an overhand grasp. With the assistance of two spotters, one in front and one in back of pupil, the pupil raises her body off the floor to a position where the chin is above the bar, the elbows are flexed, and the chest is close to the bar. The pupil holds this position as long as possible.

Rules: 1. The stop watch is started as soon as the subject takes the hanging position.

2. The watch is stopped when (*a*) pupil's chin touches the bar, (*b*) pupil's head tilts backwards to keep chin above the bar, (*c*) pupil's chin falls below the level of the bar.

Scoring: Record in seconds to the nearest second the length of time the subject holds the hanging position.

Starting position for flexed-arm hang.

Flexed-arm hang.

TEST 3—SIT UPS

Equipment: Mat or floor.

Description: The pupil lies on his back, either on the floor or on a mat, with legs extended and feet about two feet apart. His hands are placed on the back of the neck with the fingers interlaced. Elbows are retracted. A partner holds the ankles down, the heels being in contact with the mat or floor at all times. The pupil sits up, turning the trunk to the left and touch-

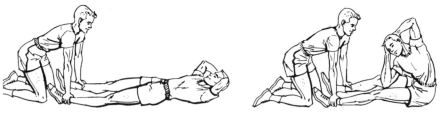

Starting position for sit-up.   Sit-up.

ing the right elbow to the left knee, returns to starting position, then sits up turning the trunk to the right and touching the left elbow to the right knee. The exercise is repeated, alternating sides.

Rules: 1. The fingers must remain in contact behind the neck throughout the exercise.

2. The knees must be on the floor during the sit-up but may be slightly bent when touching elbow to knee.

3. The back should be rounded and the head and elbows brought forward when sitting up as a "curl" up.

4. When returning to starting position, elbows must be flat on the mat before sitting up again.

Scoring: One point is given for each complete movement of touching elbow to knee. No score should be counted if the fingertips do not maintain contact behind the head, if knees are bent when the pupil lies on his back or when he begins to sit up, or if the pupil pushes up off the floor from an elbow. The maximum limit in terms of number of sit-ups shall be: 50 sit-ups for girls, 100 sit-ups for boys.

TEST 4—600 YARD RUN

Equipment: Track or area and stopwatch.

Description: Pupil uses a standing start. At the signal "Ready? Go!" the pupil starts running the 600-yard distance. The running may be interspersed with walking. It is possible to have a dozen pupils run at one time by having the pupils pair off before the start of the event. Then each pupil listens for and remembers his partner's time as the latter crosses the finish. The timer merely calls out the times as the pupils cross the finish.

Rules: Walking is permitted, but the object is to cover the distance in the shortest possible time.

Scoring: Record in minutes and seconds.

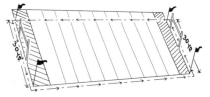

Using football field for 600-yard run-walk.

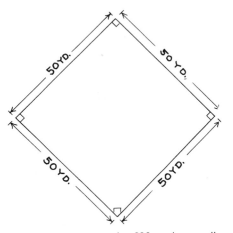

Using any open area for 600-yard run-walk.   Using inside track for 600-yard run-walk.

TEST 5—50 YD. DASH

Equipment: Two stopwatches or one with a split-second timer.

Description: It is preferable to administer this test to two pupils at a time. Have both take positions behind the starting line. The starter will use the commands "Are you ready?" and "Go!" The latter will be accompanied by a downward sweep of the starter's arm to give a visual signal to the timer, who stands at the finish line.

Rules: The score is the amount of time between the starter's signal and the instant the pupil crosses the finish line.

Scoring: Record is seconds to the nearest tenth of a second.

Starting the 50-yard dash.

TEST 6—STANDING BROAD JUMP

Equipment: Mat, floor, or outdoor jumping pit, and tape measure.

Description: Pupil stands with the feet several inches apart and the toes just behind the take-off line. Preparatory to jumping, the pupil swings the arms backward and bends the knees. The jump is accomplished by simultaneously extending the knees and swinging forward the arms.

Rules: 1. Allow three trials.

2. Measure from the take-off line to the heel or other part of the body that touches the floor nearest the take-off line.

3. When the test is given indoors, it is convenient to tape the tape measure to the floor at right angles to the take-off line and have the pupils jump along the tape. The scorer stands to the side and observes the mark to the nearest inch.

Scoring: Record the best of the three trials in feet and inches to the nearest inch.

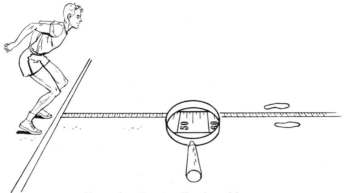

Measuring the standing broad jump.

TEST 7—SOFT BALL THROW

Equipment: Softball (12-inch), small metal or wooden stakes, and tape measure.

Description: A football field marked in conventional fashion (5-yard intervals) makes an ideal area for this test. If this is not available, it is suggested that lines be drawn parallel to the restraining line, 5 yards apart. The pupil throws the ball while remaining within two parallel lines, 6 feet apart. Mark the point of landing with one of the small stakes. If his second or third throw is farther, move the stake accordingly so that, after three throws, the stake is at the point of the pupil's best throw. It was found expedient to have the pupil jog out to his stake and stand there; and then, after five pupils have completed their throws, the measurements were taken. By having the pupil at his particular stake, there is little danger of recording the wrong score.

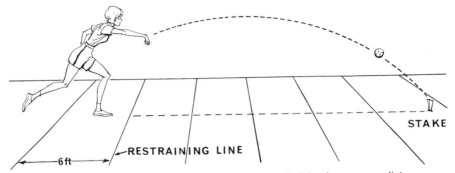

Measuring the softball throw for distance. Wherever ball lands, measure distance perpendicular to starting line.

Rules: 1. Only an overhand throw may be used.

2. Three throws are allowed.

3. The distance recorded is the distance measured at right angles from the point of landing to the restraining line.

Scoring: Record the best of the three trials to the nearest foot.

TEST 8—SHUTTLE RUN

Equipment: Two blocks of wood, 2 inches x 2 inches x 4 inches, and stopwatch. Pupils should wear sneakers or run barefooted.

Description: Two parallel lines are marked on the floor 30 feet apart. The width of a regulation volleyball court serves as a suitable area. Place the blocks of wood behind one of the lines. The pupil starts from behind the other line. On the signal "Ready? Go!" the pupil runs to the blocks, picks one up, runs back to the starting line, and *places* the block behind the line; he then runs back and picks up the second block, which he carries back across the starting line. If the scorer has two stopwatches or one with a split-second timer, it is preferable to have two pupils running at the same time. To eliminate the necessity of returning the blocks after each race, start the races alternately, first from behind one line and then from behind the other.

Rules: Allow two trials with some rest between.

Scoring: Record the time of the better of the two trials to the nearest tenth of a second.

Starting the shuttle run.

PULL-UP FOR BOYS

Percentile Scores Based on Age / Test Scores in Number of Pull-Ups

Percen-tile	Age								Percen-tile
	10	11	12	13	14	15	16	17	
100th	16	20	15	24	20	25	25	32	100th
95th	8	8	9	10	12	13	14	16	95th
90th	7	7	7	9	10	11	13	14	90th
85th	6	6	6	8	10	10	12	12	85th
80th	5	5	5	7	8	10	11	12	80th
75th	4	4	5	6	8	9	10	10	75th
70th	4	4	4	5	7	8	10	10	70th
65th	3	3	3	5	6	7	9	10	65th
60th	3	3	3	4	6	7	9	9	60th
55th	3	2	3	4	5	6	8	8	55th
50th	2	2	2	3	5	6	7	8	50th
45th	2	2	2	3	4	5	6	7	45th
40th	1	1	1	2	4	5	6	7	40th
35th	1	1	1	2	3	4	5	6	35th
30th	1	1	1	1	3	4	5	5	30th
25th	0	0	0	1	2	3	4	5	25th
20th	0	0	0	0	2	3	4	4	20th
15th	0	0	0	0	1	2	3	4	15th
10th	0	0	0	0	0	1	2	2	10th
5th	0	0	0	0	0	0	0	1	5th
0	0	0	0	0	0	0	0	0	0

FLEXED-ARM HANG FOR GIRLS

Percentile Scores Based on Age / Test Scores in Seconds

Percen-tile	Age								Percen-tile
	10	11	12	13	14	15	16	17	
100th	66	79	64	80	60	74	74	76	100th
95th	31	35	30	30	30	33	37	31	95th
90th	24	25	23	21	22	22	26	25	90th
85th	21	20	19	18	19	18	19	19	85th
80th	18	17	15	15	16	16	16	16	80th
75th	15	16	13	13	13	14	14	14	75th
70th	13	13	11	12	11	13	12	12	70th
65th	11	11	10	10	10	11	10	11	65th
60th	10	10	8	9	9	10	9	10	60th
55th	9	9	8	8	8	8	8	9	55th
50th	7	8	6	7	7	8	7	8	50th
45th	6	6	6	6	6	6	6	7	45th
40th	6	5	5	5	5	6	5	6	40th
35th	5	4	4	4	4	4	4	4	35th
30th	4	4	3	3	3	3	3	4	30th
25th	3	3	2	2	2	2	2	3	25th
20th	2	2	1	2	1	1	1	2	20th
15th	2	1	0	1	1	0	1	0	15th
10th	1	0	0	0	0	0	0	0	10th
5th	0	0	0	0	0	0	0	0	5th
0	0	0	0	0	0	0	0	0	0

SIT-UP FOR BOYS

Percentile Scores Based on Age / Test Scores in Number of Sit-Ups

Percen-tile	Age								Percen-tile
	10	11	12	13	14	15	16	17	
100th	100	100	100	100	100	100	100	100	100th
95th	100	100	100	100	100	100	100	100	95th
90th	100	100	100	100	100	100	100	100	90th
85th	100	100	100	100	100	100	100	100	85th
80th	76	89	100	100	100	100	100	100	80th
75th	65	73	93	100	100	100	100	100	75th
70th	57	60	75	99	100	100	100	100	70th
65th	51	55	70	90	99	100	99	99	65th
60th	50	50	59	75	99	99	99	85	60th
55th	49	50	52	70	77	90	85	77	55th
50th	41	46	50	60	70	80	76	70	50th
45th	37	40	49	53	62	70	70	62	45th
40th	34	35	42	50	60	61	63	57	40th
35th	30	31	40	50	52	54	56	51	35th
30th	28	30	35	41	50	50	50	50	30th
25th	25	26	30	38	45	49	50	45	25th
20th	23	23	28	35	40	42	42	40	20th
15th	20	20	25	30	36	39	38	35	15th
10th	15	17	20	25	30	33	34	30	10th
5th	11	12	15	20	24	27	28	23	5th
0	1	0	0	1	6	5	10	8	0

SIT-UP FOR GIRLS

Percentile Scores Based on Age / Test Scores in Number of Sit-Ups

Percen-tile	Age								Percen-tile
	10	11	12	13	14	15	16	17	
100th	50	50	50	50	50	50	50	50	100th
95th	50	50	50	50	50	50	50	50	95th
90th	50	50	50	50	50	50	50	50	90th
85th	50	50	50	50	50	50	50	50	85th
80th	50	50	50	50	49	42	41	45	80th
75th	50	50	50	50	42	39	38	40	75th
70th	50	50	50	45	37	35	34	35	70th
65th	42	40	40	40	35	31	31	32	65th
60th	39	37	39	38	34	30	30	30	60th
55th	33	34	35	35	31	29	28	29	55th
50th	31	30	32	31	30	26	26	27	50th
45th	30	29	30	30	27	25	25	25	45th
40th	26	26	26	27	25	24	24	23	40th
35th	24	25	25	25	23	21	22	21	35th
30th	21	22	22	22	21	20	20	20	30th
25th	20	20	20	20	20	19	18	18	25th
20th	16	19	18	19	18	16	16	16	20th
15th	14	16	16	15	16	14	14	15	15th
10th	11	12	13	12	13	11	11	12	10th
5th	8	10	7	10	10	8	7	9	5th
0	0	0	0	0	0	0	0	0	0

600-YARD RUN-WALK FOR BOYS

Percentile Scores Based on Age / Test Scores in Minutes and Seconds

Percen-tile	10	11	12	13	Age 14	15	16	17	Percen-tile
100th	1'30"	1'27"	1'31"	1'29"	1'25"	1'26"	1'24"	1'23"	100th
95th	1'58"	1'59"	1'52"	1'46"	1'37"	1'34"	1'32"	1'31"	95th
90th	2' 9"	2' 3"	2' 0"	1'50"	1'42"	1'38"	1'35"	1'34"	90th
85th	2'12"	2' 8"	2' 2"	1'53"	1'46"	1'40"	1'37"	1'36"	85th
30th	2'15"	2'11"	2' 5"	1'55"	1'48"	1'42"	1'39"	1'38"	80th
75th	2'18"	2'14"	2' 9"	1'59"	1'51"	1'44"	1'40"	1'40"	75th
70th	2'20"	2'16"	2'11"	2' 1"	1'53"	1'46"	1'43"	1'42"	70th
65th	2'23"	2'19"	2'13"	2' 3"	1'55"	1'47"	1'45"	1'44"	65th
60th	2'26"	2'21"	2'15"	2' 5"	1'57"	1'49"	1'47"	1'45"	60th
55th	2'30"	2'24"	2'18"	2' 7"	1'59"	1'51"	1'49"	1'48"	55th
50th	2'33"	2'27"	2'21"	2'10"	2' 1"	1'54"	1'51"	1'50"	50th
45th	2'36"	2'30"	2'24"	2'12"	2' 3"	1'55"	1'53"	1'52"	45th
40th	2'40"	2'33"	2'26"	2'15"	2' 5"	1'58"	1'56"	1'54"	40th
35th	2'43"	2'36"	2'30"	2'17"	2' 9"	2' 0"	1'58"	1'57"	35th
30th	2'45"	2'39"	2'34"	2'22"	2'11"	2' 3"	2' 1"	2' 0"	30th
25th	2'49"	2'42"	2'39"	2'25"	2'14"	2' 7"	2' 5"	2' 4"	25th
20th	2'55"	2'48"	2'47"	2'30"	2'19"	2'13"	2' 9"	2' 9"	20th
15th	3' 1"	2'55"	2'57"	2'35"	2'25"	2'20"	2'14"	2'16"	15th
10th	3' 8"	3' 9"	3' 8"	2'45"	2'33"	2'32"	2'22"	2'26"	10th
5th	3'23"	3'30"	3'32"	3' 3"	2'47"	2'50"	2'37"	2'40"	5th
0	4'58"	5' 6"	4'55"	5'14"	5'10"	4'10"	4' 9"	4'45"	0

600-YARD RUN-WALK FOR GIRLS

Percentile Scores Based on Age / Test Scores in Minutes and Seconds

Percen-tile	10	11	12	13	Age 14	15	16	17	Percen-tile
100th	1'42"	1'40"	1'39"	1'40"	1'45"	1'40"	1'50"	1'54"	100th
95th	2' 5"	2'13"	2'14"	2'12"	2' 9"	2' 9"	2'10"	2'11"	95th
90th	2'15"	2'19"	2'20"	2'19"	2'18"	2'18"	2'17"	2'22"	90th
85th	2'20"	2'24"	2'24"	2'25"	2'22"	2'23"	2'23"	2'27"	85th
80th	2'26"	2'28"	2'27"	2'29"	2'25"	2'26"	2'26"	2'31"	80th
75th	2'30"	2'32"	2'31"	2'33"	2'30"	2'28"	2'31"	2'34"	75th
70th	2'34"	2'36"	2'35"	2'37"	2'34"	2'34"	2'36"	2'37"	70th
65th	2'37"	2'39"	2'39"	2'40"	2'37"	2'36"	2'39"	2'42"	65th
60th	2'41"	2'43"	2'42"	2'44"	2'41"	2'40"	2'42"	2'46"	60th
55th	2'45"	2'47"	2'45"	2'47"	2'44"	2'43"	2'45"	2'49"	55th
50th	2'48"	2'49"	2'49"	2'52"	2'46"	2'46"	2'49"	2'51"	50th
45th	2'50"	2'53"	2'55"	2'56"	2'51"	2'49"	2'53"	2'57"	45th
40th	2'55"	2'59"	2'58"	3' 0"	2'55"	2'52"	2'56"	3' 0"	40th
35th	2'59"	3' 4"	3' 3"	3' 3"	3' 0"	2'56"	2'59"	3' 5"	35th
30th	3' 3"	3'10"	3' 7"	3' 9"	3' 6"	3' 0"	3' 1"	3'10"	30th
25th	3' 8"	3'15"	3'11"	3'15"	3'12"	3' 5"	3' 7"	3'16"	25th
20th	3'13"	3'22"	3'18"	3'20"	3'19"	3'10"	3'12"	3'22"	20th
15th	3'18"	3'30"	3'24"	3'30"	3'30"	3'18"	3'19"	3'29"	15th
10th	3'27"	3'41"	3'40"	3'49"	3'48"	3'28"	3'30"	3'41"	10th
5th	3'45"	3'59"	4' 0"	4'11"	4' 8"	3'56"	3'45"	3'56"	5th
0	4'47"	4'53"	5'10"	5'10"	5'50"	5'10"	5'52"	6'40"	0

50-YARD DASH FOR BOYS

Percentile Scores Based on Age / Test Scores in Seconds and Tenths

Percentile	Age								Percentile
	10	11	12	13	14	15	16	17	
100th	6.0	6.0	6.0	5.8	5.8	5.6	5.6	5.6	100th
95th	7.0	7.0	6.8	6.5	6.3	6.1	6.0	6.0	95th
90th	7.1	7.2	7.0	6.7	6.4	6.2	6.1	6.0	90th
85th	7.4	7.4	7.0	6.9	6.6	6.4	6.2	6.1	85th
80th	7.5	7.5	7.2	7.0	6.7	6.5	6.3	6.2	80th
75th	7.6	7.6	7.3	7.0	6.8	6.5	6.3	6.3	75th
70th	7.8	7.7	7.5	7.1	6.9	6.6	6.4	6.3	70th
65th	8.0	7.8	7.5	7.2	7.0	6.7	6.5	6.4	65th
60th	8.0	7.8	7.6	7.3	7.0	6.7	6.5	6.5	60th
55th	8.1	8.0	7.8	7.4	7.0	6.8	6.6	6.5	55th
50th	8.2	8.0	7.8	7.5	7.1	6.9	6.7	6.6	50th
45th	8.3	8.0	7.9	7.5	7.2	7.0	6.7	6.7	45th
40th	8.5	8.1	8.0	7.6	7.2	7.0	6.8	6.7	40th
35th	8.5	8.3	8.0	7.7	7.3	7.1	6.9	6.8	35th
30th	8.7	8.4	8.2	7.9	7.5	7.1	6.9	6.9	30th
25th	8.8	8.5	8.3	8.0	7.6	7.2	7.0	7.0	25th
20th	9.0	8.7	8.4	8.0	7.8	7.3	7.1	7.0	20th
15th	9.1	9.0	8.6	8.2	8.0	7.5	7.2	7.1	15th
10th	9.5	9.1	8.9	8.4	8.1	7.7	7.5	7.3	10th
5th	10.0	9.5	9.2	8.9	8.6	8.1	7.8	7.7	5th
0	12.0	11.9	12.0	11.1	11.6	12.0	8.6	10.6	0

50-YARD DASH FOR GIRLS

Percentile Scores Based on Age / Test Scores in Seconds and Tenths

Percentile	Age								Percentile
	10	11	12	13	14	15	16	17	
100th	6.0	6.0	5.9	6.0	6.0	6.4	6.0	6.4	100th
95th	7.0	7.0	7.0	7.0	7.0	7.1	7.0	7.1	95th
90th	7.3	7.4	7.3	7.3	7.2	7.3	7.3	7.3	90th
85th	7.5	7.6	7.5	7.5	7.4	7.5	7.5	7.5	85th
80th	7.7	7.7	7.6	7.6	7.5	7.6	7.5	7.6	80th
75th	7.9	7.9	7.8	7.7	7.6	7.7	7.7	7.8	75th
70th	8.0	8.0	7.9	7.8	7.7	7.8	7.9	7.9	70th
65th	8.1	8.0	8.0	7.9	7.8	7.9	8.0	8.0	65th
60th	8.2	8.1	8.0	8.0	7.9	8.0	8.0	8.0	60th
55th	8.4	8.2	8.1	8.0	8.0	8.0	8.1	8.1	55th
50th	8.5	8.4	8.2	8.1	8.0	8.1	8.3	8.2	50th
45th	8.6	8.5	8.3	8.2	8.2	8.2	8.4	8.3	45th
40th	8.8	8.5	8.4	8.4	8.3	8.3	8.5	8.5	40th
35th	8.9	8.6	8.5	8.5	8.5	8.4	8.6	8.6	35th
30th	9.0	8.8	8.7	8.6	8.6	8.6	8.8	8.8	30th
25th	9.0	9.0	8.9	8.8	8.9	8.8	9.0	9.0	25th
20th	9.2	9.0	9.0	9.0	9.0	9.0	9.0	9.0	20th
15th	9.4	9.2	9.2	9.2	9.2	9.0	9.2	9.1	15th
10th	9.6	9.6	9.5	9.5	9.5	9.5	9.9	9.5	10th
5th	10.0	10.0	10.0	10.2	10.4	10.0	10.5	10.4	5th
0	14.0	13.0	13.0	15.7	16.0	18.0	17.0	12.0	0

STANDING BROAD JUMP FOR BOYS

Percentile Scores Based on Age / Test Scores in Feet and Inches

Percen-tile	10	11	12	13	14	15	16	17	Percen-tile
				Age					
100th	6' 8"	10' 0"	7'10"	8' 9"	8'11"	9' 2"	9' 1"	9' 8"	100th
95th	6' 1"	6' 3"	6' 6"	7' 2"	7' 9"	8' 0"	8' 5"	8' 6"	95th
90th	5'10"	6' 0"	6' 4"	6'11"	7' 5"	7' 9"	8' 1"	8' 3"	90th
85th	5' 8"	5'10"	6' 2"	6' 9"	7' 3"	7' 6"	7'11"	8' 1"	85th
80th	5' 7"	5' 9"	6' 1"	6' 7"	7' 0"	7' 6"	7' 9"	8' 0"	80th
75th	5' 6"	5' 7"	6' 0"	6' 5"	6'11"	7' 4"	7' 7"	7'10"	75th
70th	5' 5"	5' 6"	5'11"	6' 3"	6' 9"	7' 2"	7' 6"	7' 8"	70th
65th	5' 4"	5' 6"	5' 9"	6' 1"	6' 8"	7' 1"	7' 5"	7' 7"	65th
60th	5' 2"	5' 4"	5' 8"	6' 0"	6' 7"	7' 0"	7' 4"	7' 6"	60th
55th	5' 1"	5' 3"	5' 7"	5'11"	6' 6"	6'11"	7' 3"	7' 5"	55th
50th	5' 0"	5' 2"	5' 6"	5'10"	6' 4"	6' 9"	7' 1"	7' 3"	50th
45th	5' 0"	5' 1"	5' 5"	5' 9"	6' 3"	6' 8"	7' 0"	7' 2"	45th
40th	4'10"	5' 0"	5' 4"	5' 7"	6' 1"	6' 6"	6'11"	7' 0"	40th
35th	4'10"	4'11"	5' 2"	5' 6"	6' 0"	6' 6"	6' 9"	6'11"	35th
30th	4' 8"	4'10"	5' 1"	5' 5"	5'10"	6' 4"	6' 7"	6'10"	30th
25th	4' 6"	4' 8"	5' 0"	5' 3"	5' 8"	6' 3"	6' 6"	6' 8"	25th
20th	4' 5"	4' 7"	4'10"	5' 2"	5' 6"	6' 1"	6' 4"	6' 6"	20th
15th	4' 4"	4' 5"	4' 8"	5' 0"	5' 4"	5'10"	6' 1"	6' 4"	15th
10th	4' 3"	4' 2"	4' 5"	4' 9"	5' 2"	5' 7"	5'11"	6' 0"	10th
5th	4' 0"	4' 0"	4' 2"	4' 5"	4'11"	5' 4"	5' 6"	5' 8"	5th
0	2'10"	1' 8"	3' 0"	2' 9"	3' 8"	2'10"	2' 2"	3' 7"	0

STANDING BROAD JUMP FOR GIRLS

Percentile Scores Based on Age / Test Scores in Feet and Inches

Percen-tile	10	11	12	13	14	15	16	17	Percen-tile
				Age					
100th	7' 0"	7'10"	8' 2"	7' 6"	7' 4"	7' 8"	7' 5"	7' 8"	100th
95th	5' 8"	6' 2"	6' 3"	6' 3"	6' 4"	6' 6"	6' 7"	6' 8"	95th
90th	5' 6"	5'10"	6' 0"	6' 0"	6' 2"	6' 3"	6' 4"	6' 4"	90th
85th	5' 4"	5' 8"	5' 9"	5'10"	6' 0"	6' 1"	6' 2"	6' 2"	85th
80th	5' 2"	5' 6"	5' 8"	5' 8"	5'10"	6' 0"	6' 0"	6' 0"	80th
75th	5' 1"	5' 4"	5' 6"	5' 6"	5' 9"	5'10"	5'10"	5'11"	75th
70th	5' 0"	5' 3"	5' 5"	5' 5"	5' 7"	5' 9"	5' 8"	5'10"	70th
65th	5' 0"	5' 2"	5' 4"	5' 4"	5' 6"	5' 7"	5' 7"	5' 9"	65th
60th	4'10"	5' 0"	5' 2"	5' 3"	5' 5"	5' 6"	5' 6"	5' 7"	60th
55th	4' 9"	5' 0"	5' 1"	5' 2"	5' 4"	5' 5"	5' 5"	5' 6"	55th
50th	4' 7"	4'10"	5' 0"	5' 0"	5' 3"	5' 4"	5' 4"	5' 5"	50th
45th	4' 6"	4' 9"	4'11"	5' 0"	5' 1"	5' 3"	5' 3"	5' 3"	45th
40th	4' 5"	4' 8"	4' 9"	4'10"	5' 0"	5' 1"	5' 2"	5' 2"	40th
35th	4' 4"	4' 7"	4' 8"	4' 8"	5' 0"	5' 0"	5' 0"	5' 0"	35th
30th	4' 3"	4' 6"	4' 7"	4' 6"	4' 9"	4'10"	4'11"	5' 0"	30th
25th	4' 2"	4' 4"	4' 5"	4' 6"	4' 8"	4' 8"	4'10"	4'10"	25th
20th	4' 0"	4' 3"	4' 4"	4' 4"	4' 6"	4' 7"	4' 8"	4' 9"	20th
15th	3'11"	4' 1"	4' 2"	4' 2"	4' 3"	4' 6"	4' 6"	4' 7"	15th
10th	3' 9"	3'11"	4' 0"	4' 0"	4' 1"	4' 4"	4' 4"	4' 5"	10th
5th	3' 6"	3' 9"	3' 8"	3' 9"	3'10"	4' 0"	4' 0"	4' 2"	5th
0	2' 8"	2'11"	2'11"	2'11"	3' 0"	2'11"	3' 2"	3' 0"	0

SOFTBALL THROW FOR BOYS

Percentile Scores Based on Age / Test Scores in Feet

Percen-tile	Age								Percen-tile
	10	11	12	13	14	15	16	17	
100th	175	205	207	245	**246**	250	271	291	100th
95th	138	151	165	195	208	221	238	249	95th
90th	127	141	156	183	195	210	222	235	90th
85th	122	136	150	175	187	204	213	226	85th
80th	118	129	145	168	181	198	207	218	80th
75th	114	126	141	163	176	192	201	213	75th
70th	109	121	136	157	172	189	197	207	70th
65th	105	119	133	152	168	184	194	203	65th
60th	102	115	129	147	165	180	189	198	60th
55th	98	113	124	142	160	175	185	195	55th
50th	96	111	120	140	155	171	180	190	50th
45th	93	108	119	135	150	167	175	185	45th
40th	91	105	115	131	146	165	172	180	40th
35th	89	101	112	128	141	160	168	176	35th
30th	84	98	110	125	138	156	165	171	30th
25th	81	94	106	120	133	152	160	163	25th
20th	78	90	103	115	127	147	153	155	20th
15th	73	85	97	110	122	141	147	150	15th
10th	69	78	92	101	112	135	141	141	10th
5th	60	70	76	88	102	123	127	117	5th
0	35	14	25	50	31	60	30	31	0

SOFTBALL THROW FOR GIRLS

Percentile Scores Based on Age / Test Scores in Feet

Percen-tile	Age								Percen-tile
	10	11	12	13	14	15	16	17	
100th	167	141	159	150	156	165	175	183	100th
95th	84	95	103	111	114	120	123	120	95th
90th	76	86	96	102	103	110	113	108	90th
85th	71	81	90	94	100	105	104	102	85th
80th	69	77	85	90	95	100	98	98	80th
75th	65	74	80	86	90	**95**	92	93	75th
70th	60	71	76	82	87	90	89	90	70th
65th	57	66	74	79	84	87	85	87	65th
60th	54	64	70	75	80	84	81	82	60th
55th	52	62	67	73	78	82	78	80	55th
50th	50	59	64	70	75	78	75	75	50th
45th	48	57	61	68	72	75	74	74	45th
40th	46	55	59	65	70	73	71	71	40th
35th	45	52	57	63	68	69	69	69	35th
30th	42	50	54	60	65	66	66	66	30th
25th	40	46	50	57	61	64	63	62	25th
20th	37	44	48	53	59	60	60	58	20th
15th	34	40	45	49	54	58	55	52	15th
10th	30	37	41	45	50	51	50	48	10th
5th	21	32	37	36	45	45	45	40	5th
0	8	13	20	20	25	12	8	20	0

SHUTTLE RUN FOR BOYS

Percentile Scores Based on Age / Test Scores in Seconds and Tenths

Percen-tile	Age 10	11	12	13	14	15	16	17	Percen-tile
100th	9.0	9.0	8.5	8.0	8.3	8.0	8.1	8.0	100th
95th	10.0	10.0	9.8	9.5	9.3	9.1	9.0	8.9	95th
90th	10.2	10.1	10.0	9.8	9.5	9.3	9.1	9.0	90th
85th	10.4	10.3	10.0	9.9	9.6	9.4	9.2	9.1	85th
80th	10.5	10.4	10.2	10.0	9.8	9.5	9.3	9.2	80th
75th	10.7	10.5	10.3	10.1	9.9	9.6	9.5	9.3	75th
70th	10.8	10.7	10.5	10.2	9.9	9.7	9.5	9.4	70th
65th	10.9	10.8	10.6	10.3	10.0	9.8	9.6	9.5	65th
60th	11.0	10.9	10.7	10.4	10.0	9.8	9.7	9.6	60th
55th	11.0	11.0	10.9	10.5	10.2	9.9	9.8	9.7	55th
50th	11.2	11.1	11.0	10.6	10.2	10.0	9.9	9.8	50th
45th	11.4	11.2	11.0	10.8	10.3	10.0	10.0	9.9	45th
40th	11.5	11.3	11.1	10.9	10.5	10.1	10.0	10.0	40th
35th	11.6	11.4	11.3	11.0	10.5	10.2	10.1	10.0	35th
30th	11.8	11.6	11.5	11.1	10.7	10.3	10.2	10.1	30th
25th	12.0	11.8	11.6	11.3	10.9	10.5	10.4	10.4	25th
20th	12.0	12.0	11.9	11.5	11.0	10.6	10.5	10.6	20th
15th	12.2	12.1	12.0	11.8	11.2	10.9	10.8	10.9	15th
10th	12.6	12.4	12.4	12.0	11.5	11.1	11.1	11.2	10th
5th	13.1	13.0	13.0	12.5	12.0	11.7	11.5	11.7	5th
0	15.0	20.0	22.0	16.0	16.0	16.6	16.7	14.0	0

SHUTTLE RUN FOR GIRLS

Percentile Scores Based on Age / Test Scores in Seconds and Tenths

Percen-tile	Age 10	11	12	13	14	15	16	17	Percen-tile
100th	8.5	8.8	9.0	8.3	9.0	8.0	8.3	9.0	100th
95th	10.0	10.0	10.0	10.0	10.0	10.0	10.0	10.0	95th
90th	10.5	10.2	10.2	10.2	10.3	10.3	10.2	10.3	90th
85th	10.8	10.6	10.5	10.5	10.4	10.5	10.4	10.4	85th
80th	11.0	10.9	10.8	10.6	10.5	10.7	10.6	10.5	80th
75th	11.0	11.0	10.9	10.8	10.6	10.9	10.8	10.6	75th
70th	11.1	11.0	11.0	11.0	10.8	11.0	10.9	10.8	70th
65th	11.4	11.2	11.2	11.0	10.9	11.0	11.0	11.0	65th
60th	11.5	11.4	11.3	11.1	11.0	11.1	11.0	11.0	60th
55th	11.8	11.6	11.5	11.3	11.1	11.2	11.2	11.1	55th
50th	11.9	11.7	11.6	11.4	11.3	11.3	11.2	11.2	50th
45th	12.0	11.8	11.8	11.6	11.4	11.5	11.4	11.4	45th
40th	12.0	12.0	11.9	11.8	11.5	11.6	11.5	11.5	40th
35th	12.1	12.0	12.0	12.0	11.7	11.8	11.8	11.6	35th
30th	12.4	12.1	12.1	12.0	12.0	11.9	12.0	11.8	30th
25th	12.6	12.4	12.3	12.2	12.0	12.0	12.0	12.0	25th
20th	12.8	12.6	12.5	12.5	12.3	12.3	12.2	12.0	20th
15th	13.0	13.0	12.9	13.0	12.6	12.5	12.5	12.3	15th
10th	13.1	13.4	13.2	13.3	13.1	13.0	13.0	13.0	10th
5th	14.0	14.1	13.9	14.0	13.9	13.5	13.9	13.8	5th
0	16.6	18.5	19.8	18.5	17.6	16.0	17.6	20.0	0

Index

AAHPER test, 50, 332, 355–367
Academic achievement, motor therapy and, 15
  physical education and, 12, 14–15
Acceptance, 26. See also *Peers.*
Accident. See *Injury.*
Accident report, 107 f.
Accuracy, technique and, 119
  tests for, 336
Ace of diamonds, 312
Achievement, 26
Act of God, 110
Activities, active vs. passive, 68
  classes for, 100
  fundamental skill, 123–142
  structured vs. unstructured, 67
Agility, 20, 61
  exercises for, 299
All-purpose polka, 315–316
All the way kickball, 271
All the way over, 221
Alternate knee touch, 228
American Association of Health, Physical Education
    and Recreation, 105. See also *AAHPER test.*
American children, physical fitness of, 9–10, 46–49,
  50
American heel-and-toe polka, 316
Animal walk relays, 234
Apparel, 52–53
Appetite, 59
Arguments, 120
Arm circles, 297
Around the bases relay, 238–239
Around the bases volleyball, 259
Artificial ventilation, 106–107
Athletics, 6, 66
  interschool, 7
Automatic skill pattern, 25

Back arch, 215
Back hyperextension, 296, 333
Back to back, 289

Backward circle, 226
Backward roll, with extension, 208–209
  Pike position, 208
  Tuck position, 208
Backward walk, 228
Balance, 20, 61, 169–170
  exercises for, 298
Balance beam, 227–229
Ball. See also *Baseball; Basketball games; Football games;*
    Softball entries; *Volleyball games.*
  basic movement problems, 150
  bouncing, 135–136
  catching, 131–132
  control of, 153
    with feet, 137
  curve, 167
  dodging, 154–155
  kicking, 136–137
  retrieving of, 153
  rolling, 129
  slow motion, 154–155
  spin on, 166–167
  striking, 132–135
  throwing, 129–131, 186
    for distance, 175–176
Ball games, 184–192
Ball pass relays, 234–235
Ball patrols, 111
Balloon volleyball, 255–256
Bamboo hop dance, 323–328
Barley break, 204–205
Basal metabolic rate, 174, 175
Base tag, 203–204
Baseball, 184–185
  games, 269–271
Basketball games, 260–269
Bat around kick ball, 187
Baton pass, 274, 275
Beam stand, 334
Beam walking, 227, 228, 229
Bear walk, 287
Bench step, 294, 334

Bent leg sit up, 296
Bicycle ride, 295
Bicycle safety, 278
Big man volleyball, 260
Bingo, 308
Bleking, 313
Blood loss, 106
Body levers, 163
Body parts, movement of, 86–89, 144–149
Body position, 61
Body proportions, 35
Body stability, 163–164
Body support, 149–150
Bombardment, 261–262
Bones, 34–36
Bounce, one hand, 136
    two hand, 135
Bounce and bat, 269–270
Bounce ball across the beam, 229
Bounce over the hole, 220
Boundary ball, 186
Box ball, 189–190
Boys, bone mineralization in, 35
    50-yard dash, 364
    growth of, 32
        intellectual, 43
    Meredith height-weight chart, 350–351
    motor ability, 41
    motor fitness, 40
    muscular development, 36, 39
    physical fitness norms, 37–40
    pull-ups, 355, 361
    shuttle run, 367
    sit-ups, 362
    600-yard walk-run, 363
    softball throw, 366
    standing broad jump, 365
Brace test, 40–41
Broad jump, 275–276
    standing, 275, 359, 365
Brownies and fairies, 194–195
Bugs, 203
Burpee, 295
Butterflies and flowers, 196

Caged lion, 198
Caged tiger, 197
Calisthenics, 8, 66, 67, 113, 294–297. See also *Exercise;*
    Gymnastics.
    physical fitness and, 11
Calories, 21, 56, 167–168, 173–175
Camel walk, 286
Capture the gold, 204
Carotid pulse, 173
Carpenter tests, 346–349
Carry-over objective, 59–60, 339
Cartwheel, 210
Cartwheel vault, 219
Catching, with arms, 131–132
    with hands, 132
Center of gravity, 163, 164
Centering a ball, 245–246
Chase the ball, 188

Chariot relay, 238
Chest balance, 213
Children, differences between, 29
    responsibility of, 110
Chinese wall, 182
Circle, 115, 151
    double, 115, 193–194
Circle call ball, 188
Circle change, 193
Circle games, 193–194
Circle relay, 232, 274–275
Circuit training, 290–291
Citizenship, 28
Class, 101, 102
    activity in, 120
    discussion in, 66, 100
        questions for, 160–179
    excuse from, 105
    experiments for, 160–179
    organization of, 75
    time allotment for, 113
Coffee grinder, 285
Cognitive-affective objective, 59, 62, 69t, 97–98
    program organization for, 101–102
Come let us be joyful, 312–313
Comin' round the mountain, 319–320
Competition, 7, 28, 114
Conceptual knowledge, 59, 99t
Cooperation, 28
Coordination, 20
Cork screw, 296
Counting off, 116
Crab soccer, 248–249
Crab walk, 286
Crawl the beam, 228
Creativity, 84, 85
Crows and cranes, 200
Curiosity, 84
Curl the arm, 300
Curriculum, 67–68. See also *Programs.*
Curve, 167

Daily plan, 77, 79
Dance, 303–329
Dance of greeting, 310
Dependence, 29
Development. See *Growth.*
Diet, 21, 57
Dip walk, 229
Direction exploration, 148
Disability, 9
Distance test, 336
Dive roll, 207
Diver's balance, 298
Diver's stance, 169
Dodge ball, 154–155, 190–191
Dodge call ball, 192
Dodging, 154–155
Double circle, 115, 193–194
Double forward roll, 213
Double tag, 196–197
Down and back relays, 233–234
Dribble relays, 240

Dribble tag, 263–264
Drills, fundamental skill, 139–142
"Drop off," 118
Drums, 152
Dual stunts, 288–289

Education, physical education and, 1, 8, 12, 14–15
Ego, 26
Elephant walk, 287
Emotional development, 25–28, 44, 49, 51–54
  objectives for, 61–62, 69t
Emotional needs, 335, 337t
Emotional problems, 25
Emotional release, 26
Endurance, 20, 36–39, 168–169. See also *Strength.*
  exercises for, 169, 294–296
English movement education, 82–83
Environment, 32, 81
Equipment, 74, 75, 110, 111–112. See also *Facilities.*
  legal liability and, 109
  official, 111–112
Europe, physical fitness of children, 9
Evaluation, 3, 75, 330–341
  definition, 330–331
  purposes of, 331
Excuses, 105
Exercise, 98, 113, 294–297. See also *Calisthenics;*
    Gymnastics.
  for agility, 299
  for balance, 298
  calories used in, 167–168
  choice of, 177
  contraindications for, 22
  corrective, 67
  endurance and, 169, 294–296
  for flexibility, 297
  growth and, 34, 36
  heart and, 22, 23, 36, 172–173
  isometric, 300
  for muscular endurance, 296
  muscle development and, 36
  overload and, 171–172
  positions for, 295
  for strength, 296
  time for, 105
  weight control and, 57
Experiments, 66, 100–101, 102, 160–179
  balance performance, 169–170
  ball spin, 166–167
  body stability, 163–164
  calorie use, 167–168, 173–175
  endurance performance, 168–169
  exercise and heart, 172–173
  exercise choice, 177
  feedback, 164–165
  friction, 165–166
  heart and exercise, 172–173
  lifting, 162–163
  overload, 171–172
  pacing performance, 176–177
  posture, 160–162
  pulling, 162–163
  pushing, 162–163

Experiments, reaction time evaluation, 170–171
  throwing for distance, 175–176
  weight control, 173–175
Explosive power, 20

Facilities, 74, 102, 110. See also *Equipment.*
  legal liability and, 109
Falling, 127–128
Fat, body, 36, 167
Fatigue, 26, 98
Feedback, 25, 118–119, 164–165
50-yard dash, 358, 364
Figure-eight run, 299
Fire engine, 195–196
First aid, 98, 99t, 106–107, 110, 178
Fish flop, 209
Flag forward pass, 244–245
Flexed arm hang, 356
Flexibility, 20
  exercises for, 297
  Kraus-Weber test for, 332
Flip the lid, 201
Fly away ball, 264–265
Folk dance, 303–329
Follow the leader, 181, 280–281
Football games, 241–247
Football position play, 246–247
Force exploration, 145, 146
Formations, 114–117
  relay, 231–232
Forward circle, 226
Forward pass, 244–245
Forward roll, Pike position, 207–208
  Tuck position, 207
  on tumbling table, 219
Forward roll over the hole, 222
Forward to backward roll, 209
Four squares, 252–254
Friction, 165–166
Frog jump, 286
Frog stand, 209
Front support, 225
Full eagle, 216
Full twist spring, 222

Galloping, 126
Games, 28, 67, 98. See also *Sports.*
  ball, 184–192
  baseball, 269–271
  basic skill, 181–184
  basketball, 260–269
  development of, 158
  football, 241–247
  highly organized, 66
  lead up, 241–279
  low organized, 66, 180–205
  for physical fitness, 280–285
  risk in, 110
  running, 194–205
  softball, 269–271
  volleyball, 252–260
Get movin', 200

Girls, bone mineralization in, 35
  50-yard dash, 364
  flexed arm hang, 356, 361
  growth of, 32
    intellectual, 43
  Meredith height-weight chart, 352–353
  motor ability, 40, 41
  muscular development, 36, 39
  obesity in, 57
  physical fitness norms, 37–40
  shuttle run, 367
  sit-ups, 362
  600-yard walk-run, 363
  softball throw, 366
  standing broad jump, 365
Glow worm, 316–317
Go fetch it relay, 236
Goals. See *Objectives*.
Golf, 277–279
Gorilla walk, 287
Grades, concepts for, 99t
  objectives for, 61
Grading, 339–341
Groups, movement in, 151
  rope jumping in, 138–139
  size of, 120
  skill drills for, 142
Growth, 9, 21, 32–36
  Wetzel grid for, 335, 354
Guard the basket, 185–186
Guard the pin, 183
Gymnastics, 66, 67, 206–230
  legal liability in, 109
  spotting in, 109

Habit, 165
Half eagle, 216
Half twist spring, 222
Handspring, 211
Handspring vault, 220
Handstand, 210
Hanging front leg raises, 296
Head, 35
Headover, 224
Headspring, 210–211
Headspring over the tube, 223
Headstand, 210
Health, 1–2, 8, 9, 36–39
  movement and, 98, 99t
  physical fitness and, 20
Heart, 36, 169
  exercise and, 172–173
  injury to, 22
  textbook fallacies about, 22, 23
Height, 32, 36
Height-weight charts, 335, 350–353
Hemorrhage, 106
Heredity, 32
High jump, 277
Highland schottische, 315
Hit pin kickball, 271
Hit the deck, 281
Hit the pole, 265–266

Hitting, moving object, 135
  stationary object, 134
Hokey pokey, 305
Hook on, 202
Hoops, basic movement problems, 151
  rhythmic patterns, 152
Hop-kick golf, 277–279
Hop-step-jump, 276
Hop the tires, 299
Hopping, 125
  one foot, 125
Horizontal bar stunts, 224–227
Hot time in the old town tonight, 320–321
Hula hoop ball, 262–263
Human ball, 288
Hurdling, 273

Identification, 29
Illness, 106
Implements, 90
  movement of, 150–151, 153
In the air four square, 257–259
Inch worm, 287
Indian dance, 304
Indian squat, 298
Injury, 7, 21, 105, 106, 109, 110
  accident report, 107–108
Insurance, liability, 109, 110
Intelligence, 43
Interests, 75
Interval training, 289–290
Intramurals, 6, 7
Iowa Brace tests, 334, 346–349
Isometric exercises, 300

Jack spring, 218, 221, 299
Jump the ditch, 182–183
Jump the line, 282
Jump to seat, 222
Jump to table, 218, 219
Jumping, 126, 275–277
Jumping half turn, 170
Jumping rope, 137–139
Juvenile delinquency, 49

Kick, instep, 136
  punt, 137
  toe, 136
Kickball, 270–271
Kinderpolka, 311
Knee dip, 298
Knee hang, 225
Knee-shoulder balance, 214
Knee to feet, 299
Knee to roll, 223
Knee to seat, 223
Kraus-Weber tests, 47, 48, 61, 332, 344–346

"L" ladder balance, 216
La raspa, 317–318

Laboratory. See *Experiments.*
Ladder balancing, 215–216
Lead up games, 241–279
Leader-squad relays, 239–240
Leadership, 7, 28, 44, 49, 114
Leap to leap, 229
Leaping, 126
Learning, 29, 31–45, 75
  blocks to, 25
  guidelines for, 19–30
  inhibition of, 25
  prerequisites for, 74
  principles of, 117–119
  readiness for, 25
  reinforcement of, 25, 118
  rewards and, 25
  skill curves, 117–118
  transfer of, 25
Leg cross, 300
Leg growth, 35
Leg hang, 215
Leg hyperextension, 334
Leg straightener, 300
Leisure, 28, 56. See also *Recreation.*
Lesson objectives. See *Objectives.*
Levels exploration, 147
Leverage, 163
Liability insurance, 109, 110
Lift the toe, 297
Lifting, 128, 162–163
Line soccer, 250–251
Locomotion, 89, 144–145, 146, 147, 148, 149–150
Log roll, 206
  three man, 213
Looby loo, 305–306
Lower the legs, 333

Many ball, 189
Mat tumbling, 206–212
Materials. See *Equipment.*
Maturation, 26, 32
Measurement, 330
Medical examination, 105, 110
Medicine ball put, 333
Medicine ball volley, 257
Meredith height-weight charts, 335, 350–353
Metabolic rate, 174, 175
Midnight, 195
Mini-tramp, 217–220
Mistakes, 119, 120
Monkey hang, 225
Monkey play relationships, 51–54
Motivation, 24, 39
Motor ability, 40–41
Motor fitness, 40
  AAHPER test for, 332, 355–367
Motor therapy, academic achievement and, 15
Movement. See also *Motor therapy; Skills.*
  of body parts, 86–89
  capabilities for, 97, 99t
  decisions, 98, 99t
  definition of, 81–82
  dimensions of, 85–90

Movement, efficient, 98, 99t
  elements of, 86, 89
  guideliness for experiences, 91
  health and, 98, 99t
  of implement, 89, 90
  integrating dimensions of, 90
  learning, 85, 97, 99t
  limitations of, 85
  of objects, 89–90
  patterns of, 152–153, 154
  potential for, 90–91
  utility of, 85
  with others, 90, 151
Movement education, English, 82–83
Movement exploration, 66, 81–95, 143–159
  demonstration, 92–94
Mulberry bush, 307
Mule kick, 285
Muscular endurance, 20
  exercises for, 296
Muscular strength, Kraus-Weber tests for, 332, 344–346
Muscles, 36
  development of, 61
  overload and, 171–172
Music, 66
  movement to, 153

National Safety Council, accident report, 107–108
Neck resistor, 300
Negligence, 109–110
Newcomb, 256–257
Noise, 120
Noon hour, 109
North Pole, 181
Norwegian mountain march, 311–312
Norwegian polka, 316
Number call relay, 237–238

"O" ladder balance, 216
Obesity. See *Weight control.*
Objectives, 2, 9–10, 24, 46–64, 80. See also *Programs.*
  carry-over, 59–60, 339
  evaluation of, 338
  experiences for meeting, 121
  lesson, 75
  operational, 60–62
Objectivity, 331
Objects, 90
  movement of, 150–151, 153
Obstacle course, 292–293
Obstacle relays, 235–236
Oh, Johnny, 322
Oh, Susanna, 322
On all fours, 183
One foot stand, 169
One foot turn, 228
One leg back circle, 227
One leg forward circle, 227
One leg kick up, 226
One leg swan stand, 298
Oregon motor fitness test, 11

Over the rope, 284–285
Overlearning, 25
Overload, 19, 21, 22, 36, 105, 171–172
Oxygen consumption, 167–168

Pacing performance, 176–177
Paralysis of analysis, 118
Parent-consent forms, 110
Parents, excuses from, 105
  injured child and, 107
  reporting to, 339–341
Partners, 151
Path exploration, 148–149
Patrols, 111
Patterns, of movement, 152–153, 154
Paw paw patch, 306–307
Peers, 26, 28
  play relationship, 52–53
Personality, development of, 28
  guidelines for, 25–28
  play and, 26, 51–54
Physical development. See *Growth.*
Physical education, 1–4. See also *Teaching.*
  academic achievement and, 12, 14–15
  adapted program, 105
  children's understanding of, 96–103
  definition of, 5–9
  experiences for meeting objectives, 121
  general guidelines for, 29
  requirements for, 48
  values of elementary, 10
Physical fitness, 1, 8, 9–12, 26, 36–40, 41, 46–49
  activities, 66, 280–302
  of American children, 46–49, 50
  calisthenics and, 11
  definition, 20
  of European children, 9
  guidelines for developing, 19–22
  need for, 332–333
  norms for, 37–40
  objectives of, 61, 69t
  records of, 301–302
  special programs for, 289–293
  stunts for, 285–289
  tests of, 332, 333–334t
Physical prowess, 26, 28, 52, 53
Pictures, movement as, 158
Pin bombardment, 260–261
Planning. See *Programs.*
Play, 28
  calories used in, 167–168
  learning and, 26
  monkey play relationships, 51–54
  peer relationships and, 52–53
  personality development and, 51–54
  race and, 52
  social interaction and, 52
Playground duty, 110
Poems, movement with, 155–157
Pogo jump, 294
Poison pin, 282–283
Policies, 104–112
Polish polka, 316

Polka, 315–316
Polly wolly doodle, 309–310
Pop goes the weasel, 321
Positions, for exercises, 295
Posture, 7, 123, 124
Posture exploration, 148
Practice, 24–25, 117–118
Prejudice, 28, 49
President's Council for Physical Fitness, 9, 47, 104
Press together, 300
Priorities, 68, 70–71, 73t
Prisoner base, 200–201
Problem solving, 66, 82, 83, 84, 100–101, 143–159
Programs, 3. See also *Objectives.*
  change in, 338–339
  content, 71, 73t
  daily, 77, 79
  improvement, 77–79
  planning, 65–80
  yearly, 73–75, 74t, 79
  unit, 75–77, 79
Prone position, 295
Protective measures, 109
Prowess, 26, 28, 52, 53
Puberty, 32, 36, 39, 40
Pull the tail, 181–182
Pull-ups, 355
Pulling, 128, 162–163
Pulse, 173
Punt, 137
Push and pull, 288–289
Push ball, 283
Push the wall, 300
Push-up position, 295
Pushing, 128, 162–163
Pyramids, 214–215

Race, play and, 52
  prejudice, 49
Railroad relay, 237
Reaction time, 20, 170–171
Readiness, law of, 25
Reading, motor skills and, 12, 14
Recess, 6, 11, 109
Recreation, 6
  skills, 24, 43. See also *Leisure; Skills.*
Red light, 198
Relaxation, 21, 68
Relays, 66, 231–240
  circle, 274–275
  development of, 159
  shuttle, 273–274
Report card, 340
Rescue relay, 236–237
Respiration, 167
  artificial, 106–107
Rest, 21
Retarded child, 14
Rhythmic activities, 66, 152, 303–329
Ring around the ring, 193
Risk, 110
Rocking horse, 288
Roll call, 113

Rolling, 129
Rope, basic movement problems with, 150–151
Rope jumping, 137–139, 294
Rotation forward pass, 245
Roundoff, 211–212
Roundoff vault, 220
Rules, 98, 99t, 102, 119, 120, 178
Run sheep run, 198–199
Running, 125
Running broad jump, 275–276
Running games, 194–205
Running in place, 294

Safety, 98, 99t, 102, 119
  bicycle, 178
Safety line tag, 202
Scandinavian polka, 316
Schottische, 315
Seal walk, 229, 286
Self-image, 26, 28, 53
Self-regulation, 29
Semi-circle relay formation, 232
Set back, 241–242
Seven jumps, 308–309
Sexual maturation, 32, 36
Shadows, 155
Shock, 107
Shoot the rapids, 187
Shuttle relays, 232, 239, 272–274
Shuttle run, 360, 367
Sickness, 106
Side leg raises, 296
Side shuffle, 228
Signals, for squads, 114
Single file line, 116
Sit-ups, 356–357, 362
Six count Burpee, 299
600-yard run-walk, 357, 362
Skills, 20, 96–97
  automatic performance of, 25
  demonstration of, 119
  friction and, 165–166
  fundamental, 66, 123–142
  drills for, 139–142
  games for developing, 181–184
  guidelines for, 22, 24–25
  Iowa Brace test for, 334, 346–349
  learning, 114
    curves, 117–118
    years for, 24, 43
  mastery, 26
  measure of potential, 41
  motor, reading and, 12, 14
  need for, 334–335
  objectives, 54–56, 61, 69t
  senses and, 164–165
  tests of, 334, 335, 336, 346–349
Skin the cat, 224
Skip the beam, 228
Skipping, 127
Sleep, 26, 28
Slow motion, 154
Soccer games, 247–252

Soccer kick ball, 251–252
Soccer throw in, 249
Social acceptance, 52
Social attitudes, 28
Social development, 49, 51–54
  objectives, 61–62, 69t
Social-emotional needs, 335, 337t
Social interaction, 26
  play and, 52
Social learning, 25–28
Softball games, 269–271
Softball throw, 359–360, 366
Space exploration, 144–145
Speed, 20
Spider walk, 288
Spiders and flies, 194
Spin, 166–167
Sports, 49, 56, 66, 67, 96–97, 98, 102, 241–279. See
    also *Games.*
  arguments about, 120
  risk in, 110
  spectator, 179
Sportsmanship, 9, 28, 44, 49
Spotting, 109, 212
Springing, 221–223
Sprinters stride, 295
Sprinting, 271–273
Squads, 113–114
Squat vault, 219
Squirrels in trees, 197
Stability, 163–164
Stampede ball, 191–192
Stance, 163–164
Stand in pairs, 199
Stand up, 299
Standing, 123–124
Standing broad jump, 275, 359, 365
Standing start, 272
Start, 272
Steal the bacon, 184
Steal the bacon basketball, 266–267
Stoop stretch, 297
Stop and start, 282
Stork stand, 229, 298
Straddle around, 222
Straddle jump, 294
Straddle vault, 219
Straight line relay formation, 231
Straight lines, facing, 117
  facing teacher, 116
Strategy, 98, 99t, 178
Strength, 20, 21, 36–39. See also *Endurance; Physical
    prowess.*
  exercises for, 296
Stride jump, 294
Striking, 132–135
  with implement, 134, 135
  one hand, 132, 133
  overhand, 133, 134
  two hands, 133, 134
  underhand, 132, 133
Student interests, 332
Student knowledge, 338
Student needs, 332

Stunts, 212–215
  dual, 288–289
  horizontal, 224–227
  physical fitness, 285–289
Subjectivity, 331
Success, 26
Supervision, 29
  legal liability and, 109
Supine position, 295
Supplies. See *Equipment.*
Swan spring, 221
Swan stand, 170
Swing, 224

Tantoli, 314
Task tests, 336
Teaching. See also *Evaluation; Objectives; Programs.*
  details of, 104–112
  formation for, 114–117
  guidelines for, 19–30
  legal liability and, 109
  point of view, 5–18
  suggestions for, 113–121
  techiques, 98, 100–101
Teaching-learning process, 2–3. See also *Learning.*
Teams, 113, 114
Technique, accuracy and, 119
  new, 117–118
Ten little Indians, 304
Tether ball, 254–255
Tests, 338
  AAHPER, 50, 332, 355–367
  Brace, 40–41
  Carpenter, 346–349
  Iowa Brace, 334, 346–349
  Kraus-Weber, 47, 48, 61, 332, 344–346
  for physical fitness, 332, 333–334t
  of skill, 334–335, 336
  for weight control, 335
Thigh stand, 213–214
Throwing, for distance, 175–176
  one hand, 130, 131
  overhand, 130–131
  softball, 359, 366
  two hands, 129, 130–131
  underhand, 129–130
Three leg crawl, 285
Three man basketball, 268–269
Three man log roll, 213
Thinking, 81, 84
Time allocation, 71, 73, 74, 75, 78
  for class, 113
  for physical education, 104–105
  squad organization and, 114
Time exploration, 146, 147
Time test, 336
Tinikiling, 323–328
  basic step, 323–324
  cross-over step, 326–327
  pole variations, 327–328

Tinikiling, straddle step, 325
  turn step, 325
Tip up, 170, 209
Tire end ball, 243
Toe raises, 296
Toe to head, 298
Track and field, 271–277
Train tag, 199
Trampolette, 217–220
Travel, 110
Tube tumbling, 220–224
Tug-o-war, 284
Tumbling, 66, 206–230
  dual, 212, 215
  group, 212–215
  individual, 206–212
  tube, 220–224
Tumbling table, 217–220
Tunnel ball, 185
Tunnel crawl, 299
Two foot turn, 228

Unit plan, 75–77, 79
United States. See *American* entries.
Use and disuse, law of, 19

V sit, 300
Vaulting, 218–220
  from table, 218, 219
Ventilation, artificial, 106–107
Vertical jump, 333
Virginia Reel, 318–319
Volleyball games, 252–260

Walk the line, 298
Walk the plank, 298
Walking, 98, 124
  balance beam, 227, 228, 229
Walrus walk, 287
Weather, 74, 102
Weight, 32, 36
Weight control, 21, 56–59, 61, 69t, 173–175, 335
Wetzel grid, 335, 354
Wheat, the, 311
Whiffle end ball, 267–268
Whistle, 119
Wolfe vault, 219
Wring the rag, 289

X-ray, of wrist bones, 35

Yearly program, 73–75, 74t, 79

Zone soccer, 247–248

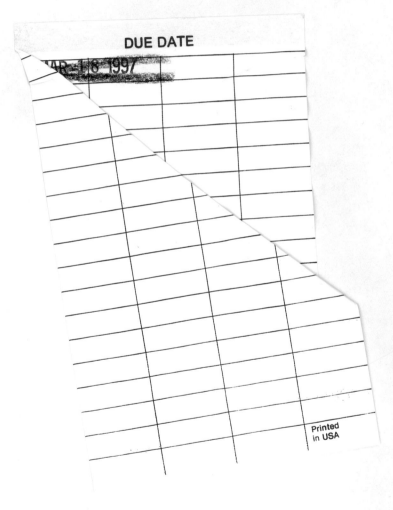

DUE DATE

MAR 18 1997

Printed
in USA